THE FINAL FEW

THE FINAL FEW

THE LAST SURVIVING PILOTS
OF THE BATTLE OF BRITAIN
TELL THEIR STORIES

DILIP SARKAR

AMBERLEY

To members of the Battle of Britain Fighter Association, past and present.

First published 2015

Amberley Publishing
The Hill, Stroud
Gloucestershire, GL5 4EP

www.amberley-books.com

Copyright © Dilip Sarkar, 2015

The right of Dilip Sarkar to be identified as
the Author of this work has been asserted in
accordance with the Copyrights, Designs and
Patents Act 1988.

ISBN 978 1 4456 4236 9 (hardback)
ISBN 978 1 4456 4255 0 (ebook)

British Library Cataloguing in Publication Data.
A catalogue record for this book is available
from the British Library.

Typesetting and Origination by Amberley
Publishing
Printed in the UK.

CONTENTS

AUTHOR'S NOTE & GLOSSARY

The aviation-minded reader will notice that I have referred to German Messerschmitt fighters by the abbreviation 'Me' (not 'Bf', which is also correct), or simply by their numeric designation, such as '109' or '110'. This not only reads better but is authentic; during the Battle of Britain, Keith Lawrence, a New Zealander, flew Spitfires and once said to me, 'To us they were just 109s or 110s, simple.'

In another attempt to preserve accuracy, wherever possible I have also used the original German regarding terms associated with the Luftwaffe, such as:

Adlerangriff	'Attack of the Eagles'
Adlertag	'Eagle Day'
Eichenlaub	The Oak Leaves, essentially being a bar to the Ritterkreuz
Erprobungsgruppe	Experimental group, in the case of *Erprobungsgruppe* 210 a skilled precision bombing unit
Experte	A fighter 'ace'. Ace status, on both sides, was achieved by destroying five enemy aircraft
Freie hunt	A fighter sweep
Gefechstand	Operations headquarters

Geschwader	The whole group, usually of three *gruppen*
Geschwaderkommodore	The group leader
Gruppe	A wing, usually of three squadrons
Gruppenkeil	A wedge formation of bombers, usually made up of vics of three
Gruppenkommandeur	The wing commander
Jagdbomber ('Jabo')	Fighter-bomber
Jagdflieger	Fighter pilot
Jagdgeschwader	Fighter group, abbreviated JG
Jagdwaffe	The fighter force
Jäger	Hunter, in this context a fighter pilot or aircraft
Kampffleiger	Bomber aircrew
Kampfgeschwader	Bomber group, abbreviated KG
Kanal	English Channel
Katchmarek	Wingman
Lehrgeschwader	Literally a training group, but actually a precision bombing unit, abbreviated LG
Luftflotte	Air fleet
Oberkannone	Literally the 'Top Gun', or leading fighter ace
Oberkommando der Wehrmacht (OKW)	The German armed forces high command
Ritterkreuz	The Knight's Cross of the Iron Cross
Rotte	A pair of fighters, comprising leader and wingman, into which the *schwarm* broke once battle was joined
Rottenführer	Leader of a fighting pair
Schwarm	A section of four fighters
Schwarmführer	Section leader

Seelöwe	Sealion, the code name given to Hitler's proposed seaborne invasion of England
Stab	Staff
Stabschwarm	Staff flight
Staffel	A squadron
Staffelkapitän	The squadron leader
Störflug	Harrassing attacks, usually by lone Ju 88s
Stuka	The Ju 87 dive-bomber
Sturkampfgeschwader	Dive-bomber group, abbreviated StG
Vermisst	Missing
Zerstörer	Literally 'destroyer', the term used for the Me 110
Zerstörergeschwader	Destroyer group, abbreviated ZG

Each *geschwader* generally comprised three *gruppen*, each of three *staffeln*. Each *gruppe* is designated by Roman numerals, i.e. III/JG 26 refers to the third *gruppe* of Fighter Group (abbreviated 'JG') 26. *Staffeln* are identified by numbers, so 7/JG 26 is the seventh *staffel* and belongs to III/JG 26.

Rank comparisons may also be useful:

Unteroffizier	Corporal, no aircrew equivalent in Fighter Command
Feldwebel	Sergeant
Oberfeldwebel	Flight Sergeant
Leutnant	Pilot Officer
Oberleutnant	Flight Lieutenant
Hauptmann	Squadron Leader
Major	Wing Commander
Oberst	Group Captain

RAF Abbreviations

AAF	Auxiliary Air Force
AASF	Advance Air Striking Force
A&AEE	Aeroplane & Armament Experimental Establishment
AFC	Air Force Cross
AFDU	Air Fighting Development Unit
AI	Airborne Interception radar
AOC	Air Officer Commanding
AOC-in-C	Air Officer Commanding-in-Chief
ATA	Air Transport Auxiliary
ATS	Armament Training School
BEF	British Expeditionary Force
CAM	Catapult Assisted Merchantship
CAS	Chief of the Air Staff
CFS	Central Flying School
CGS	Central Gunnery School
CO	Commanding Officer
DES	Direct Entry Scheme
DFC	Distinguished Flying Cross
DFM	Distinguished Flying Medal
DSO	Distinguished Service Order
E/A	Enemy Aircraft
FAA	Fleet Air Arm
EFTS	Elementary Flying Training School
FIU	Fighter Interception Unit
FTS	Flying Training School
ITW	Initial Training Wing
LAC	Leading Aircraftman
MRAF	Marshal of the Royal Air Force
MSFU	Merchant Ship Fighter Unit
NCO	Non-Commissioned Officer
ORB	Operations Record Book

OTC	Officer Training Corps
OTU	Operational Training Unit
PDC	Personnel Distribution Centre
RAFVR	Royal Air Force Volunteer Reserve
RFS	Reserve Flying School
RN	Royal Navy
RNAS	Royal Navy Air Service
SASO	Senior Air Staff Officer
SOO	Senior Operations Officer
SSC	Short Service Commission
UAS	University Air Squadron
U/S	Unserviceable

INTRODUCTION

On Saturday 20 September 1997, I was honoured to be the Battle of Britain Fighter Association's guest at that year's Annual Reunion Dinner – held at Bentley Priory, Air Chief Marshal Sir Hugh Dowding's Fighter Command HQ in 1940. The invitation had been kindly extended by the (then) Chairman, Air Chief Marshal Sir Christopher Foxley-Norris, and Secretary, Wing Commander Pat Hancock (both now sadly deceased), as the result of my long involvement with their members – all of whom are Battle of Britain aircrew. That evening left, needless to say, an indelible impression.

As a child growing up in the 1960s, I was very conscious that the Second World War had been an event of great significance, and, indeed, seemed omnipresent: one's older relatives and neighbours had been personally involved, or some relative or other killed, and war films made for constant weekend viewing. Scale plastic models were popular, and my interest in the Battle of Britain was initially inspired by an uncle who made large-scale flying models. In 1969, the film *Battle of Britain* was released, with flying scenes recreated for the big screen using *real* aircraft, and during the months leading up to and for some time after the film's premier associated merchandising material abounded: collectors' cards, posters, books, models and even a die-cast Dinky *Stuka* that dropped a cap-firing bomb! When I was eighteen, however, I came to understand that war was not a game – and I was *deeply* moved by the realisation that most of those who lost their lives during the Battle of Britain were around my own age, or not very much older. So it was that I began researching the stories of casualties, in an effort to ensure that this important personal record was not lost. As my quest developed, I soon came into contact with their families, and survivors who had flown with these unfortunates. Back then, during the early 1980s, I was not yet trained as an historian and lacked appropriate resources, but I was on a mission and possessed boundless enthusiasm and energy. The desire to make this contribution became an obsession, about which I became, it must be said, quite single-minded. As this personal quest gathered pace, I found myself entering into an increasing amount of correspondence and meetings with the surviving Few, whose stories I also began recording. Wing Commander Hancock was ever helpful in forwarding letters to Association members on my behalf, and supplied a letter of recommendation, confirming my antecedents and good intent.

It really was as much of a pleasure as it was a privilege to spend time in the company of these august but modest men. In 1990, the Battle of Britain's fiftieth anniversary year, my first book, *Spitfire Squadron*, was published – and launched at the RAF Museum, Hendon. Present were around twelve of the Few. Further publications and larger-scale events followed over the years, held at such places as Worcester Guildhall and the Imperial War Museum's working airfield at Duxford – a former Battle of Britain sector station. Indeed, at Westland Aircraft, no less than thirty-eight of the Few attended the launch of *Angriff Westland* in 1994. These really were incredible and very popular occasions, providing the general public with a rare opportunity to meet personalities directly from the pages of history books. Indeed, hitherto the majority of these veterans had all but disappeared, happily, into anonymous obscurity, meeting up with their own kind to talk about the past at the Association's annual reunion and commemorative service at Westminster Abbey. In the winter of their lives, there can be no doubt that this activity provided many with a rekindled interest in their past, which was most stimulating. In the years since, various others have followed suit, hosting similar events, all of this activity generating a cult around the Few, the signatures of whom are avidly collected by enthusiasts, proud of the 'score' they have notched up of veterans met. Annually, the Few now also gather at the Battle of Britain Memorial Trust's National Memorial at Capel-le-Ferne for a moving service of remembrance. All of this, of course, helps keep the Battle of Britain's memory evergreen – which is as it should be.

That evening back in 1997 at Bentley Priory, I watched a Spitfire fly overhead and dined with one hundred of the Few, who had attended from all over the world. Today, at the time of writing, there are only twenty-seven survivors still alive of nearly 3,000 Fighter Command aircrew who fought – and won – the Battle of Britain. Sadly but inevitably, given that these men are all now in excess of ninety-three, by the time this book is actually published that figure will be less.

This book essentially presents, in context, the stories, largely in their own words, of certain survivors, all but three of whom are alive at this time (sadly, two of those alive and who contributed their memories died before publication; one passed away previously). These accounts therefore provide the fine detail concerning the personal, human, experience involved, thus splashing rich colour on what would otherwise be the dull canvas of history. This is possible because we live in a literate society – other famous battles of yesteryear, of course, such as Agincourt (1415) and Trafalgar (1805), do not enjoy such a legacy. In that respect the Few are fortunate, and there is no doubt in my mind that the Battle of Britain's bibliography is now so prolific that their deeds are in no danger of being forgotten. That said, it is crucially important that future generations are educated about the Battle. To this end, it is incredibly significant that the Battle of Britain Memorial Trust succeeded in creating 'The Wing', the new visitor and education centre at the Battle of Britain Memorial site at Capel-le-Ferne, which was opened by Her Majesty the Queen on 23 March 2015. Equally important, in my view, is the dedication of Bob Jeffries and other willing volunteers like him in proudly showing visitors around the underground former 11 Group Operations Room at Uxbridge. Collectively, all of this generates interest in the Battle of Britain and promotes an appreciation of the debt we owe.

However, the intention of all this commemoration and remembrance – and it must be stressed – is not to glorify war; far from it. That war is a dreadful thing is, sadly, only too evident when viewing the cemeteries, full of white headstones, where those of the Few who failed to return now lie. Moreover, the survivors themselves seek no personal glory or recognition. Anyone trying to understand why the recording and sharing of their memories is so important, in fact, needs only to read the last paragraph of *The Final Few*.

For me personally, this book represents the end of a long journey. As explained, this began many years ago, when the Few were more numerous; indeed, I came to know many of them well. Regardless of the difference in our ages, we became friends, and to some I became particularly close. In fact, it became very depressing at one point, attending an increasing amount of funerals, at some of which I was asked to speak. Being maudlin is not now my intention, but concluding this book is poignant as I reflect on the aircrew – and ground crews – I knew but who are no longer with us. This book, though, is a celebration – of the Few and what they collectively achieved, and in particular those representative pilots whose stories are told within. *The Final Few* also provides those airmen, after all these years, a stage from which to share their experiences and reflections on those now far-off, but no less epic, days of 1940. Writing another book like this would, I think, given the advanced ages of the remaining pilots, be either very difficult indeed or impossible. Although sound and document archives exist, providing an important primary source for historians from which doubtless future books will be produced, the dispassionate selection of such material is not the same as *knowing* the men involved – and I am privileged to *know* those who now speak to us all through *The Final Few*. The preparation of it has entailed numerous research trips, correspondence and telephone calls with them, every one a pleasure. It is perhaps worth emphasising that my work has never received any funding from any university or other organisation, so has always been run on a comparative 'shoestring' from my own pocket; anyone so inclined, therefore, could have done this – confirming that a significant contribution can be made by enthusiasts. There cannot be, however, to my mind, another book like this – I certainly have no plans to write one – so *The Final Few* represents the pinnacle of my personal years spent among the Few. It is, therefore, 'Journey's End' in more ways than one.

Dilip Sarkar MBE FRHistS BA (Hons)

Worcester, 3 August 2015

Prologue

THE BATTLE OF BRITAIN

After Britain and France declared war on Nazi Germany on 3 September 1939, the dreaded 'knock-out blow' that it was feared the Luftwaffe would make on Britain failed to materialise. Indeed, for the first few months of 1940, little happened. The Soviets finally overwhelmed the Finns, U-boats continued to attack Britain's North Atlantic shipping, but elsewhere the 'Phoney War' persisted. With the exception of the Poles and Czechs, few people had unduly suffered from the conflict thus far. In early April, Hitler invaded Denmark and Norway, drawing Anglo-French forces into a hopeless campaign in Norway's inhospitable terrain. A month later saw the long-awaited attack on France, the Allies being completely overwhelmed by modern *Blitzkrieg* tactics, and shocked by German aerial superiority. Indeed, in this new global conflagration, air power would play an unprecedented part. Ever since Christmas Eve 1914, in fact, when the first German bomb was dropped on England, Britain could no longer rely upon being an island for protection. Air power changed everything, and from that point onwards Britain itself was potentially just as much a battlefield as the corner of any foreign field.

Britain's aerial defence was the responsibility of Fighter Command, formed in 1936, and specifically that of Air Chief Marshal Sir High

Dowding. Between the wars, however, priority was given not to fighters but to the bomber force. It was believed that 'the bomber will always get through', and that the 'only defence is offence', through retaliatory bombing. While acknowledging the aeroplane to be 'the most offensive weapon ever invented', the 'Father of the Royal Air Force', Marshal of the RAF Sir Hugh Trenchard, explained in 1921 that in his view aircraft were nonetheless 'a shockingly bad weapon for defence'. So little did Trenchard think of fighters that he considered them necessary only to 'keep up the morale of one's own people'. Little wonder, then, that during the 1920s and '30s the bomber force was expanded at Fighter Command's expense. When Hitler became Chancellor of Germany in 1933, the RAF remained equipped with biplanes similar to those with which it had fought the First World War. The Schneider Trophy air race, however, had emphasised the superiority of monoplanes – and in 1935 the new German single-engined fighter, the Messerschmitt 109, flew for the first time. Three years later, when British Prime Minister Neville Chamberlain flew to Munich in response to the crisis over Czechoslovakia, the RAF was only just starting to upgrade to the new Hawker Hurricane and Supermarine Spitfire monoplane fighters – it was just in the nick of time.

Fortunately, Dowding did not share Trenchard's views, and robustly argued the case that unless security of base came first, the bomber force would be unable to deliver a 'knock-out blow':

> The best defence of the country is fear of the fighter. If we are strong in fighters we should probably never be attacked in force. If we are moderately strong, we shall probably be attacked and the attacks will gradually be brought to a standstill ... If we are weak in fighter strength, the attacks will not be brought to a standstill and the productive capacity of the country will be virtually destroyed.

Technically minded, Dowding also fully appreciated the

early-warning benefits of radar, integrating this new science into his System of Air Defence. This, and the new monoplane fighters, proved crucial. Fighter Command was organised into four fighter groups, each, for tactical purposes, subdivided geographically into sectors. A sector consisted of the main sector station and airfield, sector headquarters and operations room, and one or more satellite or forward airfields providing for good dispersal. South-east England, including London, was covered by 11 Group, reinforced when required by adjacent groups. Other groups also maintained a regular supply of fresh squadrons to relieve those worn down by intensive air fighting. Between the wars, it was anticipated that any German aerial attack would approach England from across the North Sea, from bases in Germany, but even so Dowding did not concentrate his squadrons in 11 and 12 Groups, the latter defending the industrial Midlands and North. Unable to discount an aerial attack from a direction of Norway, Dowding was therefore obliged to maintain appropriate strength in northern England too.

In addition to this clever shepherding of limited resources, key to Dowding's system were the operations rooms at command, group and sector level. The operations rooms physically portrayed the status and deployment of RAF fighters, and the track of enemy raids. Squadrons were, therefore, 'scrambled' to respond to any incoming threat, and once airborne were controlled by radio-telephony. This system, of course, relied entirely upon good intelligence – which is where radar came in. Dowding was instrumental in creating a chain of radar stations around the British coastline, providing early warning of enemy aircraft approaching. This early warning was vital, especially when, as it turned out, the Luftwaffe was located just twenty-two miles from the British south-east coast – only four or five minutes' flying time away. Over land, this information was supplemented by visual sightings from the Observer Corps, all of this detail being transmitted to Fighter Command headquarters. After passing the information through a 'filter room', orders were decided and relayed immediately by telephone to command, group and sector operations rooms. In all operations rooms was a large map table upon which air-raid intelligence was plotted. Seated around the table were 'plotters', each connected by landline to the appropriate reporting centre. From these centres plotters received up-to-the-minute reports of the enemy's direction, number and height. The plotter displayed symbols on the map, representing friendly and hostile plots. Consequently every RAF commander, at all levels, had a visual representation before him of the ever-developing aerial battlefield. A 'Totalisator' board, indicating the availability and deployment of RAF fighter squadrons, meteorological information and anti-aircraft gun liaison, completed the overall picture. During the creation of this system, which harnessed the latest technology, Dowding had no precedent to assist him – but it had been researched in minute detail, and ultimately would not be found wanting.

The RAF had been formed on 1 April 1918, a new service independent of both the Army and Navy. The Air Force Cadet College at Cranwell provided training for regular officers; staff officers were trained at the Air Force Staff College at Andover; the Technical Apprenticeship Scheme at Halton produced the RAF's engineers; and the Central Flying School at Upavon produced service pilots. Trenchard's view was that all his pilots should be officers. Admission to Cranwell, however, depended upon two things: a fee-paying public school background, which was only available to 5.2 per cent of the population, and the ability to pay fees (£150 upon entry and £100 per annum for two years). A 50 per cent failure rate in flying training, however, confirmed that a socially elite background was no guarantee to ultimately achieving the coveted pilot's flying brevet. Indeed, it soon became clear that Cranwell was unable to generate the quantity of trained pilots required by Trenchard's new service, so he did two things. Firstly, in spite of his original ruling that all pilots would be officers, and in the interests of creating a trained reserve, in 1921 the flying training began of a small number of non-commissioned officers (NCO), who were expected to fly for five years before resuming their original trades while remaining eligible for recall to flying duties in the event of an emergency. The initiative was both popular and economic, although numbers were small: in 1925, only 13.9 per cent of pilots were NCOs, rising to just 17.1 per cent in 1935. Trenchard's second initiative was equally far-sighted: Short Service Commissions (SSC). In the services, officers generally served for the duration of their working lives, hence the term 'permanent commission'. This, however, led to a 'dead men's shoes' syndrome that Trenchard, understandably given that flying is a young man's activity, wished to avoid. To do so, and in order to create another substantial reserve of trained pilots, he inaugurated a scheme whereby SSC officers served a fixed contract of four years' active service followed by six on the reserve list. Such officers were only eligible for maximum promotion to flight lieutenant, but could apply for a permanent commission. Together with direct entrants from University Air Squadrons (UAS), SSC officers were not trained at Cranwell but at Service Flying Training Schools (SFTS). Direct entrants, however, were few: of the 2,408 pilots who fought the Battle of Britain, only thirteen came direct from universities.

Another sound initiative was creation of the Auxiliary Air Force (AAF), based upon the territorial concept, in 1924. By 1930, auxiliary squadrons represented 5 per cent of the regular air force. In 1939, the AAF, arguably an exclusive, elite gentleman's club comprising wealthy and well-connected individuals who flew for pleasure, had twenty squadrons. This initiative was soon followed, in 1925, by creation of another elitist reserve: the Cambridge UAS, aimed at encouraging undergraduates to take up flying and become 'air-minded'. London and Oxford soon followed suit, but collectively this represented only a very small reserve: on 3 September 1939, the Oxford UAS provided just five hundred trained officer pilots for the RAF. In 1934, however, the first Expansion Plan began, intended to raise the strength of Home Defence forces to fifty-two fighter squadrons by 1940. The most significant feature of Expansion Scheme 'F', in 1936, was the recognition that a substantial trained reserve was now essential, leading, significantly, to creation of the RAF Volunteer Reserve (VR).

The official monograph on RAF flying training during the Second World War states that the VR would 'have a wide appeal based upon the Citizen Volunteer principal, with a common mode of entry and promotion and commissioning on merit'. This was significant as it meant that in future not only the socially elite would be exclusively considered for commissions, albeit this only applied to the reserve. All VR trainee aircrew were automatically made sergeants, and this was, in effect, a grammar schoolboys' air force. All of this, of course, very much reflects the distinct hierarchical society of Britain between the wars – on the ground, officers, NCOs and other ranks being segregated in their own messes – but the volume of casualties once the shooting started soon dictated that ability and experience, not background, were the most important factors in leadership selection; no longer were all pilots officers, and nor were they all professional airmen. When war broke out, Britain's armed forces were mobilised and reservists returned to the colours. By then, the RAF also included the amateurs of the AAF and UAS, and the 'citizen volunteers' of the VR. Regular and auxiliary squadrons, therefore, while maintaining their identities, received an influx of pilots from various sources. The Fighter Command which fought in 1940, in fact, was very different to the new service created in 1918, and its pilots had taken various routes to their cockpits.

In 1939, the Air Ministry decided that Dowding required fifty-three fighter squadrons to defend the British mainland, the fleet at Scapa Flow, and coastal merchant shipping. When war broke out, Fighter Command's strength was thirty-nine squadrons. Although eighteen new squadrons were formed, Dowding was obliged to release four of these precious units to support the British Expeditionary Force (BEF) on the Continent – reducing the strength available for Home Defence to a mere thirty-six squadrons. When Hitler invaded the west on 10 May 1940, it rapidly became clear that the Allies faced a military catastrophe of unparalleled proportion. Far-sightedly, Dowding had only committed Hurricane squadrons to France, preserving his superior but fewer Spitfires for the defence of Britain ahead. Under political pressure from the French, British Prime Minister Winston Churchill promised that even more RAF fighters would cross the Channel – a potentially disastrous scenario which Dowding fully recognised and determined to prevent. On 16 May 1940, therefore, Fighter Command's Air Officer Commander-in-Chief wrote to the cabinet, making out the strongest possible case to prevent further fighters being drained in a battle already lost. This view was respected, but even so, by July 1940, Fighter Command's strength was but fifty-two squadrons. Of them, thirty-three were Hurricane-equipped; only nineteen flew Spitfires.

There were other squadrons involved, but these were equipped with either the twin-engined Bristol Blenheim, or single-seater Boulton-Paul Defiant. The Blenheim was in no way comparable to the Me 109 and completely unsuited to fighter combat. Instead, the Blenheim was pressed into service as a stop-gap night fighter. The Defiant was a disaster. With no forward-firing armament, the aircraft carried an air-gunner in a hydraulically controlled rear-facing turret. The problem was that pilot and air gunner lacked the essential and immediate eye-to-hand reflex required in fast, modern fighter combat, and, given that the aircraft was powered by the same Rolls-Royce Merlin engine propelling Spitfires and Hurricanes, performance was compromised by the extra weight.

Over Dunkirk, the Defiant had initially scored well, German pilots getting a nasty shock from its rear-facing machine-guns, but they soon wised up. When committed to the Battle of Britain, the Defiant squadrons were virtually annihilated – valiant young men needlessly sacrificed due to Air Staff's incompetence. So, the brunt of battle was borne by Hawker Hurricanes and Supermarine Spitfires, which were also the types flown by the pilots interviewed for this book; it is with those types, therefore, that we are concerned.

An RAF fighter squadron, commanded by a squadron leader, consisted of twelve operational aircraft and pilots (plus reserves), divided into two flights, 'A' and 'B', each led by a flight lieutenant. The flights were subdivided into two colour-coded sections of three aircraft: typically red and yellow for 'A' flight, blue and green for 'B'. Each pilot had a number, from one to three, one indicating the section leader. Blue 1, therefore, was the section leader of 'B' flight's Blue Section. Each squadron was identified by its own code letters, painted in large, grey letters on the fuselage, forward of the national roundel. Individual aircraft were given their own unique identification letter, A–K for 'A' flight, and L–Z for 'B'. 'QV-K', therefore, would be a Spitfire of 19 Squadron's 'A' Flight. Every squadron also had a code name: 'Maida Blue 1', for example, being the leader of 152 Squadron's 'B' Flight's Blue Section. During the Battle of Britain, promotion to command still revolved around seniority on the Air Force List, so squadron commanders could be appointed to lead fighter squadrons in the heat of battle on that basis – even though they had no combat experience whatsoever. These men were all pre-war officers and men invariably in their thirties. Monoplane fighter combat, however, proved to be very much a young man's game, and it soon became clear that it was combat experience, not seniority on the list, that counted. Consequently, as casualties mounted, promotions often came either from within the squadron concerned or from combat-blooded senior pilots from other fighter squadrons. As this went on, the average age of

RAF fighter squadron commanders decreased, usually involving pilots aged in their mid-twenties, while their youngest pilots were frequently eighteen or nineteen.

In 1940, RAF fighter pilots faced a very uncertain future. They never knew when the order to scramble would come; the atmosphere was one of suspense. If the weather was fine, the chances were that battle would be joined, the time and place, of course, dictated by the enemy. This could come both unexpectedly and suddenly, perhaps in the middle of a game of chess or cards, or while lighting a cigarette – perhaps the last. The telephone became the pilots' master, its ring often heralding violent aerial action. The operational centre of a squadron was 'dispersal', usually a wooded hut in which was situated an orderly clerk and the all-important telephone, in addition to twelve beds on which the pilots rested between sorties. Outside, the aircraft were dispersed as a precaution against bombing, always facing the airfield's centre so that the pilot could take off with the minimum of delay. During the daytime, pilots usually left their cumbersome parachutes on top of the port wing, straps hanging down below the leading edge and ready to be donned quickly. Leather flying helmets, radio lead plugged in, were left in the cockpit. There was no cockpit heating, so pilots wore thick socks to insulate against cold at high altitude, and leather flying boots (although some preferred shoes, to achieve a better feel of the controls). Flying over the sea dictated that the pilot must also wear a bulbous, orally inflated life preserver, painted yellow and known, for obvious reasons, as a 'Mae West'. In action, the pilot's head was covered by his flying helmet, his face by a canvas mask providing a radio-telephony microphone and delivering oxygen, his eyes by goggles. Hands were protected by leather gauntlets. Sometimes pilots wore flying overalls, but often flew in uniform trousers and tunics – rarely in the bulky sheepskin Irvin flying jacket. The brightly coloured fighter pilot's silk scarf, however, was not a pose, but very necessary: buttoned, stiff uniform shirt collars caused chafing as the pilot constantly searched the sky, all around, above and below, and neckties had been known to shrink in saltwater.

Fire was the pilot's greatest fear, unsurprisingly given that in both the Hurricane and Spitfire the main fuel tank is situated immediately in front of the cockpit. For that reason, pilots often flew into action with their canopy hoods unlocked, to facilitate a quick escape from a blazing aircraft. On 3 September 1940, Pilot Officer Richard Hillary's Spitfire was fitted with a new canopy, which would not slide smoothly back. That morning, Hillary, a young Oxford undergraduate, and his airframe fitter worked frantically, with a file and oil, to rectify this defect. Although progress was made, the hood still stuck halfway – then the call to scramble came. Hillary shot down a 109 but was then attacked by *Hauptmann* Erich Bode, *Kommandeur* of II/JG 26. Later, in his deeply moving memoir *The Last Enemy*, Hillary wrote:

> I felt a terrific explosion which knocked the control column from my hand, and the whole machine quivered like a stricken animal. In a second, the cockpit was a mass of flames; instructively I reached up to open the hood. It would not move. I dropped back in the seat and reached for the stick in an effort to turn the plane on its back, the heat was so intense and I could feel myself going. I remember a second of sharp agony, thinking 'So this is it!' and putting both hands to my eyes. Then I passed out.

Hillary was thrown clear, floating down by parachute, and was fortunately rescued by the Margate lifeboat. The young Spitfire pilot was grievously burned, however, and there followed many agonising months of operations and treatment, as one of pioneering plastic surgeon Sir Archibald McIndoe's 'Guinea Pigs'. Tragically, Hillary, badly scarred, recovered only to die in a flying accident in 1943.

On the ground, the fighter pilots' classic pose was leaving their tunic's top button undone – indicating membership of an elite club. Fighter pilots generally worked a four-day cycle. The first would be 'standby', ready to fly within one hour; on the second, he would be 'available' and ready to fly with fifteen minutes' notice; day three at 'readiness' and immediately able to take off; finally, day four was 'stand down', on which most pilots could leave the airfield.

RAF fighter squadrons were directly controlled by the Controller at their Sector Operations Room. Each such facility was linked by landlines and tannoy systems to the aircraft dispersal points. The Sector Controller brought his available units to readiness, or scrambled them, in accordance with the instructions he received from Group. Once the squadrons were up, the Controller was responsible for guiding the interception and placing his fighters in the best tactical position, and could speak to pilots using radio-telephony. This, of course, relied on a code, for security reasons: 'Scramble' meant to take off urgently; 'Pancake' to land; 'Angels' referred to height measured in thousands of feet (thus 'Angels One Five' meant 15,000 feet); 'Vector' the required compass heading, expressed in degrees; 'Liner' to travel at normal cruising speed, 'Buster' to make haste; a 'Bogey' was an unidentified, possibly hostile, aircraft, while 'Bandits' were confirmed enemy aircraft. When the aerial formation leader shouted 'Tally Ho!' the Controller knew that the enemy were in sight and about to be attacked. Famously, the clock code was used to identify and communicate the presence of enemy aircraft: 'Bandits six o'clock high', therefore, meant that enemy aircraft were approaching from dead astern and above. The warning for the need to take violent evasive action in the event of an attack was simply '*BREAK!*' – which inevitably saw the RAF fighters describing the tightest possible turns, to left or right.

The British fighters' standard armament was eight .303 Browning machine guns, each with 300 rounds, fired at a rate of 1,200 rounds per minute. Ammunition belts were typically made up of a variety of bullets: ball, armour piercing and incendiary. The Browning gun was generally accurate up to 300 yards, after which gravity imposed 'bullet drop'. Many pilots, therefore, harmonised their guns to converge at 250 yards, producing a lethal cone of fire. That said, rifle-calibre ammunition was found wanting so far as the destruction of increasingly armoured German bombers were concerned. The Me 109, of course, was armed with two nose-mounted 7.92 mm machine guns, synchronised to fire through the propeller arc, and a pair of wing-mounted 20 mm Oerlikon cannons. The latter had a slower rate of fire, requiring greater accuracy, but the larger round inflicted far greater damage. The 109, however, like the Spitfire, had a very strong but thin wing; when the Germans discovered Britain's intention to arm each of its new fighters with eight machine-guns, massively outgunning their fighter's two, this presented a dilemma: the wing was unable to accommodate a multiple battery of guns. It was therefore decided to put a single cannon in each wing, faring the bulbous ammunition drum within upper and under-surface blisters. In the event, this weapon proved to be an advantageous expedient, which the RAF was slow to emulate due to technical difficulties with mounting their Hispano cannon. In RAF fighters, guns were sighted via a reflector gunsight, which projected illuminated cross-hairs onto a prism, and automatically calculated the angle of deflection required, taking into account the target's speed and range. In reality, however, given the speed of modern fighter combat, this proved impractical, and so the sight was typically pre-set concerning the wingspan of the enemy aircraft type most likely to be encountered.

Connected to each fighter was a mobile starter battery, and 'erks', RAF slang for ground crew, who serviced engines, airframes, instruments and armament. Firefighters, anti-aircraft gunners, intelligence officers, service police, medics, cooks and cleaners, all supported the effort of fighter pilots and the operations rooms. Collectively these men and women represented Britain's front line and were essential to the country's defence in 1940.

It is fair to say that during the spring and summer of 1940, the world changed forever. The Nazi conquest of Belgium, Holland, Luxembourg and France, beginning on 10 May, was one of the most shocking and unanticipated victories in military history. On that fateful day, on which Germany attacked the west, Winston Churchill succeeded Neville Chamberlain as British Prime Minister; Churchill lost no time telling the House of Commons that all he could offer the British people was 'Blood, tears, toil and sweat'. Rescue of the British Expeditionary Force (BEF) from the beaches of Dunkirk was arguably a miracle, but Churchill was quick to point out that 'We must be very careful not to attribute to this deliverance the attributes of a victory. Wars are not won by evacuations.' Although it has been argued that Britain still stood on the shoulders of its Empire and Commonwealth, the fact remains that in a military sense, Britain was now alone – and only its shores, not those of colonies such as Canada or Australia, or India, the jewel in the Empire's Crown, were within range of German bombers. In that – the most important – sense, Britain was truly *alone*. America, still smarting from casualties suffered during the closing stages of the First World War, although largely sympathetic, steadfastly pursued its policy of isolationism and non-involvement in European problems. Given Hitler's breathtaking military success to date, it was naturally assumed that Britain would be next – and there was little, except Churchill's rhetoric, to suggest that Britain's David would beat the Goliath of Germany in the contest ahead. On 4 June, Churchill once more spoke to the House with a clear statement of intent, and concluded with a subtle appeal to America:

Even though large tracts of Europe and many old and famous states have fallen or may fall into the grip of the Gestapo and all the odious apparatus of Nazi rule, we shall not flag or fail. We shall go on to the end, we shall fight in France, we shall fight on the seas and oceans, we shall fight with growing confidence and growing strength in the air, we shall defend our island, whatever the cost may be, we shall fight on the beaches, we shall fight on the landing grounds, we shall fight in the fields and in the streets, we shall fight in the hills; we shall never surrender, and even if, which I do not for a moment believe, this island or a large part of it were subjugated and starving, then our Empire beyond the seas, armed and guarded by the British Fleet, would carry on the struggle, until, in God's good time, the New World, with all its power and might, steps forth to the rescue and the liberation of the old.

After the Fall of France, described by Churchill as 'a colossal defeat', there was a lull while Hitler made plans and regrouped. The situation now presented to the Führer was an unanticipated one: the opportunity for a seaborne invasion of England. Hitler's infamous Directive Number 16 stated his aims clearly:

As England, despite her hopeless military situation, still shows no sign of willingness to come to terms, I have decided to prepare, and if necessary to carry out, a landing operation against her.

The aim of this operation is to eliminate the English motherland as a base from which war against Germany can be continued and, if necessary, to occupy completely.

Thirteen divisions of the German army, each some 19,000 strong, moved to the Channel coast as the vanguard of a landing force comprising thirty-nine divisions. Plans were made to disembark 125,000 men in Kent and Sussex during the first three days of the proposed invasion – code-named 'Operation *Seelöwe*' (Sealion). To transport this force across the *Kanal*, the German navy assembled a makeshift invasion fleet of 170 large transport vessels, 1,500 barges, and several hundred tugs, trawlers, motorboats and fishing smacks. As the *Kriegsmarine*, however, was hopelessly inferior to the Royal Navy in warships of every category, the German service chiefs agreed that the operation could only succeed providing the Luftwaffe defeated Fighter Command and gained aerial supremacy prior to the fleet setting sail. The Luftwaffe would then dominate not only the skies above the battlefield, but, crucially, the beachhead's sea approaches and thus repulse any counter-attack by the Royal Navy. Not unnaturally, *Reichsmarschall* Hermann Göring was supremely confident: 'My Luftwaffe is invincible ... And so now we turn to England. How long will this one last – two or three weeks?'

On 18 June 1940, Churchill again stirred the British people:

What General Weygand called the Battle of France is over. I expect that the Battle of Britain is about to begin. Upon this battle depends the survival of Christian civilisation. Upon it depends our own British life, and the long continuity of our institutions and our Empire. The whole fury and might of the enemy must very soon be turned on us. Hitler knows that he will have to break us in this Island or lose the war. If we can stand up to him, all Europe may be free and the life of the world may move forward into broad, sunlit uplands. But if we fail, then the whole world, including the United States, including all that we have known and cared for, will sink into the abyss of a new Dark Age made more sinister, and perhaps more protracted, by the lights of perverted science. Let us therefore brace ourselves to our duties, and so bear ourselves that, if the British Empire and its Commonwealth last for a thousand years, men will still say, 'This was their finest hour.'

Churchill's 'Battle of Britain' officially began on 10 July 1940. The air forces of both sides, however, had been skirmishing over the Channel for some days beforehand, and enemy reconnaissance bombers had been active over England. On 1 July, German troops invaded and occupied British sovereign soil – the Channel Islands – giving a clear indication of what lay in store for the mainland.

Being an island, of course, Britain was dependent upon supplies imported from abroad by sea, so inbound convoys became the focus for German air attacks. These battles over the Channel, in fact, represented significant danger for the pilots of Air Vice-Marshal Keith Park, Air Officer Commanding 11 Group, because air-sea rescue remained in its infancy. German seaplanes, however, ranged far and wide, recovering Luftwaffe airmen, although many from both sides would nonetheless be claimed by the Channel.

On 1 August, Hitler issued another, significant, directive: 'The Luftwaffe will use all the forces at its disposal to destroy the British air force as quickly as possible. August 5th is the first day on which this intensified air war may begin, but the exact date is to be left to the Luftwaffe and will depend on how soon its preparations are complete, and on the weather situation.'

Now the enemy changed tack, no longer focussing on Channel-bound convoys but instead targeting coastal radar installations and forward aerodromes. This was the *Adlerangriff* – 'Eagle Attack' – and 13 August was chosen as *Adlertag* – 'Eagle Day'. The weather, however, was poor, the operation a muddle. Nonetheless, it was clear to all that the tempo of fighting was increasing. On one occasion, Churchill visited Air Vice-Marshal Park's underground Group Operations Room at Uxbridge – 'The Hole' – and watched, with War Cabinet Secretary General Sir Hastings Ismay, 11 Group's response to waves of German bombers. Afterwards, as Churchill and Ismay were driven away, the Prime Minister turned to the general and said, 'Don't speak to me. I have never been so moved.' Five minutes passed, and Churchill said, 'Never in the field of human conflict has so much been owed by so many to so few.' Four days later, on 20 August, Churchill included the now famous phrase in another speech to the House:

The enemy is, of course, far more numerous than we are. But our new production already, as I am advised, largely exceeds his, and the American production is only just beginning to flow in. It is a fact, as I see from my daily returns, that our bomber and fighter strength now, after all this fighting, are larger than they have ever been. We believe that we shall be able to continue the air struggle indefinitely and as long as the enemy pleases, and the longer it continues the more rapid will be our approach, first towards that parity, and then into that superiority in the air, upon which in a large measure the decision of the war depends.

The gratitude of every home in our Island, in our Empire, and indeed throughout the world, except in the abodes of the guilty, goes out to the British airmen who, undaunted by odds, unwearied in their constant challenge and mortal danger, are turning the tide of the world war by their prowess and by their devotion. Never in the field of human conflict was so much owed by so many to so few.

With those words, Churchill immortalised the aircrew of Fighter Command who fought the Battle of Britain – and who, even as those words were spoken, remained locked in a desperate fight for survival. However, with typical self-effacing irreverence, of the Prime Minister's moving tribute Squadron Leader Brian Lane DFC remarked, 'I thought he was talking about our Mess bills!'

Although the *Adlerangriff*, due to poor intelligence, expended effort bombing certain airfields unconnected with Fighter Command, some essential sector stations were hard hit, not least Kenley and Tangmere on 18 August. The battle's outcome, however, remained indecisive. Growing impatient, Göring called his principal officers to *Karinhall*, where he harangued them, singling out the fighter pilots for particular attention. It was clear that in spite of protracted heavy fighting, little impression had been made upon Fighter Command's strength or ability to resist. The *Reichsmarschall* concluded, 'We have reached the decisive period of the air war against England. The vital task is to turn all means at our disposal to the defeat of the enemy air force. Our first aim is the destruction of enemy fighters. If they no longer take to the air, we shall attack them on the ground, or force them into battle by directing bomber attacks against targets within range of our fighters ... Once the enemy air force has been annihilated, our attacks will be directed against as ordered against other vital targets.' Much of this made sense, but a fundamental principal of warfare is maintenance of aim – and Göring would change tack too often.

On the same day, Air Vice-Marshal Park also took stock and issued new instructions to his Controllers:

a) Despatch fighters to engage large enemy formations over land or within gliding distance of the coast. During the next two or three weeks, we cannot afford to lose pilots through forced landings in the sea;

b) Avoid sending fighters out over the sea to intercept reconnaissance aircraft or small formations of enemy fighters;

c) Despatch a pair of fighters to intercept single reconnaissance aircraft that come inland. If clouds are favourable, put a patrol one or two fighters over an aerodrome which the enemy are approaching in clouds;

d) Against mass attacks coming inland, dispatch a minimum number of squadrons to engage enemy fighters. Our main objective is to engage enemy bombers, particularly those approaching under the lowest cloud layer;

e) If all our squadrons around London are off the ground engaging mass attacks, ask No 12 Group or Command Controller to provide squadrons to patrol aerodromes Debden, North Weald, Hornchurch;

f) If heavy attacks have crossed the coast and are proceeding towards aerodromes, put a squadron or even the Sector Training Flight, to patrol under clouds over every sector aerodrome;

g) No 303 (Polish) Squadron can provide two sections for patrol of inland aerodromes, especially while the older squadrons are on the ground refuelling when enemy formations are flying overland;

h) No 1 (Canadian) Squadron can be used in the same manner by day as other fighter squadrons.

As ever, the astute Air Vice-Marshal Park was carefully preserving his resources, these instructions being sensibly directed at preventing wastage through pilots being lost in the sea, or the use of large formations which might be wiped out en masse. Also, and as per his Commander-in-Chief's specified System of Air Defence, 12 Group was to be called upon to patrol his airfields north of the Thames when their fighter squadrons were engaged further forward.

With both sides reappraised and briefed, on 24 August another new phase began, with the Luftwaffe bent on the destruction of Fighter Command's airfields in south-east England. Air Vice-Marshal Park faced repeated attacks by heavily escorted bombers on vital sector stations. Hornchurch sector station, north-east of London, was badly hit on 31 August, for example, as the station's diary describes:

Mass raids continued to be made against our aerodromes, again starting early in the morning. The first two attacks were delivered at 0830 and 1030 hours respectively and were directed at Biggin Hill, Eastchurch and Debden. The third attack was delivered at Hornchurch, but although our squadrons engaged, they were unable to break the enemy bomber formation, and so about 30 Dorniers dropped some 100 bombs across the airfield. Damage, however, was slight, although a bomb fell on the new Airmen's Mess, which had almost been completed. The only vital damage, however, was to a power cable, which was cut. The emergency power equipment was brought into operation until repair was effected. Three men were killed and eleven wounded. No 54 Squadron attempted to take off during the attack and ran through the bombs. Three aircraft were destroyed, one being blown from the middle of the landing field to outside the boundary, but all three pilots miraculously escaped with only slight injuries.

The diary of one of Hornchurch's Spitfire squadrons, 54, added that

a large formation of enemy bombers – a most impressive sight in vic formation at 15,000 feet – reached the aerodromes and dropped their bombs (probably sixty in all) in a line from our original dispersal pens to the petrol dump and beyond into Elm Park. Perimeter track, dispersal pens and barrack block windows suffered but no other damage to buildings was caused, and the aerodrome, in spite of its ploughed condition, remained serviceable. The Squadron was ordered off just as the first bombs were beginning to fall and eight of our machines safely cleared the ground; the remaining section, however, just became airborne as the bombs exploded. All three machines were wholly wrecked in the air, and the survival of the pilots is a complete miracle. Sergeant Davis, taking off towards the hangars was thrown back across the River Ingrebourne two fields away, scrambling out of his machine unharmed. Flight Lieutenant Deere had one wing and his prop torn off; climbing to about 100 feet, he turned over and, coming down, slid along the aerodrome for a hundred yards upside down. He was rescued from this unenviable position by Pilot Officer Edsall, the third member of the Section, who had suffered a similar fate except that he had landed the right way up. Dashing across the aerodrome with bombs still dropping, he extricated Deere from his machine. All three pilots were ready again for battle by the next morning.

The fourth attack of the day was also directed at Hornchurch, and, once again, despite strong fighter opposition and AA fire, the bombers penetrated our defences. This time, however, their aim was most inaccurate, and the line of bombs fell from then towards the edge of the aerodrome. Two Spitfires parked near the edge of the aerodrome were written off, and one airman was killed. Otherwise, apart from the damage to dispersal pens, the perimeter track and the aerodrome surface, the raid was abortive and the aerodrome remained serviceable. Our squadrons, which had a very heavy day, accounted for no less that nineteen of the enemy and a further seven probably destroyed. 603 Squadron alone were responsible for the destruction of fourteen enemy aircraft. Although we lost a total of nine aircraft, either in combat or on the ground, only one pilot was lost.

Between 24 August and nightfall on 6 September, Fighter Command lost 286 aircraft; five forward airfields and six sector stations were so badly damaged that Park feared another week of such attacks could be decisive. The Germans, however, had lost 380 machines, and replacement aircraft were not quickly coming. By early September, *Luftflotten* 2 and 3, the air fleets drawn up on the Channel coast, were weakened by combat losses. For the RAF, casualties had created the shortage of replacement pilots that Dowding had feared. Training units drastically cut courses, but pilots fresh from them typically had just ten hours' flying time on Spitfires or Hurricanes, and no air-to-air firing experience. The enemy, which had defeated the air forces of other countries in short order, learned to respect their opponent – and the Spitfire in particular. Twenty-two-year-old *Leutnant* Hans-Hellmuth Osterman flew Me 109s with JG 54 *Grunherz*, and, during a huge dogfight over London, saw a comrade pursued by a Spitfire:

At once I flung my machine around and went down after them. Now I was about 200 yards behind the 'Tommy'. Steady does it – wait. The range was much too far. I crept slowly nearer until I was only one hundred metres away, and the Spitfire's wings filled my gunsight. Suddenly the Tommy opened fire and the Me 109 in front of him went into a dive. I too had pressed the firing button, having taken careful aim. The Spit caught fire at once, and with a long grey plume of smoke dived vertically into the sea.

The Me 109, however, like the Spitfire and Hurricane, was designed and intended as a short-range defensive interceptor; it was not a long-range offensive or escort fighter, which roles it now fulfilled. Concerned with mounting bomber losses, Göring had inflexibly shackled the fighters to the close escort role, denying his *Jagdfliegern* the opportunity to hunt freely, which they deeply resented. As it was, the 109 only had sufficient fuel for ten minutes' combat over London, and jiggling throttles to keep pace with their slower charges exacerbated the situation. *Oberleutnant* von Hahn, of I/JG 3, reported that 'there are only a few of us who have not yet had to ditch in the Channel with a shot-up aircraft or a stationary airscrew'. Ostermann wrote that 'utter exhaustion from the English operations had set in. For the first time, I heard pilots talk of the prospect of posting to a quieter sector.' Indeed, a survivor, *Oberleutnant* Ulrich Steinhilper, of JG 52, more recently described *Kanalkrankheit* – 'Channel sickness' – the symptom of which was the feigning of mechanical failure so as not to join combat over England. It must be remembered that enemy aircrew had by now been in action for several months – and combat fatigue was inevitably taking its toll.

While enemy fighter pilots had to endure two sea-crossings and operate at the limit of their machines' endurance, Fighter Command enjoyed a distinct advantage in fighting over home ground. Essentially, while German aircrew who survived being shot down over England were out of the war, RAF pilots who baled out or forced-landed were reunited with their squadrons and could fly again. When the *Battle of Britain* film was made in 1969, one of the German historical advisers, General Adolf

Galland himself, was most anxious for one thing in particular not to be portrayed: the shooting by German pilots of defenceless RAF pilots descending by parachute. 'To the best of my knowledge,' he insisted, 'and that of all people I have asked who were involved, this has never happened.' A British consultant, Squadron Leader Ben Bowring, who had been a flight commander on 111 Squadron flying Hurricanes during the Battle of Britain, disagreed: 'One of my Polish officers called up that he was baling out. Almost immediately two *Messerschmitts* attacked him, when he was on his parachute.' The pilot to whom Bowing referred was Pilot Officer Janusz Macinski, who was shot down off Folkestone on 4 September 1940; the twenty-four-year-old Pole remains missing. There were other such incidents reported, so there is no doubt that General Galland was quite wrong in his insistence that this was untrue. There were, though, occasional glimpses of chivalry in the air. Wing Commander Bob Doe flew Spitfires with 234 Squadron in the summer of 1940:

> I suddenly saw a Messerschmitt going back towards France, a few hundred feet above the sea, so I set off after him. Eventually I got close enough, well out to sea, and started shooting, out of range at first, but I closed in. I hit him, he had to jettison his hood, his engine stopped. I thought 'That's it', and pulled alongside him to see what I'd been shooting at. I always remember this: the only occasion I actually saw the human enemy. He was a big blond man, wearing sky blue flying overalls; he just sat in the cockpit, turned round, looked at me, and went down and landed in the sea. I left him there, nothing I could do about it.

Although Doe was unable to do anything once the 109 crashed into the sea, he could easily have made sure of his kill by continuing to pour rounds into the disabled German fighter. On balance, it is likely that the enemy airman was *Oberleutnant*

Martin Trümpelmann of II/JG 27, who, in spite of the Spitfire pilot's mercy, was killed.

The 'home team' also had something else spurring them on: flying and fighting over and in defence of England. 'Sailor' Malan:

> Fear and intense physical danger and the discomfort of battle were more than compensated by the very positive feelings nearly all of us had of satisfaction at being the only human beings who were able to stand between Hitler and world freedom. We knew that any day we might be shot down to death, but I swear that this feeling of being the only spearhead, the only instrument between German domination and democracy was the one thing that kept us going and beat the Luftwaffe. It gave us an elation that far transcended all else.

'Fear,' wrote Polish Battle of Britain survivor Wing Commander Jurek Poplawski, 'was always there. We were all afraid, of course we were. The man who denies this is a liar. We lived our lives by a code, not to let our friends down, so we learned how to conquer and control our fear.'

The possibility of sudden and very violent death was, of course, the constant companion of all fighter pilots; Pilot Officer Richard Hillary: 'In a fighter plane, I believe, we have found a way to return to war as it ought to be, war which is individual combat between two people, kill or be killed. It's exciting, it's individual, and it's disinterested.' Group Captain Peter Townsend commanded 85 Squadron during the battle, and told me, 'We were not trying to kill the man. It was the machine that we were trying to destroy. That is not to say we had any qualms about killing Germans, we didn't, but the point is that we were trying to knock down their machines. We had no particular personal hatred for the German aircrews, although we naturally objected rather strongly to them bombing our country and people, but they, like us, had a job to do.'

Many pilots whose homelands were occupied by Nazi Germany, but who had escaped to fly with the RAF and fight another day, felt very differently, however. Poles, Czechs, Belgians and Free French were all represented in Fighter Command during the Battle of Britain. The Poles, in fact, had had a particularly hard time. Theirs was the first country to fall, after which many Polish airmen escaped and continued the fight with the French. After the Fall of France, they were on the run again, arriving in England by various means. These were all trained pilots that were sorely needed. The problem, though, was the language barrier. Some were converted to RAF fighter types and sent directly to RAF fighter squadrons. Other Poles and Czechs, being the greater number, served in squadrons specially formed of their fellow countrymen – excepting that there were British squadron and flight commanders. 303 (Polish) Squadron was formed at Northolt on 2 August 1940 to fly Hurricanes. On 30 August, 'B' Flight was engaged on a training flight with Blenheim bombers over St Albans when Sergeant Ludwik Paszkiewicz sighted a formation of raiders. While his five comrades remained with the Blenheims and escorted them to safety, Paszkiewicz was unable to contain himself, breaking formation to attack and destroy a Do 17. The following day, 303 Squadron was declared fully operational. They concluded the Battle of Britain with an unparalleled record: 126 enemy aircraft destroyed against the loss of 8 pilots killed. Although we now know that combat claims were exaggerated due to the confusion involved, this figure nonetheless confirms the ferocity with which 303 Squadron fell upon the enemy. Pilot Officer Tadeusz Nowierski flew Spitfires with the British 609 Squadron of the AAF; in his excellent first-hand account, *Spitfire Pilot*, Pilot Officer David Crook wrote of 'Novi' and an action fought near Southampton on 15 October 1940:

Novi was also attacked, but managed to shoot down another 109, which crashed near Bournemouth. When the machine was near the ground, the pilot got out and just managed to open his parachute in time, but landed very heavily and lay on the ground, probably winded by the fall. Novi circled round and said afterwards, in his rather broken English, 'I circle round, bloody German lies down, he is dead, OK. But I look again, he is now sitting up. No bloddy good!' He was very disappointed; in his opinion, the only good Germans are dead Germans.

It was actually, in effect, an international air force which opposed the Luftwaffe during the Battle of Britain. In addition to men like 'Novi' from the enemy occupied lands, Fighter Command also included pilots from the Commonwealth, and even eleven American volunteers.

Casualties were something else that Fighter Command's pilots had to learn to deal with. Sergeant Norman Ramsey, a Spitfire pilot, commented, 'People missing or killed at that stage of the battle meant little to me. I had joined 222 from 610 Squadron at Biggin Hill after we had lost ten – yes, ten – pilots, so I was well-used to the disappearing faces. Having been shot down myself, I had learned to survive, to gain the experience necessary for survival.' Another Spitfire pilot, Sergeant Bernard 'Jimmy' Jennings: 'Casualties? Well, when it came to that sort of thing, we just didn't talk about it much, didn't dwell on it. It was just a case of "Old so and so's copped it", and that was that.'

On the night of 24 August 1940, German bombers, bound for the aircraft factory at Rochester and oil refinery at Thames Haven, made a navigational error and accidentally bombed Central London. Churchill immediately ordered Bomber Command to mount reprisal raids against Berlin, and, over the next ten days, four such raids were made. Hitler was furious, and told the *Reichstag*, 'Since they attack our cities, we shall wipe theirs out.' On the afternoon of Saturday 7 September, Göring stood on the French cliffs at Cap Blanc Nez with *Generalfeldmarschall*

Kesselring and watched a massive formation of fighters and bombers droning overhead towards England. Fighter Command anxiously monitored this latest threat, naturally assuming sector airfields to be the target – fully aware that an attack on this unprecedented scale could deliver the telling blow. At 1617 hours, eleven RAF squadrons were scrambled, and by 1630 all twenty-one squadrons in the London area were airborne. East of Sheppey, the defenders intercepted the incoming raid – nearly 1,000 aircraft flying in a formation over a mile high and occupying some 800 square miles of airspace. The Germans fought their way up the Thames Estuary but did not, as anticipated, separate into smaller groups, bound for different airfields. It then became obvious to Air Vice-Marshal Park that his airfields were to be spared: the target was London. Soon, hundreds of bombs were falling on the docklands east of Tower Bridge. As this new fire of London later illuminated the night sky, the raiders returned in a round-the-clock and incessant stream. When the guns at last fell silent, 1,800 Londoners were dead. In failing to direct such a substantial force against 11 Group's sector stations, Göring had, however, made a tactical error that would ultimately cost him victory. Moreover, his belief that London was the only target likely to force Dowding to commit all of his fighters to battle, for destruction en masse, was, in the event, unfounded. That night, Air Vice-Marshal Park looked out over London: 'It was burning all down the river. It was a horrid sight. But I looked down and said, "Thank God for that", because I knew that the Nazis had switched their attack from our fighter stations, thinking that they were knocked out; they weren't, but they were pretty groggy.' The critical 'Battle of the Airfields' was now over.

German bombers returned to London on 9, 11 and 14 September, on which latter date Hitler, having been advised by his staff that aerial superiority had yet to be won, postponed *Seelöwe* until 17 September. With this in mind, Göring and Kesselring launched what proved to be their final maximum effort to gain a decision in daylight over London on Sunday 15 September. Dawn on that day found southern England shrouded in mist, which evaporated as the sun climbed higher. By 0800 hours, visibility was excellent. Before 1100, German reconnaissance aircraft had probed the Straits of Dover and east coast of Kent. From first light onwards, standing patrols of Spitfires and Hurricanes were up from Harwich to Land's End. At 1050, radar detected German formations assembling over the Pas-de-Calais, south-east of Boulogne, and five minutes later every squadron in 11 Group was brought to readiness. At 1133, the first enemy formation crossed the Kentish coast between Dover and Folkestone, followed three minutes later by two more hostile plots incoming between Dover and South Foreland. This time, the raiders' targets were London's gasworks and other industrial objectives. Twenty of Park's squadrons were scrambled, reinforced at midday by 12 Group's so-called 'Big Wing' of five squadrons, led by the legless Squadron Leader Douglas Bader – the arrival of whose sixty Spitfires and Hurricanes over London dealt a crushing blow to the morale of enemy airmen. Such was the ferocity of Fighter Command's attack on the one hundred Do 17s of KG 76 that the formation was broken up before reaching their target. Two random bombs, however, fell on Buckingham Palace – placing the popular king and queen, who had refused to leave the capital, firmly in Britain's frontline alongside humble East Enders.

Hardly had the first mass attack been dispersed, though, before radar detected further enemy formations assembling over France. Between 1410 and 1434 hours, eight or more German formations approached London. Visiting 'The Hole' at Uxbridge, Churchill enquired of Air Vice-Marshal Park what reserves he had available: 'None, sir,' the New Zealander replied. Churchill himself later wrote, 'The odds were great; our margins small; the stakes infinite.' Thirty-one RAF squadrons, in fact, were committed to battle over London that afternoon. Among them was Squadron Leader Brian

Lane DFC, the twenty-three-year-old Commanding Officer (CO) of 19 Squadron; in his personal combat report, he later recorded the number of enemy aircraft engaged as 'infinite'. Having lit fires in Woolwich, Barking, Stepney, Stratford, West Ham and Penge, the Luftwaffe withdrew, constantly harried by Spitfires and Hurricanes. Further west, twenty-seven He 111s attacked naval installations at Portland, but were seen off by just six Spitfires. Six RAF squadrons and accurate anti-aircraft fire then thwarted an intended raid on Supermarine's all-important Spitfire factory at Woolston. That unsuccessful enemy foray, in fact, marked the end of fighting on what has gone down in history as 'Battle of Britain Day'.

On the great day, Fighter Command claimed the destruction of 158 German aircraft. At the time, the newspapers reported these statistics along the lines of a sporting contest: 'RAF still batting.' Such claims were also accepted with little cross-reference, thereby providing a distorted view. We now know, for example, that the actual figure on this most significant day was closer to fifty-eight enemy machines destroyed. Nevertheless, Fighter Command had only lost twenty-eight fighters – and the day's events confirmed beyond question that the Luftwaffe was nowhere even close to achieving its mission. Two days later, instead of launching *Seelöwe*, Hitler postponed it – indefinitely. Arguably, therefore, 15 September represented the battle's climax – and 17 September the conclusion. The Air Ministry, however, decided that the Battle of Britain did not end until 31 October 1940 – which has been the subject of debate ever since. We also know now that on 27 September, Hitler ordered that preparations should be made for the invasion of Russia. Eastward expansion, in fact, had always been Hitler's real war aim. The opportunity to invade Britain had been unexpected. Hitler expected Britain to sue for peace, but when it did not, with Germany riding high on the tide of victory, invasion appeared a possibility. Ultimately, the Germans were denied that opportunity by Fighter Command – and the English Channel. From Hitler's perspective, continuing to pursue this objective was pointless, because as a small island Britain had not the natural resources or living space required by his Nazi empire. Alone, without essential American military support, Britain was not in a position to continue any significant resistance – so could be left, isolated, without undue risk, whilst Russia, the infinitely greater prize, was conquered; Britain, therefore, could be dealt with later. Nonetheless, although *Seelöwe* was called off, offensive air operations against England did not cease when the *Führer* turned his attentions eastward.

By September 30, the German bomber force was unable to continue suffering such heavy casualties, and switched to attacking British cities at night. By then, a small number of Me 109s had been turned into fighter-bombers, meaning that daylight fighter sweeps could not be ignored, because Controllers could never be certain as to whether these formations included such aircraft. Consequently, Fighter Command found itself mounting standing patrols, dawn to dusk – this was another exhausting period. Enemy air attacks by day now focussed on targets connected with the British aircraft industry. There were several notable successes, most notably the virtual destruction of the Supermarine factory at Woolston on 26 September, which brought Spitfire production there to a standstill – but this was far too late in the day.

Although, as previously explained, it was decided that 31 October 1940 represented the Battle of Britain's official conclusion, German bombers, continued to pound Britain by night until May 1941, and the fighters of both sides clashed until the weather finally brought the 'season' to a natural end in February 1941. Wing Commander Hubert 'Dizzy' Allen DFC, a Spitfire pilot during the Battle of Britain, recognised that there was no clear-cut victory or defeat of the Luftwaffe, which remained an effective fighting force. In his 1975 book *Who Won the Battle of Britain?*, Allen levelled scathing criticism at the Air Staff and was first to argue that the Royal Navy was actually the real deterrent. Others have advanced these arguments, tirelessly debating the points, but the fact remains that, because of Fighter Command, Britain remained in the war. Quite simply, the Battle of Britain was a contest for control of the air over south-east England, and the Germans were denied. This, surely, is evidence enough that they *lost*. The outcome was also important psychologically, because hitherto Hitler's war machine had been unstoppable. The Battle of Britain, then, was Nazi Germany's first reversal – its first defeat, although not necessarily in the traditionally accepted military sense. This crucial British *victory*, unexpected across the Atlantic, marked a new level of American commitment and closer support of the war effort. Roosevelt was broadly supportive, and after his election as president pursued his policy of assisting Churchill through the Lend-Lease Bill – which solved the problem of Britain's inability to pay for war materials by providing the president power to transfer American war materiel to a foreign power. On 22 June 1941, Hitler finally invaded Russia; on 7 December 1941, the Japanese made a devastating surprise air attack on the American Pacific fleet at Pearl Harbor. That night, Churchill wrote of how he had been 'saturated and satiated with emotion and sensation, I went to bed and slept the sleep of the saved and thankful'. On 11 December 1941, Hitler, already fighting on two fronts, sealed the fate of Nazi Germany: the Führer declared war on the United States of America. Without the Battle of Britain, in a sense, none of this would have mattered, certainly not to a Britain enslaved as part of a racist Nazi empire.

Ultimately, America poured men and material into Britain, from where, on 6 June 1944, the Allies launched the liberation of occupied Europe. With the Russians in Berlin, in April 1945, Adolf Hitler committed suicide in his underground bunker. On 8 May, Germany surrendered – unconditionally. In the Far East, the war against Japan continued until the Emperor too surrendered unconditionally – by which time the United States had avenged the ignominy of Pearl Harbor by dropping atomic bombs on

Hiroshima and Nagasaki. During the war, Britain suffered 300,000 dead, including 60,000 civilians; 292,000 Americans made the ultimate sacrifice; how many Russians died is unknown, but is reportedly in excess of 20 million. As it celebrated total victory in Berlin, the Red Army brought with it years of Soviet domination and Communism to Eastern Europe, which remained until the Iron Curtain fell in 1989. Britain emerged into Churchill's 'broad sunlit uplands' victorious – but bankrupt. No longer, however, would America isolate itself from European affairs – it would dominate them, through the North Atlantic Treaty Organisation (NATO), and, indeed, the international stage. America was richer in 1945 than when Japanese bombs rained down on Pearl Harbor less than four years before; war had arguably achieved financially what the so-called 'New Deal' had not. There can be no doubt, therefore, that the events of 1940 shaped the world in which we live today – our democratic way of life preserved due in no small part to Fighter Command's victory during the Battle of Britain. The crucial significance of that fateful summer, simply put, cannot be ignored or underestimated – and nor should those who fought out that great contest for freedom be forgotten.

Nearly 3,000 aircrew of Fighter Command were combatants during the Battle of Britain. Of them, 544 lost their lives during the Battle; 791 more would perish before the war was won. After the war, various campaign and other medals were struck, to recognise an individual's service. In 1944, Sir Ronald Boss, Londonderry's Unionist MP, had argued that Churchill's 'Few' – given their 'signal victory over Germany' – should be specially recognised. In May 1945, news was released of various medals to mark an individual's service and contribution to the war effort, including the 1939–45 Star. Acknowledging the validity of Boss's argument, it was agreed that Battle of Britain veterans would be afforded the special honour of adding the 'Battle of Britain Clasp' to their Star. The only problem was that no definitive list existed of who they were. Applicants applied to their COs, who were instructed only to approve claims not open to any doubt. There had, however, been various reunions of veterans since 1945, and in 1958, the Battle of Britain Fighter Association was founded – membership of which remains open only to the Few themselves. The first Chairman, Air Commodore Charles Widows, CO of 29 Squadron during the Battle of Britain, stated that the new Association's objectives were to ensure the welfare of members, preserve the memory of those comrades who had died in the Battle of Britain, to extend, via the Association, the spirit of comradeship experienced in summer 1940, and represent the Association at various functions and services. The Association's first newsletter reported good news: Lord Dowding of Bentley Priory had agreed to be President, and Air Vice-Marshal Sir Keith Park Life Vice-President.

The Association's records owed much to the work of Flight Lieutenant John Holloway, who had been a wireless fitter with 615 (Hurricane) Squadron during the Battle of Britain. When the film of Paul Brickhill's best-seller concerning Douglas Bader's inspirational story, *Reach for the Sky*, was made, Holloway was still serving in the RAF, at Kenley – where some scenes were shot – and began collecting the autographs of visiting Battle of Britain survivors. Indeed, this became an obsession, as Holloway painstakingly researched a list of combatants. In 1960, the Air Ministry clarified the necessary qualification to wear the Battle of Britain Clasp: the applicant must have flown at least one operational patrol between 10 July and 31 October 1940, with one of the sixty-nine units under Fighter Command's orders (two Fleet Air Arm units being added to that number in 1961). Applications to wear the Clasp, or see it awarded posthumously to a loved one, are still made today. After Holloway's death, the Association, working alongside the Ministry of Defence's Air Historical Branch, took the lead in verifying these and continuing Holloway's efforts to produce a definitive list of combatants.

The following chapters concern the stories and recollections of some of 'The Final Few', the last of the survivors. It is important to appreciate from the outset, however, that none of these men conform to the handlebar-moustachioed, devil-may-care fighter pilot of popular culture. Moreover, the important thing was not individual, glory-hunting aces but teamwork. The most famous pilot, even today, of course, was the legless Douglas Bader, a household name during and after the Second World War. Although Bader demonstrably enjoyed more than his fair share of personal publicity, it is noteworthy that he commented thus:

> The Battle of Britain was won not by Malan, Stanford-Tuck and me, who got all the accolades. It was won by kids of nineteen or twenty, who maybe shot down nothing, or just one, before being killed themselves. They were the blokes who really won the Battle of Britain, make no mistake there. They were determined, by going off to fight and being prepared to die if necessary.

Indeed, writing in 1969, Lord Dowding, as the great man became, wrote,

> I do not think that one should consider what happened in the battle in terms of individuals and personalities. It is more fitting to think of us as a team – men and women, aircrews and ground crews, and operations and staff at all levels – in which everyone played an integral part. But for all the warmth of my feeling for those with whom I was associated in the fighting of the battle, I think that we should remember, with a very special esteem, those who did the actual fighting: the aircrews.

In that assessment, Lord Dowding was surely right – and the tenacity of 'Dowding's Chicks' was never doubted by their enemy. Indeed, Fighter Command Intelligence Summary 182, concerning the interrogation of a captured Me 110 pilot of ZG 76, includes the German's opinion that his RAF foes fought with '*kolossalen Verbissenheit*' (tremendous stubbornness). *Oberleutnant* Julius Neumann of II/JG 27, who was shot down by Spitfires and forced-landed on the Isle of Wight on 18 August 1940, later acknowledged this: 'We had the highest respect for the British fighter pilots. They were well trained and knew what they were fighting for.'

If ever today or in the future a point of reference is required to confirm exactly what was at stake during the Second World War, this is amply provided by the following extract from a speech made in 1942, by Walter Darre, Hitler's Minister of Agriculture:

> As soon as we beat England, we shall make an example of you Englishmen, once and for all. Able-bodied men and women will be exported as slaves to the Continent; the old and weak will be exterminated. All men remaining in Britain as slaves will be sterilised. A million or two of the young women of the Nordic type will be segregated in a number of stud farms where, with the assistance of picked German sires, during a period of ten or twelve years, they will produce annually a series of Nordic infants to be raised in every way German. These infants will form the future population of Britain. Thus, in a generation or two, the British will disappear.

Thanks to the RAF fighter pilots whose stories are recounted in this book, Darre's evil designs remained nothing but hot air – as was so much Nazi rhetoric. His speech does, however, provide a chilling glimpse of what would have happened to Britain had Dowding's young aircrews faltered or failed – and underlines the debt we owe.

All of the foregoing provides the essential background to accurately contextualise the following RAF Battle of Britain fighter pilots' accounts. These are not simply tales of derring-do, but important historical documents, windows through which we can still reach out and touch the summer of 1940 – provided by members of Dowding's home team.

I

WING COMMANDER P. L. PARROTT
DFC* AFC

Peter Lawrence Parrott was born at Aylesbury on 28 June 1920. In March 1938, he successfully applied for an SSC, and reported for duty at 1 EFTS, at De Havilland's, Hatfield, on 26 June that year. There he flew Tiger Moths, gaining his 'A' Licence (the equivalent of a Private Pilot Licence today). 21 August 1938 saw Acting Pilot Officer (on probation) Parrott at 1 RAF Depot, Uxbridge, 'drill training, kitting out, issue of uniform, books and flying clothing'. The following month he successfully completed flying training at 11 FTS, Shawbury, where 'advanced flying included fixed-gun firing at air-to-air and air-to-ground targets, flying the Hawker Fury'. On 30 March 1939, Pilot Officer Parrott was towing drogues for 1 Armament Training School (ATS), while trainee Bomber Command air gunners blasted away. More target-towing followed at Manby, until, on 28 December 1939, he was posted to 11 Group Fighter Pool, St Athan, for 'Hurricane fighter training'. Having successfully converted to the Hawker Hurricane, on 28 January 1940, Peter joined 607 'County of Durham' Squadron of the AAF, at Vitry-en-Artois, near Arras and Douai, in northern France:

On 10 May 1940, the real war started at about 0415 hours – when He 111s streamed over the airfield returning to base after bombing the British Army and RAF HQ at and around Arras. After a hectic seven days, there were far too many pilots, including reinforcements, for the amount of Hurricanes still serviceable; the previous evening, on 16 May, the Germans were reportedly just thirty miles away.

What Peter, typically, fails to mention is that on 10 May he was credited with the destruction of two He 111s and two probables, and on 13 May safely returned his shot-up Hurricane to base after being bounced by 109s over Louvain.

On 17 May, I had been granted a rest day, but was awoken by Pilot Officer Peter Dixon, telling me that he and I were going on leave, and that an Air Transport Auxiliary (ATA) Avro Ensign was waiting to take us back to England – but didn't intend hanging around for very long. We started with a low-level cross-country flight to the Channel, where the captain felt brave enough to climb from 500 feet to 2,000 feet, before arriving at Hendon. This flight was, in fact, a very risky one. The ATA lost five out of their seven ex-Imperial Airways Ensigns in France (there were half-a-dozen pilots from other squadrons also aboard).

We had not been given time to pack our kit, so I arrived back in England with just an overnight bag, which was barely adequate for a weekend; I never saw my kit again. I still feel resentful that I lost £64 of clothes, but the Air Ministry allowed me only £24; £3 per month to Burberry's went on for a long time thereafter! The Station Adjutant at Hendon rang the Air Ministry and the Staff Officer who answered told him to give us ten days leave. I was staying with family when, on Sunday morning, 19 May, I received a telegram ordering me to report to 145 Squadron at Tangmere – immediately. In fact, I arrived on Monday 20 May. The following day I was busy getting a new helmet, parachute, Irvin flying suit, flying boots etc.

I was glad to find that Peter Dixon, who had been a good friend in 607, was also posted to 145, although he was in 'A' Flight, commanded by Roy Dutton, and I was in 'B', led by Adrian Boyd (known to all as 'Boydy').

Our squadron CO was 'Dusty' Miller. He had formed the squadron in October 1939, firstly equipped with Blenheims, but in spring 1940 converted to Hurricanes. He was older by some years than his flight commanders, let alone we young, nineteen-, twenty- and twenty-one-year-old, junior pilots. He had led the squadron on a couple of sweeps over northern France, but had not pleased the flight commanders, who persuaded him not to do so any more. Before the war, squadron commanders had been administrators rather than operational, flying, leaders, and were not then expected to lead their squadrons in the air, or even fly at all, which was their choice. Our Squadron Leader Miller was of that ilk. In effect, therefore, our flight commanders grounded the CO, who shortly afterwards was promoted and posted to Jersey as a Wing Commander.

145 Squadron was dispersed on the south-west side of Tangmere sector station. Each flight had two Nissen huts, one for the pilots, the other for 'Chiefy' and his ground crews. To the east of us was 601 Squadron, with similar accommodation. Most of the pilots had been with the squadron from its formation, so knew each other well. They had all flown sweeps over France and had combat experience. Apart from the flight commanders, we were all pilot officers or NCOs, and got on well together.

I did my first operation with 145 Squadron on 22 May, a sweep of the Arras/Bethune area, and recorded further patrols over France on 23 and 24. On 26, we were patrolling near Dunkirk, where the evacuation was in full swing. Roy Dutton, who was leading, spotted a possible bandit, and led the squadron to the west and down towards it. I was flying as No 2, in the rearmost vic of three, and saw another possible bandit flying to the north of Dunkirk. I called on the radio but got no response, so went ahead of my Section Leader and rocked my wings. I was hoping he would follow me as I peeled off to the north – but he didn't. I gave chase to the 'possible', which I soon identified as a He III. I closed to firing range and loosed off several bursts, and hit his port engine, which emitted a thick trail of black smoke, his starboard undercarriage extended. Suddenly, I found myself in thick fog, engulfing my cockpit. I could only see one instrument, the oil pressure gauge in the top right corner of my instrument panel. The Heinkel's rear gunner had obviously hit my radiator. I had limited, misty, vision through the windscreen. I broke off and turned 180°, heading for England, home and security. The fog continued, but opening the canopy failed to disperse it. I was half way across the Channel, when the rest of the squadron joined me, having seen the white plume I was trailing behind. I had no idea how long the engine would run, but decided to keep going and ditch when it stopped. I was at 4,000 feet and Roy kept me on course. The fog finally cleared, but the engine, surprisingly, continued running for a few seconds – then stopped dead as I crossed the beach at Deal; I made a wheels-up landing on the Downs, about a mile-and-a-half from the shore.

The time was about 8 p.m. on a cloudless, warm, summer evening. There were quite a number of people out for a Sunday evening stroll, but no one approached me. I was in the middle of a large field with footpaths on either side, and was thinking of walking to a house about a third of a mile away, for help. Then I saw the local bobby approaching on his bicycle, so explained my presence to him. I was just asking said PC to guard the aircraft while I went to telephone Manston for help, when we saw the farmer approaching in his horse and trap. Unfortunately, the Hurricane's wings had killed two sheep. The farmer's words to me were, 'Who's going to pay for them sheep?' I responded that the Air Ministry would, at which he about-turned and went back to his nearby house. I then asked the constable where the nearest telephone was: the farmer's house! He did allow me to use his phone, but not to share a very handsome ham salad supper. I spent the night at Manston, and Michael Adderley, who had been a fellow pupil at FTS, flew me back to Tangmere in a Tiger Moth being used for radio control of aircraft experiments.

We continued patrolling over Dunkirk – and casualties mounted. On 27 May, three pilots went missing; they had, in fact, been killed in action on their first patrol. Three more, Forde, Wakenham and Ashton, were also shot down but returned by sea. On 31 May, my friend Peter Dixon was killed. In all, we lost four pilots and eight Hurricanes. We flew patrols on 1, 2 and 3 June, over Dunkirk, then south along the French coast and over the Channel ports. By then, we were down to only seven serviceable Hurricanes, although we still had fourteen pilots; on at least two occasions, we made up a composite squadron with 601. These final patrols were partly, I think, to see if there were any further soldiers requiring rescue; the Luftwaffe did not show up at all. We continued this uneventful patrolling until at least 15 June. On 17 June, we were ordered to Warmwell, to provide escort to France for Churchill, but the trip was cancelled. Shortly afterwards, France surrendered.

We then started a period of comparative ease, my log book showing flights training replacement pilots. In the past three weeks, we had become a close-knit flight. We now had our camp-kits at Dispersal, and, in the fine weather, enjoyed sleeping in the open air. The squadron worked at readiness roster of twenty-four hours. Readiness was at five, fifteen and thirty minutes. The latter period allowed us time to return to the Mess for a bath, change of clothing, and, if lucky, a meal – which were otherwise brought to Dispersal in hay boxes. We were now up to twenty pilots in the squadron, so could take it in turns to have a day off. We were then transferred to the Tangmere satellite at Westhampnett. Again the flights were dispersed, well apart, with just one Nissen hut each. Again we used our camp-kits. The Mess was a marquee, where we met for meals, which at first were brought over from Tangmere, again in hay boxes. We knew that the big air battle was yet to come and that this would doubtless be accompanied by an attempt by the Germans to invade.

Such, then, was Peter's experience and that of 145 Squadron when the Battle of Britain officially began on 10 July 1940. At lunchtime on 18 July, 'B' Flight was ordered to patrol base at 10,000 feet, then told to make 'Vector 240°, Angels 10'. Fifteen miles south of Selsey Bill, Blue Section sighted and attached a He 111. Pilot Officer Parrott reported,

> I led Green Section below the cloud, which was at 600 feet. The E/A dived below cloud and I went into a beam attack; No. 2 came in on a beam attack on my right. As I broke away, I saw the E/A dive into the sea and break up. There were two survivors, one of whom sank almost immediately. I gave Control a 'fix' on the remaining survivor, who was still swimming when we returned to base. No return fire was observed when he came below cloud, although two of Blue Section were hit by enemy machine gun.

The raider belonged to *Stab*/KG 27; three crewmen were killed, including the *Geschwaderkommodore*, *Oberst* Georgi.

On 8 August, Convoy PEEWIT attempted to steam through the Dover Strait, provoking a massive air attack by *Luftlotte 3*. Pilot Officer Parrott was up, flying as Yellow Two:

> At about 0830 hours I saw about seventy enemy aircraft approaching the Needles from the south. Yellow 1 led the Section into the sun and I delivered an astern attack in company with Yellow 1 on two Ju 87s. After two short bursts I broke away, as I saw there were enemy fighters in the vicinity. I climbed up. As I was climbing, an Me 109 passed in front of me, about 100 yards away. I followed him round and gave him a full deflection burst of about two seconds. He then

pulled up in a steep climb and fell away in a spin, with a little smoke coming out of his engine. My windscreen was then oiled up by oil from my airscrew, and I saw three Me 109s coming down on my tail. I therefore broke away and dived into cloud, as I could not see anything through my windscreen.

That afternoon, the battle for PEEWIT still raging, Peter was in action again, against 'large numbers' of enemy aircraft:

We were ordered to patrol Swanage at 15,000 feet, at 1600 hours. I was flying No 2 in Yellow Section. When over the Needles a large number of E/A were seen dive-bombing the convoy. Yellow 1 led the Section to attack two Me 109s. I broke away and found a Ju 87 pulling out of its dive, after bombing. I attacked E/A from beam and he immediately turned-tail and headed north. I continued to attack from astern, and E/A finally crash-landed in a field on the edge of the sea, about two miles west of St Catherine's Point. The pilot appeared to be alright, and the aircraft, which struck a tree at the end of its landing run, did not appear badly damaged.

This was a *Stuka* of 4/St 77, which the pilot, *Unteroffizier* F. Pittrof, forced-landed at St Lawrence, on the Isle of Wight; his gunner, *Unteroffizier* R. Schubert, was killed.

On that day, 145 Squadron claimed twenty-one enemy aircraft destroyed, and more possibly destroyed or damaged (although German records confirm that only seventeen were destroyed in total). We lost five pilots, among whom was Dickie Shuttleworth. He had been with us for some days, when I went over to Tangmere to collect our mail. One of the letters for him was marked from the House of Lords – and that was the first time any of us realised that he was a peer of the realm.

Following PEEWIT, we were given a day off. I did not fly on 10

August, but we were on readiness. On 11 and 12, we engaged raids on Portsmouth and Portland, in which we lost another five pilots killed and the CO wounded.

Again, what Peter omits to mention is that he made combat claims on both occasions. Immediately after the engagement on 11 August, Pilot Officer Parrott made out the following report:

At 0935 hours we were ordered to patrol base at 15,000 feet. I was flying No 2 in Yellow Section. As soon as we were off the ground we were ordered to patrol Beachy Head, at 15,000 feet. At Beachy Head we were ordered to patrol Bembridge. We saw a large number of Me 110s east of us and above. We climbed, and as we were going into attack, four Me 110s passed above us on our right, obviously trying to get on our tails. I broke away too steeply and spun. I pulled out and saw the E/A directly above me in a circle. I climbed to attack, and put a short burst into each one as I passed. I got onto the tail of the last one and fired a long burst without doing any visible damage. Three more E/A then got on my tail, and although I carried out violent evasive action, the only way I could get away was by spinning. I pulled out at about 10,000 feet, and although I tried to get back into the fight, was prevented from doing so by several enemy fighters. Knowing that I then had little ammunition left, I returned to base and landed at 1055 hours.

Of the action on 12 August, Pilot Officer Parrott reported,

At 1210 hours we were ordered to patrol Selsey Bill to Bembridge. I was flying Red 3. E/A were sighted, as soon as we took off, over Portsmouth, going south. We went into line astern, and I saw a Ju 88 break away from the main formation, being attacked by a Spitfire, which broke away and went home. The E/A appeared to be undamaged, but the rear-gunner was not firing. I delivered my attack after which E/A lost height and speed. E/A finally crashed into the sea about fifteen – twenty miles south of Selsey Bill. There were two survivors, but there was very little chance of them being picked up. As I was returning I saw a British pilot fall into the sea by parachute. I circled him and repeatedly dived on him. I led a minesweeper to him, and saw him picked up about a mile east of the Nab lighthouse. I then returned to base and landed at 1250 hours.

The Ju 88 destroyed was a machine of II/KG 51, the crew of which remain missing. There were no RAF fighter pilots recovered from the sea in this area that day, so it is likely that the airman seen picked up was actually a German airman.

By now, 145 Squadron consisted of ten Hurricanes and ten pilots available ('A' Flight: four, 'B' Flight: six). One of the pilots was Nigel Weir, who had a minor wound and sported a conspicuous white bandage around his head. On 13 August, we were stood down and prepared to move to Drem the following day. That afternoon, we were relieved by 602 (Spitfire) Squadron. Our feelings at being withdrawn were obviously relief, and some regret and sadness for those who had not survived – although we expected to be back south again soon, as soon as we had re-equipped and received replacement pilots. The ground crews were also due for a rest. Apart from the slight lull in late June to early July, they had been working day and night to carry out the re-arming and refuelling under considerable pressure. The ground crew establishment had not foreseen the number of hours flying, with a servicing requirement for the Hurricanes every ten, twenty-five, fifty and one hundred hours. The more hours flown, the greater the maintenance required, of course. They also had damaged and defective aircraft to see to, and the job of re-arming and refuelling in between seven – fifteen minutes, two, three, or sometimes four times a day. 'Chiefy' Bannister will always be remembered for his high standards, and for his care for his crew.

During our time at Drem I was only scrambled twice, and recalled almost immediately I was airborne. The only other flight I recalled was a night-flight by Boydy; it was rumoured that he had shot down a He 111, but he never talked about it. [This was true: on the night of 23 August 1940, Flight Lieutenant Adrian Boyd destroyed a *Heinkel* over Edinburgh.] On 26 September, Boydy called us together, saying that we had been asked for four experienced pilots to go as replacements to squadrons in the south. Jas Storrar, Derek Force and myself were the only experienced pilots in 'B' Flight, and Bobby Yule in 'A'. That night we were all on the 'sleeper' to London. Forde and I went to 605 Squadron at Croydon, Storrar to 73 Squadron. I was sorry to leave 145 Squadron, where I had made so many good friends.

Arriving at Croydon on 27 September, we found that 605 Squadron had taken over several abandoned semi-detached houses, all devoid of furniture. They were on the west side of the airfield, on Forest Drive, and the Hurricanes were dispersed on the other side of the hedge at the bottom of the houses' gardens. The CO was Walter Churchill, but he was in the process of handing over to Archie McKellar. I joined 'B' Flight, commanded by Jock Muirhead. At this time, the Luftwaffe was sending over Me 109s at very high altitudes, 25,000 feet and even higher. Some of these carried bombs, and were escorted by more 109s up to 33,000 feet. In an effort to meet this threat, Air Vice-Marshal Park insisted that Hurricane squadrons must climb to 25,000 feet in twenty-one minutes. That was rather optimistic: we managed that but once, and only then because we had thermals. On take-off, on the south-east edge of London, 605 had to divert away from the capital, either west or south, to climb and so as not to arrive beneath the 109s. Some local residents, however, wrote to the press, accusing us of avoiding the enemy, simply because we took off in the opposite direction.

By October 1940, Peter was a flying officer – and 'an experienced chap'. On 22 October, the *London Gazette* carried the following announcement: among those pilots awarded the Distinguished Flying Cross was Flying Officer Peter Lawrence Parrott. The citation read, 'This officer has been continually engaged in operational flights against the enemy since January 1940. He has displayed great determination and keenness, and has destroyed at least six hostile aircraft.' There is no doubt whatsoever that this was a most well-deserved award indeed.

Although the Battle of Britain concluded for official purposes on 31 October 1940, there was no abrupt end to the fighting (as suggested by the 1969 film *Battle of Britain*). Certainly the German daylight bomber offensive had been defeated (although the enemy now bombed by night with virtual impunity), and Hitler's plans to invade England long since abandoned, but the fighter forces in particular continued to clash over south-east England.

On 1 November, we attacked a number of He 111s over Kent. Archie MacKellar was shot down, our casualty since I joined the squadron. 'Bunny' Currant was made acting CO, by which time I was a Section Leader.

We were not using weavers, so Bunny introduced one. I expected the job to be shared, but found myself in an unpleasant permanent slot. As one flew from side to side behind the squadron, the weaver was using more fuel than those in the main formation.

Towards the end of November, both flight commanders and the CO were grounded for medical reasons. Gerry Edge, by then commanding 605 Squadron, called me up and told me that I was to lead 605 on the next scramble or patrol. I was by no means happy about this, but the CO had put his trust in me, which was a considerable compliment. That flight was a climb to 25,000 feet, over the Kent area. Upon arrival there, I saw half-a-dozen Me 109s about three miles to the south, flying westerly at the same height. I turned, making it very wide, as I knew we were near stalling speed. Looking over my right shoulder I saw one Hurricane descending, over my left shoulder there were two of my squadron, trying to turn too tightly, and descending. Back to weaving!

The high altitudes caused some unpleasant and dangerous possibilities. Firstly, we were breathing oxygen, through a mask. These early masks were not tight-fitting on the face, meaning much oxygen was lost, and there was no gauge to show the amount of gas remaining; some deaths, in fact, were ascribed to lack of oxygen. When breathing pure oxygen at high altitudes, the "bends" can occur in some joints – in my case, elbows and fingers. At 30,000 feet, the temperature can be minus 30° or less, so there is the possibility of frostbite. I therefore flew with eight layers of clothing: vest and pants, shirt, woollen (long-sleeved) pullover, sheepskin waistcoat, uniform tunic, Sidcot lining, sheepskin trousers and jacket, two pairs of socks, three pairs of gloves: silk, Cape leather, and gauntlets.

For 605 Squadron, Sunday 1 December 1940 proved to be, according to the unit's Operations Record Book,

A really bad day, on which everything seemed to go wrong, beginning early in the morning. The squadron had to leave the aircraft at Kenley yesterday evening, owing to fog at Croydon. We were at dawn readiness (0805 hours), so they had to leave here at 0730 hours, and which they duly did. Owing to the fact that there was some technical hitch with the starter batteries over there, we were not reported at readiness until 0825 hours. This called forth a strong rebuke from Group, which was most depressing. Ops "B" had failed to report the reason why the squadron was not at readiness at the right time, and later an apology was received from Group. There was a hard frost last night, and while taxying for take-off to Croydon, three tail-wheels were broken.

That morning, 605 Squadron was ultimately required to patrol with 253 Squadron at 27,000 feet over Canterbury; Peter remembered,

I was still the weaver, above and behind the squadron. When the squadron levelled out at 25,000 feet a few miles north of Brighton, the Controller ordered a turn east. As I turned south of the squadron, I lost some distance and was behind them. The Controller had reported that the nearest bandits were twenty miles east of us. I straightened out, to catch up, and almost immediately saw tracer passing me, and then the clatter of bullets hitting my Hurricane – something I had previously experienced in France. The aircraft was shuddering, and I immediately pulled over into a spiral dive, levelling out at 3,000 feet. My attacker had not followed me down. I was over open country, so looked for a field to land in. I opened the throttle only to get a flash of flame from the starboard cowling. At this point I pushed the hood open, undid the safety belt, stood up in the cockpit and blown flat on my back, onto the hood. I seemed to be stuck, then realised that I had not disconnected the oxygen and radio lead. I managed to pull both free. I was still travelling at around 180 mph. Almost immediately I slid along the top of the fuselage and hit the tail-fin with an almighty thump on my right shoulder, bouncing off, free of the aircraft. I was spread-eagled when I tried to pull the 'D' ring with my right hand. My right arm refused to move, so I hastily shoved with my left thumb. I had time to think that the parachute was not going to open. Suddenly it did and I swung three times – then was on the ground. I just lay in the grass. It was a cold, frosty, Sunday morning, cloudless except some ground mist; not a sound. Then I heard steps swishing through the grass. When they stopped, I opened my eyes to see a Mr Blunt, the farm labourer. Having assured him as to my nationality and condition, he told me that they had 'had one of them Germans down here last week'. Then he said that he thought I had left it too long that time – I'd also had the same thought before him! I'd landed heavily on my right leg, had already damaged my shoulder and broke my collar bone when hitting the fin. I had also severed a nerve in my arm, which numbed the right biceps. The result was that my right arm was too weak to operate the undercarriage and flaps levers, so I was unable to resume flying Hurricanes until January 1941.

The Hurricane involved was Z2323, the fourth Mk II off the production line, but there was a mystery regarding who had shot me down. The tracer bullets but no cannon rounds suggested that one of the (machine-gun only armed) RAF fighters had made a mistake. I never did discover, though, who had shot me down, friend or foe.

What we now know and accept as an understandable occurrence in war as 'friendly fire' was not uncommon either in fighter combat – which, given the speeds and suddenness involved, is unsurprising. Various incidents have come to light, in fact, whereby pilots were shot down by their own side, due to either confusion or incorrect aircraft recognition in the heat of the moment. During this particular action, 605 Squadron's Sergeant Howe was also shot down, safely crash-landing at Gravesend. The squadron made no combat claims. 253 Squadron also lost a Hurricane, and claimed the destruction of three Me 109s. Although Fighter Command lost no Spitfires that morning, one was claimed by *Oberleutnant* Hermann-Friedrich Joppien of *Stab* 1/JG 51; *Feldwebel* Erwin Fleig of 1/JG 51 claimed a Hurricane, as did *Hauptmann* Richard Leppla of *Stab* III/JG 51. Although the locations of these claims is unknown, all three Germans were experienced fighter pilots, these victories bring their respective scores to twenty-eight, eight and thirteen respectively. What happened to Peter Parrott, therefore, remains unclear. German pilots were able to select either machine gun and cannon combined or each weapon individually, so the lack of cannon shells alone does not necessarily confirm that Z2323's assailant was another British fighter. The jury, as it were, remains out.

Shortly after this incident, 605 Squadron moved to Martlesham Heath, to evaluate their new Hurricane Mk IIs. On 3 March 1941, the squadron was rested and flew to Tern Hill in Shropshire. The following month, Flying Officer Parrott was posted to the CFS, for a flying instructor's course – ending what had been a very intensive period of operational flying, lasting nearly a whole year.

In June 1943 Peter returned to operations, flying Spitfires with 501 Squadron, again based at Martlesham, 'engaged on low-level shipping recces over the French Channel ports, up to the Netherlands and down to Cherbourg'. Two months later, Flight Lieutenant Parrott was off to Malta, before joining 324 Wing in Sicily. After a supernumerary spell with 72 Squadron, he became a flight commander on 111 Squadron, 'flying Spitfire Mk Vs with 90 gallon drop-tanks', covering the Salerno landings. On 13 October 1943, Peter was promoted to squadron leader and posted to command 43 Squadron, at Capodicino, Naples: 'many patrols over the Anzio landings'. That tour concluded on 3 April 1944, when Squadron Leader Parrott was posted to El Ballah, Egypt, for a gunnery instructor's course, followed by a period of instruction at 73 OTU. On 28 October he was given command of 72 Squadron 'Spitfire IXs, with bomb racks. Close support of army, and armed reccos in northern Italy. Bombing with 500 lb bombs under belly of Spitfire; targets asked for by army, or of opportunity, such as trains and transport.' In February 1945, Peter was promoted to wing commander and received a bar to his DFC: 'Group Training Spector, Fighters. Later transferred to Wing Commander Operations, Cesena, Forli, Imsla, Udine. Accepted Permanent Commission in RAF, but rank dropped to squadron leader.'

Thereafter, Wing Commander's Parrott's long post-war career saw him serving as a test pilot, earning an AFC, as 'OC Flying Wing, RAF Nicosia, Cyprus, responsible for search and rescue, eastern Mediterranean' and as a staff officer at home and in Germany. In July 1965, Peter retired from the RAF:

Passed exams for commercial licence for helicopters, and exams for

Air Transport Pilot's Licence (Fixed Wing). Employed for contract with Libyan government to fly Learjets, as Royal Flight (King Idris) for two years. Returned to UK and flew scheduled domestic routes on Handley Page Heralds, for a year, until Heralds were withdrawn. Although the Gadaffi revolution was a problem, the Libyan contract continued, so I returned there, flying business jets. I flew such VIPs as Colonel Gadaffi, President Sadat, and even Idi Amin. Once we stopped for fuel in the Central African Republic, but got arrested as a suspected agitator! In 1967, my Learjet was destroyed at Damascus during an Israeli air attack on International Airport. In November 1973, I returned to the UK, to take up post of Flight Operations Manager, but the company went into liquidation in 1974: end of aviation career.

In retirement, it was Peter who famously arranged the sending of a telegram 'From the Few to the few', congratulating Sea Harrier pilots on their combat achievement during the 1982 Falklands Conflict. He was also a driving force behind the Battle of Britain Fighter Association's efforts to see a statue erected in London to honour Lord Dowding – and which was achieved when HM Queen Elizabeth The Queen Mother, the Association's patron, unveiled Faith Winter's bronze outside the Strand's famous Church of St Clement Dane. In 1990, when some friends and I opened our exhibition at a Worcester Museum to mark the fiftieth anniversary of the Battle of Britain, Wing Commander Peter Parrott was among our honoured guests. Inevitably, in conversation no one would have guessed his distinguished past. On 27 August 2003, Peter died – aged eighty-three – and is consequently the only pilot whose story is featured in this book to be deceased at the time of writing. His story, however, spanning the Battle of France, Dunkirk and fighter operations right up to the end of 1940, is a rare insight from a pilot who survived in those very dangerous skies. In 1990, he told me, 'Oh yes, of course I'm proud of having flown in the Battle of Britain, but that's not the point: the real point is that we don't forget it, which is why the work you do is very important.' Fortunately my friend Eric Young had the foresight to record Peter's experiences – and hence why we are able to read them here. Unfortunately, many of the Few have left no written record behind, but thankfully, largely due to the unpaid, untrained work of enthusiasts, overall the Few have generated a rich archive. Every scrap of this material is crucial to providing a comprehensive interpretation for future generations – and, thanks to Eric, Wing Commander Peter Parrott has contributed to that record from beyond the grave.

2

SQUADRON LEADER M. T. WAINWRIGHT AFC

Michael Terry Wainwright was born at Harrow Weald, on 15 March 1919.

My father was a buyer of children's prams for Barker's of Kensington, where he was a departmental manager. My first school was a Roman Catholic convent in Harrow, but, after we moved to London, I first attended Collet Court Prep School before going to St Paul's, which I left in 1936.

I had always wanted to fly. I learned to fly privately at Hanworth, near Staines, but decided that the best way to make a career of it was to join the RAF. Fortunately my High Master at St Paul's gave me a good report, so I passed my interview and was immediately given a Short Service Commission. I decided not to tell the RAF that I could fly – so that when I soloed quickly they'd think me a quick learner!

I first went to Desford for *ab initio* flying training on Tiger Moths, thence to 3 FTS at South Cerney for conversion to service types. There I flew the dual control Hawker Audax, before the Hawker Fury single-engined biplane fighter – a beautiful aeroplane which had forward-firing machine guns synchronised to fire through the propeller arc. Afterwards, in 1938, I went to the Air Armament School at Eastchurch on the Isle of Sheppey, which was frankly bloody awful! There I flew Hawker Fury fighters. We also learnt everything about the various pyrotechnics and ammunition used by the RAF – the terminal velocity of a bomb, for goodness sake! During training we had a lens-trace plane which flew from one side of a table to the other, to calculate drift and wind. There was this crazy guy, an instructor, who would stand at the far side and let the plane 'fly' into an open matchbox! Then I went to Manby for more of the same. Although we had a lovely modern Officers' Mess there, the food was disgusting! Thence to Acklington, training would-be rear gunners. We used to tow drogues and fly gunners around whilst they fired at them. There I flew Overstrand and Sidestrand twin-engined aircraft. Pre-war, the RAF was really like an exclusive flying club – and I *loved* flying!

I was then posted to 72 Squadron at Church Fenton. The CO was an Australian, who took one look at my log book, saw that I had most recently flown twins and not single-engined fighters, and posted me straight off to 64 Squadron on the same station. 64 Squadron had twin-engined Blenheims, a multi-purpose aircraft with a pack of four forward-firing machine guns under the belly. I liked the Blenheim, it was a nice plane to fly, but it was really a kind of rich man's plaything, unsuitable as a warplane – but I was just happy to fly anything! Our CO was John Hervey-Percy, a very nice chap. This was in late 1938, after the Munich Crises over Czechoslovakia. Personally I didn't sense that war with Germany was imminent or inevitable, and when it came in September 1939, I just thought how bloody stupid it was to go to war over Poland. I kept that to myself, though. A week later I married Pam, still thinking that the fact we were at war was bloody stupid! We were then flying solo sweeps over the North Sea, looking out for shipping: the 'Phoney War'.

On 30 March 1940, I flew a Spitfire Mk I for the first time at

Church Fenton, after twenty minutes dual in a Miles Master. To be honest I didn't think that much of the Spitfire on that first occasion: you have to control the throttle with your left hand, but on those early Spitfires the undercarriage had to be pumped up by hand – which made things difficult. They also had a primitive ring and bead gunsight. Also, the machine guns were harmonised to converge at 400 yards – which is too far, it needed to be 200–250 yards, but because we had no combat experience on these new monoplanes no one knew that then. Anyway, I had no intention of being a hero fighter pilot, I can tell you, I was just there to do my bit. Over the next few weeks we continued to practise on Spitfires while still flying Blenheims operationally, while the latter was replaced by the Spits. It didn't really bother me what I flew. Geoffrey Wellum fell in love with the Spitfire, but for me it was just another aircraft.

After Hitler invaded the West in May 1940, by which time we were at Kenley, we'd fly down to and operate from Hawkinge, near Folkestone, or Gravesend on the Thames Estuary. Things were already going very badly for us over the Channel. Air Chief Marshal Dowding had only sent Hawker Hurricanes to France. The Germans, of course, had worked out air fighting during the Spanish Civil War and had far superior aircraft. By comparison we'd not a clue.

Abruptly, on 10 May 1940, the great storm had finally broken: Hitler invaded Belgium, Holland, Luxembourg and France. Two days later Liege fell, and panzers crossed the Meuse at Dinant and Sedan. Hitherto, in the naive hope of remaining neutral, the Belgians had refused Lord Gort's BEF permission to fortify their border with Germany. Now the Belgian king called for help, the BEF pivoting forward from its prepared defences on the Belgian–French border. The British advanced for sixty miles over unfamiliar ground to meet the German *Schwerpunkt* – point of main effort – which was expected to follow the same route as in the First World War. It did not. Holland was certainly attacked – the Dutch air force being wiped out on the first day – but the main enemy thrust was cleverly disguised. As Allied eyes were firmly focussed on the Belgian–Dutch border, *Panzergruppe* von Kleist achieved the supposedly impossible and successfully negotiated the Ardennes, much further south. German armour then poured out of the forest, bypassing the Maginot Line, rendering its concrete forts useless. The panzers then punched upwards, towards the Channel coast – ten days later the Germans had reached Laon, Cambrai, Arras, Amiens and even Abbeville. Indeed, Erwin Rommel's 7th Panzer covered ground so quickly that it became known as the 'Ghost Division'. The effect on the Allies was virtual paralysis, so shocking was the assault, unprecedented in speed and fury. Civilians in Britain were equally shocked – not least after the bombing of Rotterdam on 14 May reportedly caused 30,000 civilian fatalities (although post-war estimates put the death toll at nearer 3,000). Hard on the heels of Guernica and Warsaw, Rotterdam's fate was terrifying news indeed.

The British Advanced Air Striking Force (AASF) had flown to France on 2 September 1939. Fairey Battle light bombers went first, followed by Blenheims and Hurricanes – but no Spitfires. And Air Chief Marshal Dowding only spared Hurricanes for two reasons: firstly, due to political pressure, he had no choice but to support the French by providing a certain amount of his precious fighters; secondly, that being so, he wisely decided only to send Hurricanes, which he knew were inferior to the Spitfire. Moreover, there were precious few Spitfires available in any case – certainly insufficient to send to France, thereby weakening Britain's defences for – as Dowding would later see it – no good purpose. On 10 May 1940, though, there were six squadrons of Hurricanes in France. One week later the equivalent of six more had crossed the Channel, and another four were operating from bases on the south-east coast of England, hopping over the Channel on a daily basis but returning to England – if they could – at the end of each day. Losses in France rapidly stacked up. The Air Ministry acted as though these casualties were a complete surprise. Dowding's sharp riposte was, 'What do you expect? When you get into a war you have to lose things, including precious aircraft. That's exactly what I've been warning you about!' His fears regarding the wastage of fighters were now being realised. The crux of the problem was that the more fighters Dowding sent to France, the further he weakened Britain's defences. Already Dowding had insisted that the minimum strength required to guarantee Britain's safety was fifty-two squadrons, and yet soon he was arguing a case to retain just thirty-six. Although Churchill later wrote that Dowding agreed with him on the figure of twenty-five, the latter dismissed this statement as 'absurd'. With the French constantly clamouring for more fighters, and putting Churchill's War Cabinet under increasing pressure, things came to a head on 15 May.

On that day, Dowding joined Newall, the Chief of the Air Staff, at a Cabinet meeting. Both men spoke out against sending more fighters across the Channel. These could not, however, be entirely denied as elements of the BEF were poised to attack enemy communications near Brussels. Dowding was dissatisfied and later commented that 'there had already been serious casualties in France, and they alone had been worrying me a very great deal. I had to know how much longer the drain was going on, and I had to ask for a figure at which they would shut the stable door and say no more squadrons would be sent to France.' Unable to request an interview with the Cabinet every time a new demand for fighters was received, on 16 May Dowding sat and composed the strongest case he could to prevent further fighters being drained away in a battle already lost. The following is extracted from that letter, which remains one of the most important documents of the early part of the war:

I must therefore request that as a matter of paramount urgency the Air Ministry will consider and decide what level of strength is to be left to the Fighter Command for the defence of this country, and will assure me that when this level has been reached not one fighter will be sent across the Channel however urgent and insistent appeals for help may be.

I believe that, if an adequate fighter force is kept in this country, if the fleets remain in being, and if the Home Forces are suitably organized to resist invasion, we should be able to carry on the war single-handed for some time, if not indefinitely. But, if the Home Defence force is drained away in desperate attempts to remedy the situation in France, defeat in France will involve the final, complete and irremediable defeat of this country.

On the very day that Dowding began his stance to stem the flow of British fighters to France, the Air Ministry required that a further eight half-squadrons be sent across the Channel. Worse, Churchill himself then flew to France, subsequently requesting a further six squadrons and a night attack by heavy bombers. This was ridiculous. Taking aside the problem of fighter strength, Britain had no heavy bombers at that time. By 19 May, the situation on the Continent had deteriorated further still. On that day the War Office and Admiralty began facing the possibility of evacuating the BEF from France, and Churchill finally saw sense. The Prime Minister's decision was recorded in a minute: 'No more squadrons of fighters will leave the country whatever the need of France.' By the following day, only three of Dowding's squadrons remained across the Channel. He considered that this 'converted a desperate into a serious situation'. The importance of this change in policy cannot be overlooked.

On 16 May, 64 Squadron left Church Fenton, bound for Kenley sector station in 11 Group. According to Pilot Officer Wainwright's personal flying log book, three days later 64 flew its first offensive operation over the French coast, a patrol of Calais – Boulogne – Dunkirk. In that record, Michael wrote that 'for the first time since the war started, Yellow Section engaged. Slight damage to Yellow 2 and 3.' He added that it was 'the most unusual Sunday afternoon I have yet experienced, in which we learned quite a lot about tactics and the like'.

Although Hitler's modern tactics of using armour supported by infantry and aerial bombardment – *Blitzkrieg* – has gone down in history as the principal reason the Fall of France happened so quickly, it was only part of the story. The fact is that, for the first time in history, complete aerial supremacy over a battlefield, the absolute saturation of the combat zone by air power, had truly won the day. Some 1,200 German fighters ruled the French skies. The achievement was, therefore, very much due to the German fighter pilots – and those flying Me 109s in particular. It is, however, perhaps difficult today for us to fully appreciate just what an absolute catastrophe the Fall of France was, and how shocking the unprecedented German military success. To say that Britain was now on the back foot would be an understatement – and to Fighter Command now fell the job, with limited resources and the prospect of operating over the French coast with what were intended as short-range defensive fighters, of providing aerial protection to the intended evacuation. Air Vice-Marshal Park rapidly began preparations for Operation DYNAMO – the decision to evacuate via Dunkirk having been made on 26 May 1940. The Spitfire would soon, at last, meet the Me 109 over the French coast – and, like many other RAF fighter squadrons, that first encounter would prove traumatic for 64 Squadron:

On 29 May, we flew a squadron patrol over Calais and Boulogne. We flew in tight vics of three, in perfect formation, as if we were performing a fly past over Buckingham Palace. It was ridiculous. We couldn't search for the enemy because we were concentrating so hard on formation flying. Inevitably we got well and truly bounced by Me 109s, losing three aircraft – including our Commanding Officer – and four were damaged. My Section was 'Arse End Charlie', at the back, so we saw what was happening in front of us. I immediately shouted over the R/T, 'Break! Every man for himself!' and went into a tight right turn. That gave me more time to see what was going on, and to think. Short of fuel, we had to break off anyway and get home. It was appalling. Back at Gravesend, the Air Officer Commanding 11 Group, Air Vice-Marshal Sir Keith Park, flew his personal Hurricane in and asked us what had gone wrong; 'Everything!' I said, and told him what I thought of the stupid vic formation.

In his log book, Michael wrote, 'Patrol Dunkirk evacuation of BEF. Enemy engaged. Squadron Leader Rogers, Flying Officer George and Pilot Officer Hackney lost.' He described those violent events as 'a terrific engagement, in which we lost our CO and two brave officers. Had a near shave myself. One Me 109 spun in whilst chasing me around'.

Of tactics, Michael more recently said,

After that our squadron arranged to fly in pairs, copying the Germans, with one aircraft slightly ahead, looking for a target, whilst the other covered the leader's tail. From time-to-time we'd swap over. That worked much better. Next time I was in action, I once more found myself taking evasive action in a tight right-hand turn. No German aircraft could out-turn a Spitfire, so you couldn't be shot at in such a manoeuvre. A 109 tried to follow me, but lost control; I last saw it spinning towards the sea but don't know what ultimately happened to it. We hadn't really got feelings of hatred against the German aircrews, we just thought that they were 'chaps' like us, it was the machine we wanted to destroy, not the man inside.

The evacuation was complete by 3 June 1940, 340,000 troops

having been brought safely back to 'Blighty'. Although the propagandists managed to cement the Dunkirk evacuation into popular perception as a victory, the reality was that the Fall of France was a military disaster without parallel. The BEF had left behind 28,000 dead or missing, and 40,000 prisoners of war, in addition to all its armour and artillery. In spite of a bad start and the problems with tactical formations, the Spitfire had, however, acquitted itself well in this first test against the Me 109. At the end of Operation DYNAMO, though, Fighter Command only had a total of 331 operational Hurricanes and Spitfires; over Dunkirk, it had lost 106 fighters (the Germans lost 130 aircraft) and eighty pilots. Nonetheless, during this unprecedented aerial fighting the balance of power did, in fact, shift from the Luftwaffe to the RAF – which, Air Vice-Marshal Park later asserted, achieved 'total ascendancy over the German bombers'. Importantly, this fighting provided Spitfire pilots with essential first-hand combat experience, and exposed deficiencies both tactical and technical, which could fortunately be largely corrected in time for the Battle of Britain – which all involved now knew lay ahead. At Aston Down, near Stroud, Pilot Officer David Scott-Malden, a Cambridge graduate with a first in Classics, was training to fly Spitfires. On 17 June 1940, he wrote in his diary, 'The French give up hostilities. Cannot yet conceive the enormity of it all. I suppose it will not be long before we are defending England in earnest.'

After dark on the same day David Scott-Malden recorded that prophetic diary entry, Pilot Officer Wainwright recorded in his log book a solo operational patrol of twenty-five minutes – during which he intercepted, fired upon and 'probably damaged' He 111.

On 21 June, Pilot Officer Wainwright flew an uneventful solo reconnaissance patrol over Abbeville, Amiens, Poix and Dieppe. In his log book, he observed that it was 'too quiet to be healthy. An ominous atmosphere.' France formally surrendered on 22 June 1940; by then, Hitler had already been sightseeing in Paris.

After Dunkirk there was a lull in the fighting, as both sides retired to repair and take stock. The campaigns fought thus far had proved that an air force with superiority and possessed of the initiative could give powerful and decisive support to rapid armoured thrusts – by preparing the way ahead with concentrated bombing, and then protecting the flanks of friendly forces from enemy counter-attack. The effectiveness of airborne troops, either conveyed by glider or parachute – providing aerial superiority had already been achieved – had also been proven. In France the Germans had met the Hurricane, which had fought well but in hopeless circumstances. Over Dunkirk the Spitfire had earned the enemy's respect. Now supremely confident, Göring had unexpected bases in northern France, vastly extending the range of its bombers and, most importantly, putting even London within range of the Me 109. That changed everything. The tacticians who had written Fighter Command's Air Fighting Manual could never have predicted Hitler's unprecedented advance to the Channel coast, which had made this possible. Göring, however, did not necessarily support the proposal for a seaborne invasion. Rightly, he recognised that 'the planned operation can only be considered under conditions of absolute air superiority'. He believed that a landing under fire was unnecessary, because the war against Britain had 'already taken on a victorious course'. The essential condition, however, was destruction of the RAF. Without air defences Britain would be impotent, making an invasion, in fact, unnecessary. This, then, was the task that Göring set to: annihilation of Fighter Command. After the Fall of France, therefore, the Luftwaffe prepared for a new assault.

Michael Wainwright:

We did a bit of night-flying too. I didn't think the Spitfire was that bad an aircraft to fly at night. Because of the long nose you couldn't see anything forward when landing in the daytime anyway!

Although I didn't fight in one, I did fly the Hurricane and actually preferred it to the Spitfire, because visibility was better and it had a variable flap control, whereas the Spitfire was simply either 'up' or 'down'. I actually developed my own technique of landing a Spitfire: with the undercarriage down and flaps up, she didn't stall until sixty knots, so I'd make a gentle approach and at that speed apply the flaps – the Spitfire would then just flop down. The best thing was that you didn't then have such a long run across the ground before stopping. The Spitfire was certainly a nice aeroplane, although I felt no emotional attachment to it, as others did, and, of course, it flew higher than the Hurricane.

That the Spitfire enjoyed a high-altitude capacity, which the Hurricane did not, would soon prove crucial – because only the Spitfire was able to mix it with the lethal 109s on high, providing a protective umbrella for the Hurricanes engaging bombers lower down. Because of this, although arguably the forthcoming Battle of Britain could not have been won without the Spitfire's ability to fight at high altitude, the Hurricane and Spitfire were perfect stablemates. Again arguably, the Battle of Britain could have been won had Fighter Command been solely equipped with that type, but not had it purely been Hurricane-equipped. The problem was, there were simply insufficient Spitfires: just nineteen squadrons of them, while thirty-three operated the Hurricane. It was this combined force, supplemented by Defiants and Blenheims, which now awaited the onslaught on Britain.

On 2 July 1940, day fighting resumed between the opposing fighter forces, when the Germans began attacking Channel-bound convoys and south coastal ports. These attacks were frequent. On that day, Fighter Command flew ninety-one sorties, 282 the following day and 399 on 8 July. Dowding reacted by moving a number of Spitfire and Hurricane squadrons to the coastal airfields of Hawkinge, Manston, and Warmwell. The problem Fighter

Command faced was that these combat took place over the sea, inevitably leading to many pilots being reported 'missing'. It was clear, however, that the Luftwaffe had regrouped and had now turned its attention to Britain. Flying Officer Frank Brinsden, of 19 Squadron, summed up the mood in Fighter Command:

At squadron level I don't think that we were fully aware of what was going on. We were just keen to have a crack at the Germans, and the prevalent attitude was that we couldn't wait for them to come. Given that the French and Belgians had proved of little use during the defence of their homelands we were glad that we were on our own. We were absolutely confident that we were better than the enemy, and wanted an opportunity to bloody Hitler's nose.

Flight Sergeant George Unwin, of the same unit, added simply that 'we never considered being beaten. It was just not possible in our eyes.' If Göring wanted a fight, Fighter Command was clearly happy to oblige.

Although fierce combats began over Channel-bound convoys over a week before, officialdom decided that the Battle of Britain began on 10 July 1940. Pilot Officer Michael Wainwright was there:

We did many convoy protection patrols, and were pretty busy when the Battle of Britain began. On July 25, we engaged the enemy over the Channel, but Sub-Lieutenant Dawson-Paul, on secondment from the Fleet Air Arm and a very gallant officer, was killed. I damaged an Me 109 but my guns suffered an inexplicable stoppage.

On 26 July, Michael flew two operational sorties. On the first, he chased a Do 17 'for some time' but lost it owing to cloud cover. Later that day, 64 Squadron engaged 'a small enemy formation. An Me 109 appeared in front of me and turned – obviously not having seen me – and presented a perfect target. I shot it down easily, which was somewhere East of Portsmouth.

The following month I had a heavy nose-bleed whilst in a high-speed dive, so the medical people sent me away from Kenley to ascertain the trouble. I was then put on public relations duties, visiting factories and talking to workers. At Pilkington's in Lancashire, which made our bullet-proof windscreens, they asked me whether I was frightened. I replied that I was certainly apprehensive! It was the waiting that was always the worst. Personally I always felt a bit sorry for the He 111s, sitting ducks, like our Blenheims, and they carried hardly any bombs anyway; a nice enough aeroplane but not really a warplane – unlike their Ju 88, which was a damn good aeroplane.

After we lost the CO on that dreadful patrol over the French coast, we carried on without one. Our two flight commanders were Flight Lieutenants Henstock and Hobson, but I found neither that inspiring. Each flight just did its own thing, independent of the other. There was another chap who claimed a lot of enemy aircraft destroyed, but his gun cameras showed absolutely nothing; he was killed. Squadron Leader Don MacDonnell, the Laird of Glengarry and a Cranwellian, was posted to command. Although he hadn't seen combat personally he tried to tell us what was what, which failed to impress. We thought 'We've been through a lot, and seen action – who the hell is he to tell us?' He said we were a 'Bolshy' lot and badly disciplined; 'Bonnie Prince Charlie' we used to call him!'

'Bonnie Prince Charlie' was, in fact, the hereditary twenty-second Laird of Glengarry – Aeneas Ranald Donald. After Hurstpierpoint College, MacDonnell became a flight cadet at Cranwell in 1932. Upon graduation two years later, he was posted to 54 Squadron, to fly Gloster Gauntlet biplane fighters. In 1936, Flying Officer MacDonnell went to 802 (Fleet Fighter) Squadron, operating between Hal Far, Malta and HMS *Glorious*. By early 1939, he was an instructor at the CFS, Upavon, then served at the Air Ministry before being given command of 64 Squadron at Kenley in mid-July 1940. MacDonnell was, therefore, a professional RAF officer and Cranwellian. He was also a fighter pilot – but with biplane experience. The Laird of Glengarry was, therefore, very much the product of his class, education and the pre-war RAF; he also proved to be an excellent fighter pilot, destroying eleven enemy aircraft during the Battle of Britain, for which he was awarded the DFC. The following year, he was shot down on a sweep over France, and captured. After the war, he remained in the service, retiring as an air commodore in 1964, and served as the Battle of Britain Fighter Association's second Chairman for eighteen years (from 1960). He died, aged eighty-five, in 1999.

Shortly after returning from my factory tour in October 1940, I was posted away to be an instructor. Later I attended a fighter leader course, but the powers that be decided to send me to a transport squadron! So I went out to the Far East where I commanded the VIP flight, which was interesting, but never flew fighters operationally again.

Thinking about the Battle of Britain now, I think of it as just an experience in my life. At our level we had no influence on decisions. Whether any decisions were made from our intelligence and combat reports I don't know. I think Dowding was very good politically, especially in refusing to send any further squadrons to France – his robustness made him powerful enemies, though, and the way both Dowding and Air Vice-Marshal Park were treated after the Battle of Britain was disgraceful. Park was a wonderful chap, excellent, but we didn't like Leigh-Mallory or Sholto Douglas: awful. It was a big mistake, I think, when they changed Fighter Command's name to 'Air Defence of Great Britain'. To me, 'Fighter Command: Offence – Defence', and all that, really had a special something. The thing is, though, we didn't really *win* the Battle of Britain, did we? The Luftwaffe was not destroyed or defeated, so how did we *win*? I don't think my fellow survivors see it that way, but I do, it was not a clear-cut thing. I still attend the annual memorial services at Westminster Abbey and Capel-le-Ferne, though. I think it tremendously important that the Battle of Britain is not forgotten. The Battle of Britain Memorial Trust's initiative and appeal to build the Wing is splendid and very important to ensuring that future generations learn about those days.

Further comment on the subject would be superfluous. Sadly, however, Michael Wainwright did not live to see this book published: he died on 23 March 2015, aged ninety-six.

3

WING COMMANDER J. F. D. 'TIM' ELKINGTON

John Francis Durham Elkington – known universally as 'Tim' – was born in Edgbaston on 23 December 1920. In September 1939, having attended Bedford School, he joined the RAF; here, for the first time, we have Tim's story in its entirety:

My parents lived at Grafton in Worcestershire. I was their only child. They later divorced when I was fourteen. I had little contact with children of my age, and was very naive; I just did not know what to expect. The RAF, however, was very much a family, you *belonged*. A pre-war fighter squadron, I was later told, was like a gentleman's club – you even needed your CO's permission to marry, and you couldn't do that until aged about thirty.

In October 1939, I went to 9 EFTS, at Ansty, where I wasted a lot of time, seventy-five hours in fact, flying Tiger Moths. Then, in April 1940, I became a flight cadet at Cranwell. The course should have been three years, but due to the war courses were reduced to three months. There I flew Hawker Hart and Hind biplanes. Thereafter, I didn't go to OTU, to convert to the type of aircraft I would be expected to fly operationally. It was ridiculous, really. No one told you how difficult aircraft are to shoot down; you think that eight machine-guns are wonderful – but they're not. There was no brief whatsoever, no tactical training.

I was commissioned on 14 July 1940, and fortunately posted to Fighter – not Bomber – Command. I reported to 1 Squadron, commanded by Squadron Leader David Pemberton, at Northolt the following day. The squadron had Hurricanes – much like a Hind without the top wing, so no great problem in converting. When I arrived at Northolt, the two most important places were the Officers' Mess and squadron Dispersal Hut. The rest of the station was really irrelevant. 1 Squadron had previously fought in France. When I arrived, the veterans, people like Matthews and Hancock, just looked at me and thought, 'Oh God – a schoolboy!'

1 Squadron was a famous RAF fighter squadron, with a proud history during the First World War, and had flown operations between the wars over India and Iraq. Ominously, in 1937, the squadron displayed its Hawker Fury fighters at the Zurich International Air Meeting – where it was clear that the biplane fighter was completely outclassed by the new Me 109 monoplane and even the Do 17 bomber. Fortunately 1 Squadron was re-equipped with the new Hawker Hurricane in October 1938, and was deployed to France in September 1939 operating that fighter. Commanded by Squadron Leader 'Bull' Halahan, the squadron claimed its first victory, a Do 17, on 31 October. The following year, 1 Squadron was heavily embroiled in the Battle of France. On 24 May, Squadron Leader Halahan was posted to command 5 OTU and was replaced at the head of 1 Squadron by Squadron Leader David Pemberton. A month later, France having fallen, Pemberton's Hurricanes were back at their home base of Tangmere, and soon started flying up to and operating from Northolt on a regular basis.

My first flight with 1 Squadron was on 18 July 1940, in a dual-seat

Miles Master with Squadron Leader Pemberton. I then flew the aircraft solo. The following day I flew a Hurricane for the first time, letter 'A'. Over the next few days I practiced climbing to 29,000 feet, formation flying, dogfighting and attacks. There was no on-squadron tactical-training as such. On 23 July, we flew down to Tangmere, to operate near the south coast. Tangmere was a wonderful station and, in fact, 1 Squadron's home, which it historically shared with 43 Squadron. My first operational patrol occurred on 27 July, in Hurricane 'S' – an uneventful one over St Catherine's Point; I had but sixteen hours on type! We were flying at 1,000 feet, covering the de-beaching of a tanker. The following night I flew the Hurricane at night for the first time. I was never keen on it. I wasn't good at flying on instruments, too easily disorientated, especially in a wartime black-out. On 12 August 1940, we started operating out of North Weald, patrolling the East coast.

At that time, it was becoming increasingly clear that the enemy had changed tack: no longer was the focus of enemy attacks on convoys, but coastal radar installations and forward aerodromes. Although hundreds of reconnaissance sorties were flown over England, German intelligence had frequently misinterpreted or not appreciated the information collated. Moreover, the crucial significance of sector stations within Air Chief Marshal Dowding's System of Air Defence had been underestimated. On 13 August 1940, the day after 1 Squadron arrived at North Weald, a sector station in Essex, a new phase of very heavy fighting commenced, although the Luftwaffe expended valuable time and resources attacking targets of little significance to their actual mission: the destruction of Fighter Command. Indeed, this day saw the so-called *Adlertag* – 'Eagle Day' – unleashed, but most of the airfields attacked were not crucial to the aerial defence of England. Sector stations, though, were soon hit, not least Manston on 14 August, by the brilliant precision bombing unit *Erprobungsgruppe*

210. Faulty intelligence or not, the demonstrable fact was that the tempo of fighting was greatly increasing; Tim Elkington would soon find himself embroiled in it, flying his Hurricane painted with a nose art of 'Eugene the Jeep', ' a mystical animal, capable of foretelling the future and materialising anywhere to work its magic'.

On 15 August we were patrolling when vectored towards Harwich, which was being bombed. I attacked an Me 109, which I believe I hit, and last saw diving away, trailing smoke, disappearing through cloud. I don't know whether it was destroyed or not, but I certainly frightened it! The first time you actually saw an aircraft with a black cross on it was quite a moment – they looked deadly, sinister. I also saw another twelve 109s going out over the coast, but wasn't in a position to attack them.

That day, *Luftflotte* 2 had launched its second major offensive effort at 1415 hours. Two *Gruppen* of JG 26 swept over Kent in advance of eighty-eight KG 3 Do 17s, closely escorted by Me 109s from JGs 51, 52 and 54, tasked with attacking the airfields at Rochester and Eastchurch. While this raid materialised, a fast plot was tracked on the radar screen, incoming over Harwich, in response to which the 11 Group Controller scrambled the fighter squadrons from Martlesham Heath – the forward coastal airfield in the Debden sector. Unfortunately the fast and low-flying Me 110s and Me 109s of *Erprobungsgruppe* 210 confounded the defenders and plastered Martlesham. Assistance was requested from 12 Group, but, taking into account time and distance, there was nothing the Duxford-based squadrons could practically do to help. South of Harwich, three Hurricanes of 17 Squadron and those of 1 Squadron were bounced by Me 109s. The latter's Red, Yellow and Green sections bore the brunt of this attack: Flight Lieutenant Brown baled out but was fortunately rescued by a passing trawler;

Pilot Officer Browne and Sergeant Shanahan were both killed. Pilot Officer Matthews sighted raiders bombing Martlesham, set off in pursuit and damaged one. Pilot Officer Mann was attacked from astern by a 110, which he shook off, only to be engaged by a 109, on which he turned the tables: the Hurricane pilot blew his assailant's canopy off before setting the German alight. Pilot Officer Elkington was Green 2 that day, and credited with an Me 109 destroyed. The following day would also be significant – but for the wrong reasons.

On 16 August, the first raids, against the sector stations at West Malling and Hornchurch, were made midmorning. The third raid, comprising over one hundred aircraft, progressed towards targets further west: Tangmere sector station, the Ventnor Chain Home radar station, and the Navy air base at Lee-on-Solent. *Sturkampgeschwader* 2's Ju 87 *Stukas* dived out of the sun, executing a highly successful attack on Tangmere, damaging all hangars together with essential facilities and services. A number of Spitfires and Hurricanes were destroyed on the ground, in addition to all aircraft on charge with the Fighter Interception Unit (which included the first operational Bristol Beaufighter). The enemy did not escape unscathed, however: the Hurricanes of 1 and 43 Squadrons shot down seven of their number and damaged three more. Tim Elkington:

We were operating from Northolt when vectored towards Portsmouth. I was in Flight Sergeant Fred Berry's Section, flying as top weaver, above the squadron. Tangmere was being heavily bombed by Ju 87s, but I saw nothing of it; because my radio was out of action, I received no instructions. I looked down one second and the squadron was there. Looked again – and as so often happens – the sky was empty. I suddenly saw enemy aircraft heading for Portsmouth so gave chase. As I straightened out – BANG – and my starboard fuel tank blew up. I tried to get out but forgot to disconnect my radio and oxygen leads. Did so and fell out at 10,000 feet. I had been hit in the face and legs by shrapnel. No pain, just blood. I was floating down by parachute over the sea but hadn't inflated my Mae West. Then I passed out. Had I landed in the sea, I would have drowned, but, although being unconscious I saw nothing of it, Fred Berry used the slipstream of his Hurricane to blow me towards land. I came to in a field at West Wittering, being attended to by a pretty, freckle-faced nurse who was cutting my trousers and pants off – all very embarrassing and, as my face was a bit of a mess, unsurprisingly my charm offensive failed miserably! My mother and stepfather lived in the area, in fact, at Hayling Island. Mother was on the balcony, watching proceedings with my Step-father's naval glasses. I was admitted to Royal West Sussex Hospital a few minutes later, from where staff telephoned my Mother, incorrectly addressing her as 'Mrs Elkington'; she knew immediately that the call involved me, and was unsurprised to discover that it was her son who she had watched descending by parachute.

That day, Flight Sergeant Berry, a veteran of the Battle of France, reported,

I was leader of Green Section of 1 Squadron, which formed the fourth in line astern on the frontal attack on the second formation of He 111s. After the first burst of three to four seconds at number eight of the second vic, it fell out of formation and glided away south, in the opposite direction, towards 10/10ths cloud. I climbed again and made a fresh attack from in front and below, in rather a steep climb. I gave a burst of two to three seconds, to number two of the third vic. The ammunition appeared to enter just behind the undercarriage. The E/A glided to the right, and I half-rolled and lost sight of him. The third attack was steeper still, from below and in front, with no apparent result. My number three mentioned that I was fired at, but I did not notice it; nor did I notice any fire from the lower gunners of the E/A that I attacked.

Berry claimed two He 111 probables.

Sadly, I never had the opportunity to thank Berry, who was killed on 1 September 1940, before I returned to the squadron. I later learned that American fighter pilots used a similar technique to deflect Japanese balloon bombs, and wonder whether Berry's use of the technique to save me was the first occasion. Much more recently I had the opportunity to meet Fred Berry's family, who confirmed the story, I, as explained, having seen nothing of it at the time. Another interesting thing is that more recently the 'Uncles' of 1, 43 and 601 Squadrons, the squadrons involved that day, worked out that I had almost certainly been the eighteenth victim of none other than Major Helmut Wick – *Kommodore* of JG 2 – who was himself killed over the Channel a few weeks later.

I remained on leave at my Grandparents' in Cornwall until 16 September. Quite honestly I think I could have been bandaged up and flown again very soon afterwards, but remained on leave. Apart from holes in my face, and bigger ones in my legs, I felt okay, so could have called up and tried to get back to the squadron. But it just didn't occur to me. I had not yet developed a sense of responsibility.

I didn't fly again until 2 October, by which time 1 Squadron was at Wittering, in 12 Group. That provided the opportunity for more training flights, although we did a number of operational patrols.

By this time, Hitler's ambition to mount a seaborne invasion on England's south coast had been thwarted. Having failed to lure Fighter Command into the air for destruction en masse by bombing London, *Reichsmarschall* Göring changed tack again. By 30 September, his bomber force was unable to sustain such heavy losses, so opted instead to operate under the cover of darkness. Mainly, only small formations of fast, heavily armed, Ju 88s ventured over England in daylight hours, or lone raiders bent on harassing attacks, relying on speed and cloud cover for preservation. In all cases targets were connected with the British aircraft industry, but this was too light an effort and too late in the day to have any pronounced effect. At 1105 hours on 9 October, Pilot Officer Elkington was airborne, with another Hurricane, a few miles north-east of base, when a Ju 88 was sighted a thousand feet below, travelling on the same course. Tim subsequently claimed the raider as a probable, but it had, in fact, been destroyed. This machine, of 6/KG 30, failed to return: all four enemy crew members remain *vermisst*.

'On 27 October, whilst patrolling the east coast with Goodman and Robinson, we ran into some Do 17s over Feltwell – Goodman and I destroyed one of them. Bofors fire hindered us, however, so we only managed a few bursts. The destruction of this raider was confirmed by the *Daily Mirror*!' In fact, two Do 17s of 7 and 9/KG 3 were damaged by 1 Squadron over Feltwell, but both returned to base, one carrying a dead crewman, the other a badly wounded occupant.

Four days later, the Battle of Britain was officially considered over; Tim Elkington:

I had not realised at the time just how important was the battle that we were fighting. Briefing was non-existent and accurate news sadly lacking. I knew that the Germans were "over there", but didn't know where, really, just that they were attacking us. Surviving being shot down saved me, because I missed the heavy fighting in September.

In April 1941, Pilot Officer Elkington was posted from 1 Squadron to instruct at 55 Operational Training Unit (OTU) at Usworth, and later Ouston. Soon afterwards:

I hit a high-tension power cable over the River Tyne (whilst on authorised low flying), cutting the power to the village where I was billeted. Not popular. I was fortunate in not only surviving the encounter, but in receiving a rapid posting back to a squadron, rather than a court martial.

In July 1941, after a short spell with 601 Squadron at Manston, I went to Russia on the first convoy there – the only one to get through unscathed – and consequently missed 1 Squadron's very demanding night intruder operations. Aboard HMS *Argus*, on 18 August 1941, the First Sea Lord briefed us, telling us that we, 151 Wing, had been promised by Churchill in response to Stalin's demand for support. Our role was to be the defence of the naval base of Murmansk, and cooperation with Soviet forces in that area. We were to instruct the Soviets in the operation and maintenance of our aircraft and ground equipment, which was then to be handed over to them. And so it was that we joined the first ever convoy to Russia, together with merchantmen carrying the rest of the Wing and our crated Hurricanes. We were escorted by HMS *Victorious*, a cruiser and several destroyers. Whilst in Scapa Flow, outbound, from 20 August, we received typical naval hospitality on several of the ships anchored there. Mindful of events a few months later, it is painful to reflect on those present: HMS *Prince of Wales*, *Repulse*, *King George V*, *Victorious*, *Furious*, *Malaya*, *Sheffield* and *London*. We finally sailed for Iceland on 30 August, together with a convoy bound for North America, and were escorted by Sunderland and Catalina flying boats. For a few days, we were down to seven knots, in thick fog. On 3 September, the weather cleared, and the Martlets from *Victorious* got a Do 17; one Fulmar was lost in the engagement. Then, more days of thick fog.

Flying off *Argus* at 0600 hours on 7 September, some 200 miles north of Murmansk, our compasses were unreliable. We were told to pass over *Argus*, then a pre-positioned destroyer, and keep going! After over-flying miles of desolate tundra, we landed at Vaenga, a vast expanse of pot-holed sand which, later, became a soggy mess. Breakfast, however, was more welcoming – caviar, smoked salmon, Finnish ham, wine and champagne.

In the first month, we were unfortunate, as a squadron, to miss out on engagement with the enemy. Apart from reconnaissance, our first real work did not come until 17 September, with three patrols that day over the front line. Even then we saw nothing but flak, directed both at us and the bombers we were escorting. A few days later, close to Petsamo, one Pe2 was hit and crashed in flames after the crew had jettisoned their bombs and baled out. Their bombs came close to hitting the ships that were firing.

October opened with attacks on our airfield. Advanced warning was unsophisticated. On the first occasion, some twenty Ju88s dropped their loads, and we took off to intercept through a hail of bullets, dodging the bomb craters. One 81 Squadron pilot, whose engine was stopped by a blast on take-off, was then blown off the wing by another explosion. Of 134 Squadron, I was first away and managed to catch up with them at 7,000 feet. My Number 2 joined me and we damaged one Ju88, which later failed to reach home. The excellent DVD on the Russian episode, by Atoll Productions, has an over-generous simulation of the event showing a 'flamer', which we did not achieve. No surprise – I was rated below average in air gunnery.

The weather was now closing in and our efforts were devoted more to the conversion of Russian pilots, who seemed oblivious of fog, snow and ice, and the instruction of their technicians. On one occasion we watched with disbelief as a protégé attempted his third approach in dense fog.

Came the time for return home, and the most testing time of the expedition, for me at least, began. On 16 November, I was put in charge of an advance party of seven officers and sixty airmen, which I had to lead in deep snow, in virtual night, down the ten miles or so of treacherous track to Rosta oiling jetty. We knew when we reached our destination, at 5 p.m., when all our kit became black with oil. Our only casualty was one airman with a broken arm.

We waited there six hours for the fleet minesweepers we had to board for the voyage to Archangel – HMS *Hussar*, in our case, and *Gossamer* and *Speedy*, but they had docked at a different jetty. (If anything suggests that we had a tough assignment, read up their sea logs!) Eventually bed, without having had any food for fourteen hours, at 0200 hours. Next day, up to Polyarny, and a drink aboard the submarine *Seawolf*, before she left on patrol.

Transferring to an icebreaker, captained by a very large lady, and following the *Lenin* – the world's largest – we struggled through six inch deep ice for the last twenty miles into Archangel. On one occasion we passed a merchantman loaded with crated Hurricanes and tanks. On the icebreaker, I made the acquaintance of General Gromov – the pre-war long distance flyer.

On 24 November, we were transferred to MV *Empire Baffin*, a 10,000 ton cargo ship. Despite the icebreakers, moving yards at a time, it was not until 28 November that we were steaming past the Gorodetski light and into the open sea. We were held to 7.5 knots for the Russian boats with us – their first convoy to the UK. It was only then that we found the two Estonian stowaways who had crossed the ice at night to board us. On 29 November, HMS *Kenya*, with most of the Wing personnel on board, joined us. The following day we hove to in gale and heavy seas – our lifeboat was washed away, and slag ballast on deck shifted. We had to rope ourselves into our bunks at night. No chance of sleep. Everything heavy with frozen spray which had to be constantly chipped off with shovels. We were sleeping in our clothes in case we had to get Vic Berg – who was in full plaster after his terrible crash – to the lifeboats. On 1 December we were attacked by a U-boat, which destroyers depth charged – no casualties, but an outgoing convoy later lost several ships. Ballast shifting again. Our airmen helped to re-locate it. On 4 December, our engines cut out, with propellers racing, in the heavy seas. Steering gear damaged. Still semi-dusk all day. Several mines seen – one uncomfortably close. By 8 December we had reached Iceland, and eight days later, Scotland & home! After all the operational jazz, I must add that the expedition gave me my truest wartime friend – Vladimir Krivoschekov – the Russian general's nineteen-year-old interpreter, known as 'K the Capitalist'. His purity of English put us to shame!

In 1942 I joined the Merchant Ship Fighter Unit (MSFU). This comprised some seventy pilots divided into pools based in England, Gibraltar, Canada and Russia. The idea was that Hurricanes launched from catapults, assisted by rockets, from Catapult Aircraft Merchant Ships (CAM). After take-off and engaging the enemy it was impossible to land, so the pilot had to bale out into the sea and hope to get picked up. Some were lost, and twelve out of thirty-five CAM ships were sunk, but fortunately I had an uneventful crossing. Meanwhile 134 Squadron, with which I had flown in Russia, went to the Middle and Far East, losing many pilots.

I was then posted back to 1 Squadron, flying Typhoons, so missed the disastrous PQ Convoy to Russia. Then on to the Hurricane flight of 539 (Turbinlite) Squadron, so I missed 1 Squadron's intruder operations. Lady Luck, it seemed, was looking after me.

In 1943 I was flying Typhoons with 197 Squadron. The 'Tiffie' was a real man's machine, very powerful – although it cut you down to size when you saw a slip of a girl in Air Transport Auxiliary uniform alight from one as if it was a stroll in the park! I was then posted to India – missing the Normandy campaign in which Typhoons were heavily engaged in dangerous ground-attack sorties: Lady Luck again. Only two pilots of our original complement survived the eighteen-month tour. En route to India in 1943, I was on the first unescorted convoy through the Mediterranean – we lost some ships, but not mine. I was posted to 67 Squadron to fight the Japanese, but they were stopped at Kohima. Again, I didn't really know what was really going on, how close the Japanese actually were. I then formed Air Fighting Development Unit (AFDU) under Frank 'Chota' Carey. In 1945, I crashed a Mustang due to engine failure on take-off. Trapped in the fume-filled cockpit, I managed to smash the canopy and escape. Then I flew a Japanese Zeke 52 at the Delhi Air Display, and landed safely despite fuel spraying into my cockpit (I actually flew a number of enemy aircraft, including the Me 110 and FW 190; the latter was a beautiful aeroplane to fly). Later in the year, I became overcome by fumes whilst flying a Tempest II; tried to bale out but managed to land safely at Cawnpore with fuel venting into the engine bay! Also, that same year I had four tyres burst on take-off (one when actually 'bombed-up'). Fortunately, when I was leading six L5 spotter planes down to Ceylon for Operation Zipper in Burma, the war ended while we were airborne!

'Lady Luck', it certainly seems, had a hand in Tim's safe deliverance from the global conflagration of 1939–45. By 1945 Tim was a Flight Lieutenant, and he remained in the post-war service. He was converted to Meteor jet fighters and Varsities, and then flew a tour on Avro Shackletons with 240 Squadron at Turnhouse: 'I flew the Shackleton that photographed the first H-bomb trial at Christmas Island. Later that year I crash-landed; sparks, but no flames.' In 1959, after a tour as a Maritime Controller in Cyprus, Tim was posted to the Central Flying School (CFS) at Little Rissington, in the Cotswolds: 'I bought a house, which was not the custom in those days. It would not still be a family home had my wife, Pat, not stuck it out here whilst I commuted weekly for twelve years. Pat had to do the station runs, school runs, garden, WI market, alterations, the lot!' Tim eventually left the RAF, a Wing Commander, after thirty-five years' service in 1975: 'Failed job interviews, so set up a fine art and picture-framing business at home, which was greatly appreciated by my artist daughter.' After eventually retiring in 2005, this active and 'computer-literate' ninety-three-year-old remains a devoted family man and great company: 'Twelve fairly normal children and grandchildren, three great in-laws.' He was, I think, a natural pilot, and, the record shows, potentially a very good fighter pilot indeed – although, as self-effacing as they come, Tim would never admit it: 'I just didn't know what was going on.' Recently, he flew a Spitfire again, from the back cockpit of a two-seater out of Kidlington: 'Wasn't quite the same, in the back, very limited forward view, I like to see all around, but I did fly the thing for half an hour, straight and level.' Naturally, he retains a keen interest in the RAF, and in 2010 Wing Commander Elkington spoke at the Annual Dinner of the Joint Harrier Force:

Nowadays, I follow 1 Squadron's activities with interest and admiration, and still recall with great pleasure and pride my two short tours with the squadron. The 'Brylcreem Boys' of 1940 have had their fair share of hero worship in the media, but given the choice of your war or ours, I know which I would choose: ours, most definitely. Given the hazards of warfare today – the nature of the enemy, the environment, modern weaponry, together with the complexity of aircraft systems, I count you not only brave but wonderfully skilled to boot. It's encouraging to see the great traditions of the services in such good hands.

Left: 1. During the Battle of France, Peter Parrott appeared on an RAF recruiting poster. He survived the war, a decorated wing commander, but sadly died in 2003. *Right:* 2. A *Stuka* dive-bomber which crash-landed on the Isle of Wight, 8 August 1940, having been shot down by Pilot Officer Peter Parrott, then flying Hurricanes with 145 Squadron.

3. Ground crew of 145 Squadron with the fin of a He 111 destroyed by the unit's Hurricanes.

4. On 26 September 1940, Pilot Officer Peter Parrott was posted to 605 Squadron – this is one of their Hurricanes being rapidly 'turned around' at Croydon during the Battle of Britain.

5. Michael Wainwright pictured as a pilot officer in 1940.

Left: 6. Squadron Leader N. C. Odbert, briefly CO of 64 Squadron early in the Battle of Britain, looks on as his pilots are presented to HM King George VI. Pilot Officer Michael Wainwright was in the line-up, and can just be seen to the king's left.

Right: 7. A 64 Squadron Spitfire scrambles from Kenley in the Battle of Britain.

8. A page from Michael Wainwright's log book, recording action in the Battle of Britain.

9. Squadron Leader Michael Wainwright (second right), pictured later in the war, planning a flight while commanding the Far East Communications Squadron.

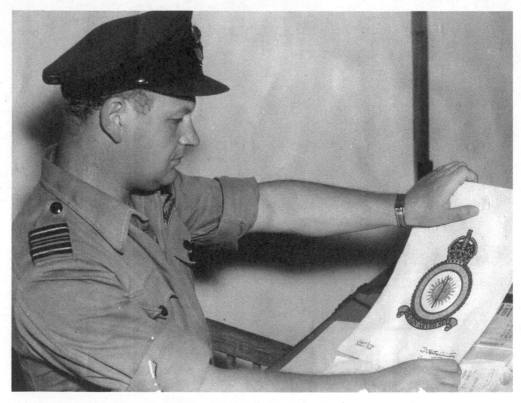

10. Squadron Leader Michael Wainwright with artwork for the Far East Communications Squadron's new crest.

11. Squadron Leader Michael Wainwright, holding his portrait, photographed at home by the author in 2012.

12. John Francis Durham 'Tim' Elkington, pictured as a newly commissioned pilot officer.

13. Pilots of 1 Squadron pictured in late 1940, Pilot Officer Elkington on wing, extreme right. Others include (front row): Pilot Officer Pat Hancock DFC (later a long-serving Secretary of the Battle of Britain Fighter Association and of great help to the author's research; sadly now deceased); Squadron Leader Mark 'Hilly' Brown DFC, Pilot Officer Charles Cetham. Middle row: 2nd Lieutenant Jean Demozay (French, extreme left); Sergeant Antoni Zavoral (Czech, extreme right). On wing, extreme left, Pilot Officer Arthur Clowes DFM.

14. Pilot Officer Tim Elkington and Hurricane, Wittering, 1940.

15. Pilot Officers Tim Elkington (in flying jacket and white silk scarf) and Pat Hancock DFC (centre) with other 1 Squadron pilots.

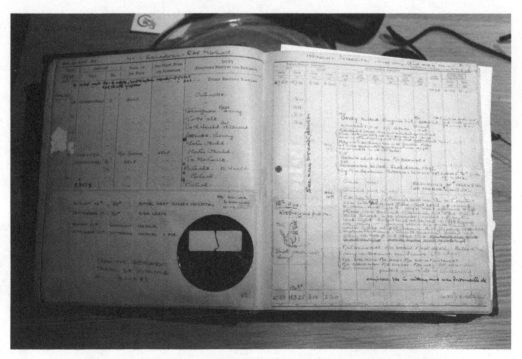

16. Wing Commander Tim Elkington's log book, recording the action on 16 August 1940; the instrument facia was recovered from the crash site of his Hurricane, recovered in 1983.

Left: 17. On 16 August 1940, Pilot Officer Elkington was shot down by the German ace Major Helmut Wick. Sergeant Fred Berry DFM, seen here at his wedding with fellow 1 Squadron pilot Sergeant Arthur Clowes, used his slipstream to blow the unconscious pilot's parachute to land. Sadly, Berry was killed in action just a few days later.

Below: 18. Pilot Officer Tim Elkington in Russia during 1941, serving with 134 Squadron.

Top: 20. An RAF Hurricane takes off from Vayhenga during the Russian adventure of 1941.

Above: 21. Recently, Wing Commander Elkington, now aged ninety-three, took control of this dual-seat Spitfire, from the rear cockpit.

Right: 22. Wing Commander Tim Elkington and log book, pictured at his Cotswold home by the author in 2012.

Opposite: 19. Tim Elkington joined the RAF expedition to support Soviet forces after Operation BARBAROSSA, flying in hostile conditions with limited resources – as indicated by this photograph from the album of (the late) Flight Lieutenant Mike Bush DFC, who flew there with 81 Squadron.

23. Ken Wilkinson, snapped while a sergeant pilot flying Spitfires with 19 Squadron at Fowlmere during the Battle of Britain.

24. Pre-Fighter Course, Montrose, June 1940: Sergeant K. A. Wilkinson second row, second right; many pictured went on to fly, fight and sadly in some cases die in the Battle of Britain.

26. Sergeant Bernard 'Jimmy' Jennings DFM, Ken Wilkinson's closest friend on 19 Squadron, who taught the fledgling fighter pilot the skills of dogfighting: 'He was a hard taskmaster.'

27. Warrant Officer Ken Wilkinson, on wing, left, pictured with 'A' Flight on 165 Squadron at Church Stanton in 1943.

28. Warrant Officer Ken Wilkinson with 165 Squadron Spitfire Mk IX, Church Stanton, 1943.

29. Ken Wilkinson and the author, pictured at a book signing in 2009.

30. LAC Bill Green – a newly qualified pilot but not yet promoted sergeant – upon his marriage to Bertha Louisa Biggs, 3 June 1940.

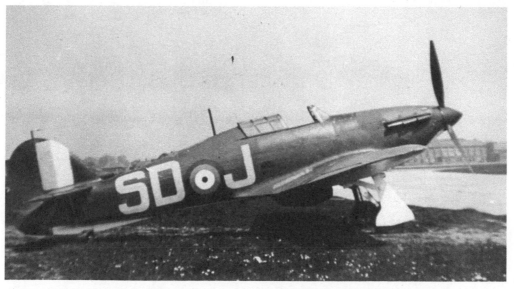

31. A 501 Squadron Hurricane pictured at Kenley in September 1940.

32. A well-known photograph of 501 Squadron pilots at Kenley during the Battle of Britain. Seated at right is Flight Commander John 'Gibbo' Gibson, who was shot down in the same action as Sergeant Green on 29 August 1940. Gibson, however, made a parachute descent from 16,000 feet, drifting out to sea, while Green's parachute opened a mere second from certain death.

33. The way it was: pilots of 501 Squadron at readiness, Gravesend, August 1940. From left: Sergeant Tony Pickering, Sergeant R. J. K. Gent, Flight Sergeant Peter Morfill, Sergeant Paul Farnes, Sergeant Anton Glowacki (Polish), unidentified, Sergeant W. B. Henn, Sergeant Tony Whitehouse, Sergeant James 'Ginger' Lacey, Pilot Officer Bob Dafforn.

34. Sergeant Anton Glowacki (Polish) makes his after action combat report to a steel-helmeted intelligence officer during the Battle of Britain.

35. Squadron Leader Harry Hogan (centre, in forage cap) with pilots of 501 Squadron – which was in the front line throughout the Battle of Britain, losing nineteen pilots.

Above left: 36. 501 Squadron Battle of Britain survivors at Colerne, 1941; from left: Pilot Officers James 'Ginger' Lacey DFM, Ken MacKenzie DFC (later a long-serving Chairman of the Battle of Britain Fighter Association), Tony Whitehouse, Bob Dafforn and Vic Ekins. Of this group, only Dafforn would not survive the war.

Above right: 37. Warrant Officer Bill Green serving with 504 Squadron at Filton in 1941. Commissioned the following year, Green had achieved a rare feat: the transition from lowly engine fitter on an AAF squadron to commissioned fighter pilot.

Left: 38. A 22 OTU Hurricane in September 1944, from the pages of Bill Green's log book.

Bottom left: 39. Flight Lieutenants Bill Green (right) and 'Shag' Hellens with a 1682 BTD Flight Tomahawk in March 1944.

Left: 40. Bill Green, photographed at his West Country home by the author in 2012.

Right: 41. Pilot Officer Geoffrey 'Boy' Wellum (right) at Biggin Hill with his flight commander and mentor, Flight Lieutenant Brian Kingcome DFC, for whom Geoffrey has only the greatest respect and affection: 'Brian Kingcome *was* 92 Squadron.'

42. On 14 September 2010, BBC2 broadcast Matthew Whiteman's docudrama *First Light*, based upon Geoffrey Wellum's best-selling memoir of that title. Here Ben Aldridge (left) and Sam Heughan are pictured during filming as Kingcome and Wellum respectively.

Above: 43. Flying Officer Alan Wright with his 92 Squadron Spitfire at Pembrey in the Battle of Britain.

Left: 44. Pilot Officer Desmond Williams of 92 Squadron, illustrating 1940 flying kit – excluding the all-important 'Mae West' life preserver worn when operating over water. Williams became an ace in the Battles of France and Britain, but was killed on 10 October 1940 when he collided with another Spitfire while attacking a German bomber near Tangmere; he was twenty years old.

45. Flight Lieutenant Brian Fabris Kingcome DFC, drawn by Cuthbert Orde in 1940. Kingcome rose to Group Captain, also awarded the DSO, and after the war ran a chauffeuring business with fellow Battle of Britain Spitfire pilot 'Paddy' Barthropp before setting up a furniture-making concern in Devon; he died in 1994.

46. Sam Heughan, as Pilot Officer 'Boy' Wellum, in the excellent BBC2 docudrama *First Light*.

47. Squadron Leader Geoffrey Wellum DFC, pictured by the author with his latest model ship project at his Cornish home in 2012.

Left: 48. Wing Commander John Scatliff Dewar DSO DFC, Station Commander of RAF Exeter and the highest-ranking RAF officer to be killed during the Battle of Britain – a very experienced and successful fighter pilot and leader, the thirty-three-year-old would doubtless have achieved great things in the service.

Right: 49. Johnny Dewar's grave at North Baddesley, Hampshire. Although the date of death is recorded as 12 September 1940, Wing Commander Dewar was actually killed the previous day – as explained in this book.

50. The 2013 service of remembrance at the Battle of Britain National Memorial, situated on the cliffs overlooking Folkestone in Kent.

Above: 51. Sally Kerson leads the commemoration of Wing Commander Johnny Dewar at St John the Baptist, North Baddesley, on 9 July 2015. The event was initiated by Dilip Sarkar (right of headstone), Wing Commander Jon Whitworth (centre) leading the RAF presence.

Left: 52. Children from William Gilpin School place flowers on Wing Commander Dewar's grave, watched by Sally Kerson and Dilip Sarkar – who drew inspiration for this moving act of remembrance from Arnhem's 'Flower Children'.

4

FLYING OFFICER K. A. 'KEN' WILKINSON

Kenneth Astill Wilkinson and I first corresponded in 1986, since when we have enjoyed many hours in each other's company, attending exhibitions, memorial services, book signings and other events – including my wedding, at which Ken was an honoured guest. One occasion that particularly stands out occurred in 1996, when we were filming a news item about Douglas Bader for Central Television: the camera was focussed on Flight Lieutenant Ron Rayner DFC, who had flown Spitfires with 41, 43 and 72 Squadrons between 1941 and 1945; suddenly, Ken interrupted, put his arm around Ron, and determinedly said to the camera, 'If you were a fighter pilot, you were a cocky so-and-so, but if you were a *Spitfire* pilot, you were cockier still!' Needless to say, Ken flew Spitfires; this is his story.

My father was in the Royal Flying Corps (RFC) during the Great War, and there are some photographs of him in uniform in our family album. At one stage, he was at Joyce Green aerodrome, east of London, which was the airfield from which Lieutenant Leefe Robinson flew when he destroyed the *Graf Zeppelin*, which was bombing the capital. Robinson received the VC for that 'signal act of valour' but sadly died of this flu virus, which killed many people in this country after the Great War. Between the wars, my father first worked in the aircraft industry for AV Roe, then Gloster's, The Experimental Establishment at Farnborough, Comperswift, Parnall, before returning to Gloster's; there he was a works inspector.

Soon after my seventeenth birthday, my father asked me if I would like to fly in the RAF. Of course there was only one answer: yes! Applications could only be made at seventeen and three-quarters, so before that father arranged for me to fly in a service aircraft, to ensure that I was OK with flying. Earlier, I'd had flights in an aircraft of Alan Cobham's Flying Circus, which cost five shillings, but that wasn't really an indication of my suitability, just involving a take-off, straight and level flying, and a landing.

So it was that I went to Brockworth aerodrome to fly with John Summers, brother of Supermarine test pilot 'Mutt', who flew the prototype Spitfire, K5054, on its first flight. We flew in a Hawker Hartebeeste, built for the South African Air Force, which was basically a Hawker Hart light day bomber; I was in the rear gunner's seat, facing backwards. The flight was certainly thrilling – even looking backwards. John carried out aerobatics, which were part of the test. After a while we landed and I expressed gratitude for the great favour I had received. Sometime later I discovered that John had been grateful to have someone in the back, as ballast, otherwise he would have flown with a sack!

In due course I was unsuccessful in my application for a SSC. That was just as well, as it turned out, because during the war I met a successful candidate who had been poorly paid during peacetime and miserable not to go into it with the rest of us when the balloon went up in 1939. The next option for me was joining the RAFVR, but as I was travelling around the country for various jobs, opportunities were limited until I was told that there were vacancies at Staverton, near my home in Cheltenham. I was then working in Birmingham, so I gave my notice, got a job in Cheltenham, and applied to the VR: again, an interview and another medical. I was surrounded by big, beefy, fellows who positively exuded fitness – whilst I had been out dancing the previous night! Strangely, I passed, they didn't; I was attested the same day.

The following morning, I went to Staverton airfield, made myself known to the instructors, and had my first flight in a Tiger Moth – thus properly starting my flying career. Within a day or so, I was told that there was a vacancy for the fifteen days of annual training, so I applied to go. Once more I gave in my notice and started full-time flying training. Obviously, as a result, I went solo fairly quickly. When we were flying, pupils sat outside, watching those in the air, and listening to the instructors and others. The days passed thus: cycle to Staverton, flying training, cycle home, then ground training at night school. Then I got a job with the test flight department at Rotol, at Staverton, working for the test pilot. My social life became Aircraft 2, Girls 0, and the girl I intended to marry ditched me and went off with a chap who worked for Cheltenham council. At that time, I had decided to become a curate, and in order to raise the necessary money for theological college, I had agreed with said girl that I should join the RAF for four to six years, after which I would have both the money and the ability to fly and navigate aircraft. Despite that agreement I was ditched, but that meant I could concentrate of flying training and ground school – which I did. I passed the elementary flying on Tiger Moths, and went on to fly Hawker Harts. Whilst working at Rotol, I got in quite a few hours flying time, including odd things like ferrying new aircraft to RAF aerodromes – where the sight of a pilot in 'civvies' was rare. Then came 1 September 1939: we were all called into the test pilot's office and told that we were in reserved occupations. When my turn came to speak, I said that I hadn't joined the RAFVR for that – and took my leave of Rotol. On 3 September 1939, war began – and I was gainfully employed again.

Staverton was a good aerodrome, being near to the Cotswolds, and a lot of well-known aviators visited the private flying club, including Jim Mollinson and Amy Johnson. Because the club had a drinks licence we VR pilots went there frequently, after flying. Some of the visiting aircraft were interesting. There was one low-winged monoplane that went out of sight in the long grass; it was powered by a Ford V8 engine and capable of taxiing in a straight line. When the pilot wanted to take-off, he got out of the cockpit, lifted the tail to face the aircraft into wind, got back in and took off. The VR had a dinner dance at the Queen's Hotel, Cheltenham, and it was interesting to see the different clothes: some farmer's sons came in suits and boots, some in uniform, some in dinner jackets, because few young men wore suits, we just couldn't afford them. Some of those farmer's boys, in fact, went on to become Master Bombers with high rank.

When the VR reported for duty at Cheltenham headquarters, one of the pilots was called Perkins. He was the MP for Stroud and told us that he had been talking to Neville Chamberlain, the Prime Minister, who thought war would be over by Christmas; how wrong he was. During the summer of 1939, pupil pilots would go off to the Severn, generally Wainlodes, drink beer, have bread and cheese, which allowed us to carry on drinking until 11 p.m. We'd then strip off, swim the Severn and go back. Some of us then had to get on our bikes and cycle twelve miles to Cheltenham. Other VR members were posted off, to continue their service flying training, but I stayed at VR HQ, assembling equipment and packing it up in cases. You get to know what makes a Rolls-Royce Kestrel engine when you have to put it back together again. Once or twice I had to take parties to places like Cambridge, for them to continue training, then return to Cheltenham. All comparatively dull, until December, when I was about the last to be posted, and went to the Initial Training Wing (ITW) at Marine Court, on the sea front at Hastings: my RAF career had finally begun.

The ITW was really intended to occupy us with Physical Training (PT), drill and sport, but there were also exams in various subjects. Marine Court was a block of luxury flats, which had been cleared out and requisitioned by the RAF. We were on the top floor (no lifts). We discovered that if we failed we would be re-mustered as air gunners. The majority passed everything. Although we were not actually flying, we were treated very well and a lot of famous people came to see us. In RAF terms, the most important was Billy Bishop, a Canadian VC and Great War fighter pilot. I was in charge of the guard, and asked him if he wished to inspect us; he took one look and declined! Len Harvey, the lightweight champion boxer, gave us lessons on the stage, and we were entertained by stars including Marlene Dietrich.

In March 1940, we were back flying again, this time at Hanworth. Although I had done a lot of flying, I hadn't passed my ground exams, so I had to start flying training all over again. It was not an auspicious start. The whole course was given the usual pep talk and an instructor tried to show off by holding the aircraft low – he failed to pull up in time, piled into a row of parked Miles Magisters, and promptly killed himself – fortunately only himself. Hanworth Park Hotel was in the middle of the aerodrome, and this was our accommodation. We shared the airfield with the General Aircraft Company, which was testing certain prototypes, nearly all with tricycle undercarriages. Part of the flying included landing at Denham, which was next door to the British film industry, so we met the young starlets there, then met them again at a pub near Staines with a Thames-side garden. On one occasion a male film star, full of his own self-importance, was making a nuisance of himself, so we frog marched him down to the river and chucked him in. Getting to the West End was easy, and so we saw new films and acquainted ourselves with the better hotels.

After Hanworth, some of us went to Yatesbury to do night flying and aerobatics on Tiger Moths for a fortnight. On one of the hills overlooking Yatesbury there is a prehistoric horse cut out and outlined in chalk. A very good landmark. We were able to go into Chippenham and Calne, but not for long, because afterwards we were posted: first off we went to Paddington, then to King's Cross, and overnight to Montrose, and 8 FTS for advanced flying training. Until then, the war had been something we read about in the papers, but at King's Cross we all had to stand aside and give priority to soldiers returning from Dunkirk. Seeing their expressions and the state of their uniforms showed us just what war entailed. It was a necessary experience for us.

Montrose aerodrome had been built in 1913, it being obvious that the German navy would be interested in the Royal Navy's nearby anchorage at Scapa Flow. We arrived to find that we were designated 'Pre-Fighter Course', which established our future: fighter pilots. It was an interesting area to fly over, with the North Sea on one side, and mountains on the other. Our training continued without hindrance until the wings exam, when the Luftwaffe decided to wake us up with a daylight raid by a Ju 88. Montrose was a legitimate target because 603 Squadron had a flight of Spitfires there. After that, night flying was carried out at Edzell, and aerodrome that was no more than a grass field. After wings exam, some were recommended for a commission, including Neil Cameron and Peter Fox ... One exercise was flying and navigating under the hood, with one pilot as lookout and the other navigating with only watch and compass. Whoever chose the route was lacking a sense of humour, because he decided that Kirriemuir should be the first turning point. When Cameron and Fox arrived over the town, the hood went up and they did some very low flying, so low that they wrote off the local telephone system. Both lost their recommendations for commissions. Cameron later got his back, and finished up a Marshal of the Royal Air Force (MRAF), Chief of the Air Staff, and Chief of the Defence Staff; Peter Fox was shot down in 1941, captured, and never commissioned.

In the meadowland around the Dee, just inland of Aberdeen, there was a nudist camp and many cine camera photos from our aircraft began with the target aircraft, but finished with nudists running for cover! Scotland was used by the Germans as a discreet landing place for submarines, so we had to be very careful what we talked about in public. One night, in a pub in Montrose, we were questioned about our activities in some detail, so one of our party found a policeman who arrested the man. Drinking in Scotland on a Sunday was very restricted in those days, so only genuine travellers could get a drink, so those of us not on church-parade would hire a taxi and go to Aberdeen or Dundee, and there be served with enormous steaks – probably a month's ration for people in England.

At the end of August 1940, the course finished. Some went to fly Hurricanes and others, including me, were posted to fly Spitfires at 7 OTU, Hawarden, near Chester. We arrived to find a big aerodrome with lots of aircraft needing ferrying to squadrons. 7 OTU, however, was basically a tented village by a stream; the catering tent was at the top end, with other activities along the stream's length; I need not add which convenience was at the end. We were billeted in Hawarden Church Hall, with solid oak pews for bunks, plus one issue blanket.

Flying was limited due to the small number of aircraft available, but there was always ground tuition, aircraft recognition, the Merlin engine, and Spitfire characteristics to learn about. The Station Commander was one Group Captain Ira Jones VC, another famous Great War fighter pilot, who had his own way of describing Germans. His powers of description would have offended most ladies of a genteel nature, but brought home to us the need to attack and best place to do it. Whilst at Hawarden I managed to get to Manchester and see my grandfather, as it happened for the last time, and we went to Liverpool to watch a Bing Crosby film; half-way through, there was an air raid alert. I heard bombs exploding but continued watching the film. Upon conclusion I realised I was the only person left in the cinema! The bombs had hit the hospital behind the cinema, in fact.

Whilst we were doing our flying in Spitfires – a wonderful aeroplane – a raid was reported: a German aircraft making its way through Wales to Liverpool. Everyone flying was alerted. Needless to say we went to Liverpool – I didn't see the enemy aircraft at all, so my first effort to defend democracy was a damp squib. That raider, however, was destroyed over Wales by another Spitfire pilot. Previously, I had had a molar extracted, and flying at height resulted in a painful cavity – treatment for which involved dripping brandy into said cavity. Very pleasant, but it held me back for a few days. Consequently I missed the first posting, which was to 611 Squadron at Ternhill, but then 'Red' Parker and I were posted to Wittering. We arrived there in the middle of an air raid. Next morning we were told that we were supposed to be with 616 Squadron at Kirton-in-Lindsey, so off we went again. At Kirton we found our first RAF station: a proper sergeants' mess, single bedrooms and, believe it or not, a cup of tea in the morning brought in by a young lady of the Women's Auxiliary Air Force (WAAF).

Sergeant Wilkinson reported to 616 Squadron on 1 October 1940, which had been formed at Doncaster in 1938, as an AAF unit. Having been called to full-time service in September 1939, 616 had participated in Operation DYNAMO before returning to Leconfield, in north-east England. On 15 August 1940, *Luftlotte* 5, based in Norway, sent a large formation of KG 26 He 111s and KG 30 Ju 88s to attack Sunderland and Driffield respectively. This attack, of course, proved Dowding's wisdom in retaining a strong fighter force in the north. 616 Squadron was among those scrambled to deal with this raid, intercepting over fifty Ju 88s, plus Me 110 twin-engined fighters escorting, ten miles off Flamborough Head – and subsequently claimed the destruction of eight Ju 88s, four more probably destroyed and two damaged, for no loss.

Four days later, however, the squadron flew south, to Kenley in 11 Group. The change in tempo of operations, from encountering lone or formations of unescorted bombers over northern England, to the intensity of fighting now involved, which included the Me 109 peril, was traumatic. On 3 September, having lost five pilots killed and many Spitfires destroyed or damaged, 616 was relieved by 64 Squadron. Squadron Leader Marcus Robinson was relieved of command by Squadron Leader Billy Burton, a Cranwell Sword of Honour winner, who settled down to rebuilding the squadron.

The following day, Air Chief Marshal Dowding's Senior Air Staff Officer (SASO), Air Vice-Marshal Evill, had provided the Air Staff figures indicating that in the four weeks ending 4 September, Fighter Command aircrew casualties numbered 338. In that time, the OTUs, however, had only produced 280 replacement pilots. In response to this crisis, Air Chief Marshal Dowding and Air Vice-Marshal Park decided upon the 'Stabilising Scheme'. This designated fighter squadrons either 'A' – fully operational and at full strength; 'B' – those being rested but with at least six combat ready pilots among their total complement of eighteen pilots; and 'C' – squadrons rebuilding and with only three or less pilots with operational experience. In this way, 11 Group could be maintained with 'A' squadrons. When depleted and downgraded to 'B' or 'C', squadrons could be withdrawn, to rebuild and refit, while squadrons having done so, and having resumed 'A' status, could replace them. Initially, 616 was given 'C' status, so badly mauled had it been at Kenley, but it was soon increased to B' – and as such contributed a flight, on several occasions, to operate with the Duxford Wing. It was on one of those operations, in fact, that the sixth and final 616 Squadron pilot to be killed in the Battle of Britain was shot down.

With 616 Squadron we were able to get more flying practice on Spitfires. The training involved concerned formation flying, firing guns, practice aerial combat, and spending time at readiness. Being in East Anglia, we were in 12 Group, and our job was to protect the industrial Midlands and north, in addition to covering 11 Group's airfields whilst Park's squadrons were up. Readiness involved the occasional scramble, looking for aircraft approaching Humberside. One difficulty was that the Anti-Aircraft gunners were unable to distinguish friend from foe, and blasted away at both RAF fighters flying east, and incoming German bombers flying west. On one occasion we found Coastal Command Hudsons returning from a patrol, instead of the Germans we sought. On another, I flew south, to join the Duxford Wing on a patrol over the Thames Estuary, but that was uneventful.

There was one incident with 616 Squadron when I suffered injustice. Red Parker and I went off to practise formation flying with our flight commander, Flight Lieutenant CAT 'Jerry' Jones. Jones was Red 1, me 2, and Parker 3. As we were returning to base, Jerry put us in echelon. Flying and landing whilst in formation involves keeping an eye on the leader, which Red and I did. Jerry bounced badly on landing, as did I but without harming the aircraft, but Red also did so and damaged his Spitfire. The injustice was that my log book was inscribed with a red endorsement, and histories of the Battle of Britain state that I broke my Spit. That wasn't the case. I landed safely and did not damage my aircraft. Red, however, landed badly and damaged his, the machine having to go off for repair. This just goes to show that the written record is not always accurate – not even written records.

On 17 October 1940, Sergeant Wilkinson was posted again, this time to 19 Squadron, at Fowlmere, in the Duxford Sector of 12 Group. 19 was a regular RAF squadron, and was, in fact, the first to receive the Spitfire in 1938. It also participated in Operation DYNAMO – losing its CO, Squadron Leader Geoffrey Stephenson, on the squadron's first full-formation combat, over Calais, on 26

May 1940; the former Cranwellian was captured, ending the war in the infamous Colditz Castle. The commander of 'A' Flight, Flight Lieutenant Brian Lane, thereafter led the squadron in the air, receiving a well-deserved DFC for his efforts over Dunkirk. Stephenson's replacement, Squadron Leader Phillip Pinkham AFC, busied himself with test-flying the unit's experimental cannon-armed Spitfires, which suffered so many stoppages that tired machine-gun-armed Spitfires from Hawarden replaced them. On 5 September 1940, Pinkham led his squadron into action for the first time since taking command, but was shot down and killed over Kent. Lane then became CO – an exceptional pilot and leader of men, highly respected by all who knew him, even tough, no-nonsense, professional NCOs like Flight Sergeant George 'Grumpy' Unwin DFM:

> Brian Lane and I, although segregated on the ground due to our ranks, were inseparable in the air. He was unflappable. In action, his voice would come over the R/T, always completely calm, no matter what the odds, and he always made the right tactical decisions. He had time for everyone on the station, treated everyone with respect, no matter how lowly their rank or trade, and was, in my opinion, a truly exceptional leader and man. We would all have followed this quiet but compelling officer anywhere – who was also an exceptional fighter pilot.

Also stationed in 12 Group was Squadron Leader Douglas Bader, who had lost both legs in a pre-war flying accident. King's regulations, however, unsurprisingly did not provide for limbless pilots, and so Bader, who refused a ground appointment, left the service. In 1939, however, he passed a flying test and returned to the service, joining 19 Squadron at Duxford, which was commanded by his Cranwell friend and contemporary, Squadron Leader Geoffrey Stephenson. Flying Officer Bader, having previously flown biplanes with fixed undercarriage and fixed-pitch propellers, had a difficult time getting to grips with the modern Spitfire, and found it difficult being junior in rank to younger pilots. Fortunately another Cranwellian, Squadron Leader 'Tubby' Mermagen, who commanded 222 Squadron, which shared Duxford with 19, agreed to help: over Dunkirk, where Bader scored his first aerial victory, he was a flight lieutenant and commander of Mermagen's 'A' Flight. Already familiar with the 12 Group commander, Air Vice-Marshal Sir Trafford Leigh-Mallory, in July, Bader was promoted to squadron leader and became CO of the Canadian 242 Squadron, based at Coltishall.

For Bader, not being at the forefront of the action was intolerable, and he became exasperated, whiling away the hours in 12 Group while 11 Group was hotly engaged. On 30 August 1940, however, 11 Group requested assistance from 12 Group, and Bader's 242 Squadron intercepted German bombers over Hatfield. His pilots made many combat claims, generating numerous congratulatory signals. Had he intercepted with more fighters, Bader argued, he would have destroyed more enemy machines. Wing Commander 'Woody' Woodhall and Air Vice-Marshal Leigh-Mallory both supported this view – and gave Bader permission to lead the Hurricanes of 242 and 310, and the Spitfires of 19, into action. This, however, was contrary to Dowding's System and the way in which he required the battle fought. In order to preserve precious fighters, for example, Air Vice-Marshal Park attacked with small tactical formations, and, in any case, time, distance and speed made a nonsense of any suggestion that 12 Group should be scrambled to intercept incoming raids on London. Instead, the so-called Duxford Wing frequently flew what amounted to fighter sweeps over London and Kent, confusing the defenders – but claiming enormous numbers of enemy aircraft destroyed. Because such figures were largely accepted with little scrutiny, the impression was that Big Wing tactics were right, Dowding and

Park wrong. Although this is not the place to provide an account of this controversy (but see *Douglas Bader* by this author), we now know that the more fighters are engaged, the more confusing is the picture – and multiple claims therefore occur for the same enemy aircraft. The truth was that on occasions the 'Big Wing' over-claimed by 7 to 1, and Dowding and Park were entirely correct in their handling of the Battle of Britain.

It took all day to get to Duxford by train. When I arrived there I reported to the Guard Room and saw a Hurricane doing hesitation rolls with great precision. The aircraft flew a barrel roll, then went straight into a slow roll – perfect. These were very difficult to execute; you had to keep the aircraft straight whilst inverted, roll from 180° to 70°, hesitate, then come back to straight and level. 'Who the blazes is that?' I asked, never having seen such astonishing flying in my life; 'Mr Bader,' came the reply. I was aware that even with two legs in fully working order, I couldn't fly as well as that. It was inspirational. Douglas made you try harder, through his own example; it really was as simple as that.

Fowlmere was the nearby Duxford satellite, and had been an airfield in the Great War. Facilities were basic, the airfield having been brought back to use. There were rows of Nissen huts; dispersal was a bell tent, in which I had the bed next to Pilot Officer Wallace 'Jock' Cunningham, an ace with the DFC, and our 'operations room' was a lean-to shed with a tarpaulin to keep the rain off. Inside were the serviceability states of our aircraft, and names of pilots who would fly them operationally. Spitfires were dispersed all over the aerodrome. My first job was to take a Spitfire from Fowlmere to Duxford. I pride myself that I never made a bad landing in a Spitfire, but on that occasion I landed fine but the wheels gave way, the oleo leg came through the wing; I banged my nose on the reflector gunsight, situated right in front of the pilot. Nothing was said, so it must have been known that the aircraft was dodgy. I then flew the 'B' Flight Commander, Flight Lieutenant 'Wilf' Clouston, to aerodromes on Salisbury Plain: Upavon and Netheravon. We were there for some time, and it was getting very dark on the return flight. I put down at Kidlington and phoned Duxford – the squadron had already written me off! I stayed the night and flew home the following day. So it was that I became 19's 'odds and sods bloke' for a while.

My closest friend on 19 was Sergeant Bernard 'Jimmy' Jennings, an experienced combat pilot with whom I practised formation and dogfighting; a hard taskmaster. In those days, formation flying was the be all and end all. Flying in a 'vic' you had to be tight, and concentrate hard. Before the war, they used to do this with Gauntlets actually tied together! In cloud, though, it was best to move away from the other aircraft, because you just can't see each other, increasing the risk of collision. That said, it was better for getting a section of aircraft from 'A' to 'B' in bad weather than the 'Finger Four', in which aircraft were more spread out and so difficult to see. The 'vic', though, was too inflexible and required too much concentration on formation flying rather than searching for the enemy – so proved useless for combat flying.

I also got on well with the other sergeant pilots, especially Johnson, 'Chaz' Charnock and Scott. Boswell was always saying that he wanted the cloud-base to be at an altitude of five feet ten inches, so he could walk underneath it. He was injured, so we went to see him in Ely Hospital. There we found some very attractive society ladies, voluntary nurses, in loose, revealing uniforms, which was too much for Boswell!

We didn't see much of the officer pilots, Pilot Officer Richard Jones, for example, who I later got to know very well, or our CO, Squadron Leader Brian Lane DFC, from whom, except at dispersal, we were segregated from on the ground. The squadron's greatest ace was Flight Sergeant George 'Grumpy' Unwin DFM, the all-powerful, the almighty, who advised from on high. He was posted away after the Battle of Britain. My 'A' Flight Commander was Flight Lieutenant Walter 'Farmer' Lawson, but he didn't seem to like me very much. Lawson had been a pre-war NCO pilot, who had worked up the hard way to become a sergeant pilot. We amateurs of the VR, however, were all sergeants straightaway. We all had similar socio-educational backgrounds and it was just the luck of the draw as to who was commissioned after getting their wings. Some were, others weren't; I wasn't. To us of the VR, though, that didn't matter, we were all equals, whether sergeants or pilot officers. So I always referred to Pilot Officer so-and-so by first names, because we had all been sergeants together. Lawson took exception to this, and therefore to me.

At the time of my arrival, the Duxford Wing had been in existence for a month or more. From Duxford we had to fly south, to the main area of fighting, which was difficult at midday, with the sun in our eyes. If we weren't allowed to 'tack', change course, we could be sitting ducks with German fighters looking down on us. We travelled from 'A' to 'B' to convoy, but the formation broke up when we went into action. There were various tactics to help in combat, the main one being the very steep turn – which was good, because both the Spitfire and Hurricane could out-turn the Me 109. Of course, there are well-recorded examples of 11 Group calling for us too late, so when Douglas arrived with us over the Thames, the Germans had gone home. That being so, we would sweep over south-east England, just in case more enemy aircraft came over for a look-see. However, on one occasion, my cine-gun camera sequence clearly showed Sergeant Wilkinson attacking an Me 109 – which appeared completely unmoved by my attentions. Douglas was a bit of a law unto himself; we'd be flying south and, although there was supposed to be radio silence, he'd call up our Controller and say, 'Any business, Woody?' I think the Big Wing's greatest contribution was psychological, when, on Battle of Britain Day, Douglas appeared over London with sixty Spitfires and Hurricanes.

The German aircrews had been led to believe that we were finished, so the effect on their morale must have been devastating.

November and December 1940 were fairly quiet for us, but 19 Squadron left Fowlmere and returned to Duxford. Previously, we had only been able to get back to Duxford once a week – for a bath. On one occasion we flew over the North Sea, and I clearly saw Me 109s approaching. Lawson, however, insisted, 'It's alright, they're yellow-nosed Hurricanes.' There were no such aircraft and it was impossible to see the colour of their noses; they were 109s alright.

Into winter and dark nights, with a lot of social to-ing and fro-ing. There were social occasions in the Sergeants' Mess, and at one of them I was sitting on a three-seater settee, and Squadron Leader Douglas Bader and his wife, Thelma, sat next to me for a while. In getting up, however, he landed one of his tin legs on my in-step, but after what he had been through what could I do but smile bravely? There was then an investiture at Duxford, with many fighter pilots receiving decorations, including pilots of 19 Squadron. After the investiture we were all inspected by King George VI; a Royal Canadian Air Force (RCAF) sergeant, who was actually an American, stepped forward and said, 'Hello, King' – showing that people from republic states do not know how to treat a monarch. When all that was over, Sholto Douglas, who replaced Dowding as our boss, gathered 19 Squadron together at 'A' Flight's dispersal for a pep talk. He told us that as of 1 January 1941, the RAF would be going on the offensive, taking the war to the Germans in France – and there we were thinking that we were still defending England! On New Year's Day, the Duxford Wing did fly briefly over France, but I can't recall the occasion being particularly offensive, as it were.

In January 1941, I was Duty Pilot one day, which entailed spending twenty-four hours in the Control Room. After the first sweep 19 did that day, Pilot Officer Peter Howard-Williams, who was our very own 'Pilot Officer Prune', came back but forgot to do things he should have. Instead of coming to rest in an enclosure, he carried on into the sandbags. Incredibly, Peter later became a flight commander on 118 Squadron, shot down a few Jerries, and won a DFC!

Another incident worth recalling happened during a snowstorm in early 1941, when 'A' Flight took off and escorted a motorcade on a main road. The vehicles turned into Mildenhall aerodrome, and we landed there, hoping to be refuelled. There was no one about to do so, the whole station was on parade, so we just had to stand around and wait. We then heard guns and an enemy aircraft flew low over the airfield. It was still snowing. We scrambled and chased the Hun. Going over Feltwell aerodrome, Sergeant 'Jimmy' Jennings was just a few yards behind the raider, but the snow obscured his vision. We were all short of fuel, so had no choice but to return to Mildenhall (later in the year, the king – whose motorcade we had unknowingly escorted, and who was inspecting Mildenhall that day – thanked Jimmy for his efforts when presenting him with the DFM). It was late, and our Spitfires still didn't get refuelled, so we had to stay the night. Clearly Bomber Command operated differently to Fighter Command, and just wasn't in a hurry like we were! There was a pub on the main road through Mildenhall, so we went there after eating with most of the RAF band – all well-known musicians from radio and records. We flew back to Duxford the following morning.

It turned out that my return flight from Mildenhall was my last with 19 Squadron. On 27 January 1941, I was posted to 56 OTU, at Sutton Bridge, as an instructor. Lawson didn't like me, and, I strongly suspect, had me posted. I went to see Squadron Leader Lane, however, and asked if I could return to 19 Squadron when my stint as an instructor was over; 'Of course,' he said. On one occasion I flew down from Sutton Bridge to see the boys at Coltishall, but took one look at their new Spitfire Mk IIs with the single, wing-mounted, long range tank and thought 'Bugger that!' The squadron was engaged on sweeps and bomber escorts across the

North Sea, to Holland – and lost a lot of pilots. On one occasion Lawson was killed and Jock captured, and the next day Arthur Vokes led what was left of 19 on a search for the missing – they ran into a gaggle of Me 110s and nearly all were lost. Disastrous, and very sad.

In January 1943, I was instructing with 1488 Gunnery Flight at Martlesham Heath, where we were visited by the AOC. He came into dispersal and said to me, 'How long have you been here?' 'Too bloody long, sir!' I replied. Now this was not the way for a warrant officer to talk to an air marshal, but nevertheless within a fortnight I was on a Spitfire refresher course at 61 OTU, Rednal. I then, at last, returned to an operational Spitfire squadron, 234, at Skeabrae in the Orkneys. We were flying the Spitfire Mk VI, which had extended wing tips, making the aircraft easier to fly at high altitude but difficult to land. In addition, pilots were bolted into the pressurised cockpits. Our job was to defend Scapa Flow, and intercept aircraft from Norway interfering with our convoys. Sometimes we were scrambled but there was rarely any contact. It involved, though, a great deal of sitting in our cockpits on the runway for two hours at a time. We also patrolled up to Shetland and back, dawn to dusk. On one occasion, when I was returning from a dusk patrol as Number 2, the Duty Pilot had put the wrong direction on the runway, so the section landed in darkness, downwind. The Section Leader failed to appreciate his excessive speed, went off the end of the runway and tipped up – no joke when bolted into the cockpit. I had realised how fast we were going, so it was full left rudder and brake, stick back hard, right down the runway until I managed to turn left down the perimeter track, without damage: I'd saved an aeroplane. I switched off, got out and went to the crashed Spitfire. That was okay, so I went back to my own aircraft. A senior officer then came up and said, 'You were lucky, weren't you?' When you are a warrant officer you do not say what you think to senior officers on such occasions...

The squadron moved down to Church Stanton, near Taunton in 10 Group, during June, and put on Spitfire Mk Vs. Early in July 1943, I was posted to 165 Squadron at Ibsley, where there was an increase in activity: convoy patrols, recces to the Cherbourg area and Channel Islands. One of our Australian pilots used to fly along the canal at Lannion to wave to a girl, who waved back. I landed calibration jobs, which involved flying to Guernsey at height, so that the radar could track me. On one occasion when we flew low over the sea to keep under the German radar, we were in the bay of St Malo when I was surprised to see flying fish – I told the other chaps but they told me to take more water with it!

At the end of July I was posted overseas. Actually I had been asking to go to North Africa, but before I could get on the boat I was recalled to Kenley. The reason for this was Exercise STARKEY, the intention of which was to entice the Luftwaffe up for mass destruction. The night before STARKEY, in fact, we were addressed by no less a personality than 'Boom' Trenchard, the 'Father of the RAF' himself; it was really something to see the great man. The preparatory attacks for STARKEY were nearly always with seventy-two Marauders, with 165 as escort cover. The targets attacked were spread over northern France, Belgium and Holland. These sorties were regular during the build-up to STARKEY. On one such occasion, 165 went to Courtrai, and at the briefing we were told that other targets would be attacked simultaneously. We rendezvoused with our Marauders and went across the Channel, but soon after crossing the coast we were bounced by the Luftwaffe and there followed a merry mix-up all the way to the target. At the briefing, we had been told that there was very little flak in the vicinity of Courtrai, but when we got over the target, mixing it with German fighters, there seemed to be hell of a lot of it. We were kept busy, but the main thing was to ensure that the Marauders did their job. After the raid, I settled alongside some other Spitfires only to find that it was not 165 Squadron, but I remained with them until we crossed the English coast. I then returned to Kenley where I discovered that I had not, in fact, been to Courtrai, but somehow managed to end up on the raid to Lille! I remember that the Channel was full of landing craft, containing Canadian troops, and 165 also did a lot of standing patrols over Boulogne, but the Germans did not take the bait. So, what was supposed to be the 'Greatest Air Battle of All Time' ended up a damp squib. It was, I suppose, a dry run for Operation JUBILEE, the ill-fated Canadian landings at Dieppe, over which a big air battle did take place.

Other things we had to do were covering boats containing agents escaping from France, and ditched bomber crews until rescued by ASR. Generally this period was fairly good, but I then had to return to instructing at an OTU. In June 1944, just after D-Day, I went down to Redhill on Spitfire Mk IXs, thence to Cranfield on Spitfire Mk XIVs – which was the best Spitfire, ever, in my opinion. The adjutant there was Noel MacGregor, with whom I had been a sergeant on 19, and one day he said to me, 'How do you fancy flying in the Midlands?' Well, being from the Midlands and by then being married with a baby on the way, and with the flying on offer being at Honeybourne, in Worcestershire, not far from Cheltenham, it sounded reasonable enough. The flying transpired to be fairly obscure: pretending to be a German night-fighter and training bomber crews. The obscurity was such that on 31 December 1944, I had drawn the short straw and was flying, chasing Wellingtons. After a while I became aware that there were no clients. No one had thought to tell me that there was no more work to do. They didn't tell me either that visibility had closed in and that the visibility at Honeybourne was remarkably restricted. Now going into Honeybourne over Fish Hill when you can't see any runway lights is no joke. It was New Year's Eve, there was hell of a party ongoing in the Mess and I was very frustrated. It took me three attempts before I got the aircraft down safely. I didn't even get to the party, which had finished by the time I landed. As you can imagine, I had no great need for laxatives after that!

Eventually the war in Europe was over, Honeybourne was closed, and we went to Abingdon to rethink the training of bomber crews to fly in the Far East. Then the war with Japan was over. After that, flying became a nuisance because we wanted to get back to civilian life and on with our new post-war careers. I was released from the RAF in November 1945, as a Flying Officer, but did not pursue my original ambition to be a curate. When I left the RAF, I joined my wife, Jo, in Reservoir Road, Olton, on a Saturday night. On the following morning I saw Oswald Wainwright at 0900 hours, got a job, and started work the following Monday.

In retirement Ken played golf, with Douglas Bader and George Unwin among others from his RAF days, and became actively involved in remembering the Battle of Britain. With great pride, Ken still attends reunions of the Battle of Britain Fighter Association, the annual memorial service at Westminster Abbey, and enjoys meeting former comrades in arms and enthusiasts at book signings and other events. Naturally Ken remains justly proud of his time as an RAF fighter pilot, especially, even as a replacement pilot late in the day, during the Battle of Britain. In conclusion, he says that

the Spitfire, of course, was a wonderful aircraft. I'm not being derogatory regarding the Hurricane but if you consider its side elevation it is really a monoplane version of the Hawker Hart. I flew Spitfire Is in training at Hawarden, with the original hand-pumped retractable undercarriage, then IAs, IIs, VBs and IXs, before the Griffon-engined Mk XIV. The power of the XIV was incredible. I did about 500 operational hours on Spitfires, and around 1,300 flying hours in total. Appropriately, my membership of the Spitfire Society is, coincidentally, 1940. Now I was just what my old friend Peter

Fox once described in another of Dilip Sarkar's books as an 'also ran'. I didn't shoot anything down, but nor was I shot down. That being so, I consider that my wartime efforts against the Luftwaffe, and theirs against Wilkinson, were quite simply a 'no-score draw'.

5

FLIGHT LIEUTENANT W. J. 'BILL' GREEN

In 1918, the General Staff decreed that a new air force would be formed, independent of both the Army and RNAS. The man chosen to oversee the creation of this new service – the RAF – was Major General Hugh 'Boom' Trenchard, who became the first CAS. Although in certain respects the new RAF was similar to the RN, Trenchard modelled the new air force on the Army, particularly regarding commissions – and his vision was that all pilots would be officers. This, however, was problematic. From 1905 onwards, any public schoolboy who was awarded Certificate 'A' from his OTC, had a good school report and presented a letter of recommendation signed by a colonel was entitled to a commission by right. Only 5.2 per cent of the population, however, could afford public school fees, meaning that the best in education – and thereby commissions – was essentially the domain of the upper classes. Indeed, attendance at Cranwell, where Trenchard's officers were trained, was also dependent upon the ability to pay fees. The ability to fly, however, is literally over and above the traditional function of officers: leading men, by platoons, companies and regiments, into battle, or directing seamen aboard ship. Belonging to the top 5.2 per cent of the social pyramid, therefore, did not necessarily guarantee receiving the coveted flying brevet.

As discussed earlier, it soon became clear that Cranwell was unable to generate the quantity of trained pilots required by the RAF, leading Trenchard to institute both the Short Service Commission scheme and pilot training for selected NCOs who would be retained for five years and then returned to their trades while remaining eligible for recall. However, numbers for the latter were small: in 1925, just 13.9 per cent of pilots were NCOs, rising to 17.1 per cent in 1935. A still smaller amount of pilots came from the Direct Entry Scheme (DES), whereby permanent commissions were offered to university graduates: of the 2,408 pilots who flew in the Battle of Britain, only thirteen were direct entrants.

A greater reserve was provided by the AAF, based upon the territorial concept and founded in 1924. By 1930, auxiliary squadrons formed 5 per cent of the regular force. There was no question, however, that AAF officers, and therefore pilots, would be anything other than public schoolboys. Indeed, if pre-war Cranwellians were from British society's elite, then auxiliary officers were the elite of the elite – and many of the AAF's members perceived it as an exclusive gentleman's club. By 1939 there were twenty AAF squadrons, but this remained an insufficient reserve. In 1925 the Cambridge UAS was formed, aimed at encouraging undergraduates to take up flying. London and Oxford soon followed suit, but, again, this represented another small reserve. In February 1934, however, the first Expansion Plan began, intended to raise the strength of Home Defence forces to fifty-two fighter squadrons by 1940. The most significant feature of Expansion Scheme 'F', in February 1936, was the creation of the RAFVR – based upon the citizen volunteer principal, with a common mode of entry, and – significantly – promotion and commissioning on merit. The VR, therefore, provided the opportunity for many bright and able young men from ordinary backgrounds to fly – aviation hitherto only being available to the wealthy.

William James Green was born in Easton, Bristol, on 23 April 1917, and attended St Gabriel's Church of England School. 'Bill' did not come from the top 5.2 per cent of Britain's socio-economic pyramid – but he did become a pilot in the AAF. For that reason alone, his story is remarkable.

I speak of my service career with complete humility, so when I say that I was considered 'bright' at school it is not intended in any other way. I was always in the top three, and played for the school football and cricket teams; indeed, I was given a trial as wicketkeeper for the Bristol Schoolboys' XI, but didn't get a place. One day, when riding to play for the school one Saturday morning, the football field was at the bottom of a long, grassy, slope. I was riding my bicycle down this with abandon. Unbeknown to me, our headmaster and football coach, Frankham, was watching me. When I arrived and dismounted by bicycle, he looked at me and said, 'Green, you will live to either sail battleships or fly aeroplanes.' This turned out to be a somewhat prophetic statement.

In 1931, aged fourteen, I left school. I had actually been given a scholarship application to a higher school, but my mother needed me to go out to work. By this time, I had a half-brother and two stepsisters, bear in mind. My stepfather, a time-served marine then on the reserve, worked at the Jenkins Factory, in Rupert Street, as the warehouseman, as did my mother, who made fancy cardboard boxes. Again, in all humility, I had a good school report, known as a 'Character'. Well, I came home, looked at the paper, to see what jobs were going, and saw that an errand boy was required at Hallet's, in Cheltenham Road. I cycled there, met the owner, a Mr Hallett, and gave him my 'Character', which he studied before taking a curious look at me and saying, 'This is not a very good job, you know.'

I said, 'I just want a job.' So, I began work delivering groceries. Six months later, my stepfather said, 'Give in your notice there, you're coming to work with me.' So I did, and the following week started work at a warehouse. My stepfather was hard on me, so that no one accused him of favouring his stepson, so it was hard but a beneficial experience. I worked hard and was rewarded with a percentage share in profits, which was gratifying, although I don't think I ever saw any money! When I was seventeen, the company taught me to drive and made me a salesman – a terrific boost for me, but not great for my stepfather, who was not consulted, and had to do my work whilst I was swanning around in a motor car.

By October 1936, I was working for a company that encouraged its employees to join the Territorial Army, or Navy or Air Force reserve. Therefore I joined 501 'County of Gloucester' Squadron of the AAF, at Filton, as an aircraftsman 2nd class, fitter under training. This, of course, was part-time. Every Thursday evening and at weekends I attended lectures, and fourteen months later took a practical, written and oral examination, in which I obtained over 80 per cent. Anyone getting 80 per cent or more skipped AC1 and went straight to LAC rank, and posted to a crew of two, looking after engines, which I did. There were essentially two ground crew trades: the fitter, who looked after the engine, and the rigger, who looked after everything else. We used to cycle out to the airfield every weekend, sometimes staying overnight. We had a skeleton staff of experienced regular airmen and NCOs to train us 'weekenders'. Just after Munich, in 1938, my friend Farr, who had enjoyed a better education than me at a grammar school, told me that he was moving to the other side of the airfield to become a pilot, in the RAF VR. In all honesty I was green with envy, because I felt that I was every bit as good as he was, so I wrote to the CO and applied to do likewise. I was, in due course, ushered before a regular squadron leader who said, 'Wouldn't you rather remain with the squadron and fly?'

To which I said, 'Well, yes, but that's only for commissioned officers.' The AAF flyers at that time, of course, were the 'bluebloods', whereas I had not been to public school or university, and was not from a wealthy family. So, that is why I thought my only chance to fly was with the VR, which was not a social elite. The squadron leader, however, said, 'I can tell you in confidence that I am getting an establishment for six NCO pilots, so, if you like, you can stay on and train to be one of those.'

I said, 'Well, of course, I would like to', and so began my flying career.

Although I was at the airfield every weekend, because we only had one instructor, who was also the adjutant, and this was in the winter, I notice that in my log book I only had about ten hours' dual, on the Avro Tutor, up until the time I was mobilised in August 1939.

When mobilised, called up for full-time service 'for the duration of current hostilities', I was twenty-two. We were confined to camp and not allowed to leave for some weeks. Eventually, I got a weekend off and cycled to see my girlfriend, over the other side of Bristol, and going down the bridge at Valley Road, under the suspension bridge, and seeing the autumnal tints on the leaves, I remember thinking how wonderful it was to be out of camp and en route to see her. My girlfriend was one Bertha Louisa Biggs, whom I had met at the cardboard box factory, where she was a machine operator, and I fell in love with her at first sight.

In October 1939 I was posted to the EFTS at Hanworth, at what is now Heathrow Airport, and Heston, and started training on Magisters. I remember with some pleasure my first solo, which was a wonderful day for me. We were housed in the Hanworth Airport Hotel, which was in the centre of the airfield and which, for me, was absolute luxury – I'd never had such food, or enjoyed such comfort in accommodation. We had a very hard winter in 1939, and I remember that one weekend it took eight hours to get back home to Bristol because of ice on the rails – the journey should have taken an hour and a half. Anyway, I successfully completed my elementary flying training, and after about sixty flying hours I was posted to the FTS at South Cerney in Gloucestershire. This was in March 1940. Bertha and I had been looking at houses before the war, with a view to buying upon marriage, and in spite of all the dangers Bertha was prepared to put all those aside and still marry a flyer. We therefore made plans to marry at St Luke's church in Bedminster on 3 June.

At South Cerney I was trained on Hawker Harts, a beautiful aircraft to fly. Our training included night flying, which was quite a thrill, and after another fifty hours we began advanced training, on Harts or the Audax – the same aeroplane but with a gunnery platform. I applied for leave to marry, but because of the deteriorating situation in France, all leave was stopped. Bertha and I therefore agreed to get a special licence and marry in Cirencester, near South Cerney. Since I was night flying that week, we determined that instead of sleeping that day we would marry. The CO, however, relented and gave me a forty-eight-hour pass. So on 3 June 1940 we were married, after which we jumped on the bus and went to Cheltenham for a couple of days. Afterwards we returned to 'living out' digs at Ashton Keynes, with the Walker family, who were rose growers and whose house was called the 'Rose Garden'. We were there for the short time elapsing between our marriage and me being posted back to the squadron.

Soon after being married, my promotion from leading aircraftman (LAC) under pilot training to corporal came through. Then, they gathered us all together in this so-called advanced training school and said, 'Here's your "wings". You are now sergeants.' I was then posted back to 501 Squadron, which had by then returned from the Battle of France via Jersey, assembled at Croydon and immediately posted to Middle Wallop, which is where I rejoined them. I well recall arriving there with brand-new sergeant's stripes and wings, and presenting myself to the replacement CO, Squadron

Leader Hogan, the old one having been posted. He inquired as to who I was, where I'd been and what I'd done, and asked if I'd fired any guns, used oxygen or a radio, which I hadn't. He asked if I had flown an aircraft with a variable-pitch airscrew, retractable undercarriage, flaps and enclosed cockpit, which I hadn't. He said, 'Oh, you're no use to me. Look, they are starting some things called OTUs, and there's going to be one at Aston Down, near Bristol. You go home, and in due course you'll receive a telegram telling you to report.' So, off I eagerly and happily wended my way to my mother-in-law's house, where we were staying. When I arrived, there was already a telegram awaiting, telling me to report to Uxbridge. Well, I knew enough about Uxbridge to know that there was no airfield there and that it was a recruiting station. However, I decided that I wasn't going to be denied a night with my wife, so I used a call box to phone Uxbridge and asked if I could report the same day. The voice on the other end said, 'Oh, you don't want me, you want the BBC.' I didn't know what he was talking about, so put the phone down in disgust and called again. The next person gave me the same answer, so I said to my wife, 'To hell with it, I'll go tomorrow anyway.' So I went the next day and reported to the Guard Room, where the sergeant said, 'Oh, you don't want me, you want the PDC, the Personnel Despatch Centre.' So, off I went to the PDC, hence the confusion with 'BBC'.

When I got there, there was some newly uniformed pilot officer sat there, who said, 'What did you do before you became a pilot?' I answered that I had been a fitter, and he replied, 'Oh, you'll be for Takoradi, on the Gold Coast. Go over to stores and get overseas kit, and be back here by two o'clock to go into town and be inoculated for Yellow Fever.' So, I was a bit bewildered by all of this, thinking I was going to an OTU, and suddenly I'm on my way to Takoradi, overseas kit piled high, until eventually it finished up with a pith helmet on the top, and the corporal said, 'Sign here, Sergeant.'

I said, 'Well, I don't know that I'm going to sign it.'

He said, 'What's the matter with you, don't you want to go to Africa, Sergeant?'

I said, 'No, I don't!'

He said, 'Oh, it's wonderful! You'll either enjoy wonderful health whilst you're there, in which case you'll probably die within six weeks of getting back here, or you'll die there!'

'Oh,' I said, 'Great!' So, I went back without taking any of the kit or signing for it, to see this acting pilot officer, and told him I wanted to phone my adjutant at Middle Wallop. 'Why?' he said, '*Why?*'

I said, 'Because I don't think that I'm supposed to be going to Takoradi, I'm supposed to be going to an OTU when it's formed.'

'I'll phone him,' he said, somewhat bombastically. He disappeared and came back. He said, 'You're quite right, report to the football stadium.'

This Uxbridge activity was fast becoming a farce. Firstly, I'm supposed to be going to an OTU, and I'm posted to the middle of London; secondly, I'm on my way to Africa; and now I have to report to the football stadium. Anyway, I wandered down to the football stadium, which is, in fact, a sports track with a football field in the middle of it, went across to the one and only stand and heard voices emanating from the changing room. I went in there, and there were a number of other fellas, much like me, and there was a huge plotting board, as used by the plotting stations, with a drawing of the south-east corner of England on it. When we had all mustered, we were addressed by someone who I thought was named Professor Lloyd Williams, and he was either of the BBC, or had a person of the same name, perhaps his father, who was well known in the BBC. Anyway, he said that we were there to learn how to make the best use of radar, both by improving our diction and by adopting and getting used to a given jargon. And he then went on to explain why it was necessary. He said, 'With the rapid increase in numbers of aircraft, the wavelengths are completely overburdened and becoming jammed because people are using an undisciplined

form of communication, everybody saying what they think they
need to say, and without the person at the other end having the
slightest inclination of what to expect he will say. For instance, one
person might say, "Oh, this is Fred Jones, and I'm from so-and-so,
so-and-so squadron, and I've just been here, and I've just been there,
and I want to come in to land", or whatever. Now I'm going to
play a record, and I want you to tell me what it is.' So he put this
record on, and it played for about a minute, and it sounded just like
a chipmunk. Having stopped, he said, 'Now, does anyone know
what it says?' And, of course, we all laughed, because there was no
way. So he said, 'I'm going to play it again.' He duly played it again,
and, of course, nobody knew what it was, although one or two
had a wild guess. He said, 'Now I'm going to tell you what it says
before I play it for the third time: "Mary, Mary, Quite Contrary,
How Does Your Garden Grow?"' Then he put the record on at the
same speed, and it sounded crystal clear. And it was a wonderful
demonstration of how, if the brain is, through the ears, searching
for something that is being transmitted, there are a billion items that
it might be, whereas if one has some idea of what it might be, then
one has a lesser field to cover, and therefore the brain is more likely
to interpret the message.

He then went on to say that in selling this idea to the senior
echelons of the RAF, he picked up, in their presence, a telephone
which had loudspeaker attachments, and a female voice said,
'Number, please!' And he said, 'The gentlemen of Wembley are a
motley assembly.' She said, 'I'm sorry, Sir, what was your number?'

He said, 'The gentlemen of Wembley are a motley assembly.'

She said, 'I'm very sorry, Sir, I didn't get your Wembley number.'

He then said, 'I am not saying a number', repeated it, and then
got the answer that he would have got the first time, if she hadn't
been trying to identify a number from the words he was using. I
thought that was an absolutely wonderful demonstration of the
need for a disciplined jargon in communications.

Anyway, this was all quite cleverly done in retrospect, because at one end of the football field were three 'Wall's Ice Cream Stop Me and Buy One' tricycles. Each had a TR9 radio set, identical to those used in fighter aircraft, with a helmet, earphones and plug. And at the other end of the field was a solitary bicycle, of similar type, but with no radio. The field had been marked out in white chalk, with sections like 1, 2, 3, 4, 5, 6, 7, 8, 9, 10 or whatever, and we were asked to participate in an exercise. One of us would go onto the roof of a little hut with a Verey flare pistol, and three of us would be on a bicycle each at one end, and one at the other end; the rest would be either the controller or plotters in the plotting room. The exercise would begin when the participant on the roof would fire a Verey cartridge, and the controller would 'scramble' the three bicycles by communicating through the cyclists' headphones. When the Verey light had been seen, the person who riding the solitary tricycle at the other end had already received instructions that he was to cycle towards the opposite end of the football field, changing course now and again. The controller would then give the leader of the three bicycles a course, to intercept the intruding 'bomber' tricycle, worked out from information supplied by the rooftop observer. This would then be plotted on the field, and the whole interception recorded. This was quite ingenious, because it provided participants a complete picture of how the whole radar and interception technique worked, and at the same time enabled Professor Lloyd Jones, Lloyd Williams or whatever his name might have been, to criticise the voices or diction we were using. This lasted for three days, or thereabouts.

So at the end of the three days I returned to Middle Wallop, only to find the squadron had moved to Gravesend, to where I then wound my way. Again I presented myself to Squadron Leader Hogan, and he said, 'What's been happening to you?' bearing in mind that probably a week had elapsed since I first met him. So I told him. And he said, 'Oh well, we're not bothering with the OTU, we'll train you here. Unfortunately, we don't have a Miles Master, but they have one over at Biggin Hill in 32 Squadron, so get over there.' The Master was a low-wing monoplane which pilots flew before soloing on the Spitfire or Hurricane. Biggin Hill was the parent station of Gravesend and one or two other satellites. So, a Pilot Officer Aldridge, of the AAF, and I got into a Magister and flew across to Biggin Hill. There we presented ourselves to the commander of the training flight, who said, 'Well, unfortunately, our Master's U/S, but they've got one over at Hornchurch, so you'd better go over there, tell them who you are, and they'll take you in hand.' Well, away we went to Hornchurch, and eventually Aldridge did two dual and one solo circuit in the Master, and I one dual circuit. So, the training flight commander said, 'Well, there's no time for you to do more tonight, so you'd better get back to Biggin.' So back to Biggin we go in the Magister. And the next morning I presented myself to the training officer and told him that I'd just done the one dual circuit. He said, 'Well, what aeroplanes did you have in 501 then, when you were a fitter?' I said, 'Well, we'd just got *one* Hurricane.'

'Oh,' he said, 'Well then, you know all about them. Look, there's one out there on the tarmac,' which he pointed to; 'Go and sit in it, and when you feel happy, just take it off.' 'Well, just a minute,' I said, 'What speed does it lift off at, and what is the approach speed, and what speed would I need for a loop, etc.?' So he told me these things. So I did as I was told, went and sat in it, and familiarised myself with the taps, and off I went. And I thought, 'Right, I'm going up high to do my first loop,' and up I went to about 20,000 feet, adding about 50 per cent to the speeds he'd given me, for safety purposes. Well, bearing in mind I'd only flown Hawker Harts and Magisters, with a top speed of about 110 mph, I dived this Hurricane down to about, 250, 280, 300 mph, pulled back on the stick as I would with a Hawker Hart, and immediately blacked out. And, when I came to, I was hanging in my straps and I looked over the side and saw sky, and realised I was upside down, so put the stick over to the normal position, and spun. I didn't know much about spinning, having done my spinning training in Magisters and Harts, but I had heard say that with these new-fangled Spitfires and Hurricanes, you didn't get into a spin because, if you did, you couldn't get out. So anyway, away I went, spinning away, doing the corrective action that I'd been taught, and, lo and behold, it worked. The aeroplane came out of the spin, but I was so relieved I forgot to centralise, and off it went again, spinning in the opposite direction! By the time I managed to resume the normal flying position, I was down in the clag, very humid, hazy weather, with no clear and defined horizon, and all the instruments were going round the cockpit like hummingbirds. Nobody ever told me that you had to lock the gyroscope of the artificial horizon before you spun, and as a consequence, the gyrations I had been through had toppled the gyroscope – the artificial horizon was going round and round like a washing machine.

Anyway, I felt a little bit nauseous, but managed to get back to Biggin Hill. The air was full of dogfighting activity, warnings and shouting and so on and so forth. I approached Biggin Hill, made my approach, and realised a little bit late in the game that I had overshot, by which time I was holding off well up the runway, probably halfway, so dropped down and realised that I was going to run out of runway – and hurtled towards the Hurricanes of 32 Squadron, or some of them anyway, which were scattered about the place. Using my brakes judiciously, eventually, and somewhat miraculously, and thankfully, I came to a halt without damaging my aeroplane, any other aeroplane, or myself. I had done over 170 hours at that time, and this first Hurricane flight was on 8 August 1940, in P2549. Anyway, having screamed to a halt, I was sat in my cockpit feeling very relieved, when Squadron Leader Worrall, the CO of 32 Squadron, hurtled out of his office, jumped up onto my wing and gave me the biggest telling off of all time, confining me to camp for two weeks and ordering me to report to his office immediately, which I did. He there tore off a second strip, asked me what on earth I thought I was doing etc.; I told him that it was my first flight, and related my lack of experience. At that he relented, and said, 'OK, in that case forget about being confined to camp, but for heaven's sake don't ever do such a thing again, you could have written off several aeroplanes and killed yourself, and other people, in the process.' So, that was that.

By 14 August 1940, I had done seven hours on Hurricanes, most of which was ferrying aircraft to the various airfields around Biggin Hill: Hawkinge, Croydon, Northolt etc. On 19 August, I took a Hurricane to Gravesend, and bumped into Hogan, who asked me what I'd done. I told him, and he said, 'Oh, that's fine, they're too slow over there, you come back here and we'll train you quicker than that. Come back here, to Gravesend, tonight.' Unbeknown to me, the squadron had lost five aircraft the previous day, hence the sudden need for my return. When I duly returned to Gravesend, I was shown into a room with several beds in it and given the one next to 'Ginger' Lacey. Supper was a mug of cocoa and a cheese sandwich, and away I went to bed.

501 Squadron had originally been formed on 14 June 1929, as a day bomber unit in the Special Reserve, and named 'City of Bristol', based at Filton. In 1936, to take into account a wider recruiting base, this was changed to 'County of Gloucester', and the unit became the AAF's fourteenth squadron. Two years later, 501 transferred from Bomber to Fighter Command, converting to Hurricanes in March 1940. Two months on, the squadron joined the AASF and went to France, joining in the gallant but forlorn attempt to halt Hitler's *Blitzkrieg*. After the Fall of France, 501 was actually the last RAF fighter squadron to leave the Continent, via Le Mans and St Hellier, regrouped at Croydon on 25 June 1940, on which date Squadron Leader Harry AV Hogan replaced

Squadron Leader Clube as CO. Hogan was an Old Malvernian, from Worcestershire, who had graduated from Cranwell in 1930. Thereafter, he flew biplane fighters with 54 Squadron, operated from HMS *Courageous* with the Fleet Fighter Flight, and served as an instructor and bomber pilot. In June 1940, Hogan, converted to Hurricanes, taking command of 501 that month. Hogan, therefore, was an experienced pilot, but had few hours on the modern Hurricane, and had not personally seen combat. Some of his pilots, however, had seen a great deal of action in France, among them Sergeant James 'Ginger' Lacey, of the RAFVR, who had become an ace, destroying five enemy aircraft. It was next to this august veteran, that Bill Green found himself that August night in 1940.

About 0300 hours, I was awakened by someone shaking me in the dark, an airman waving a torch in my face. I said, 'No, not me, I'm new here, I'm Green.'

He said, 'Yes, you're Green 3!' I can't recall having any breakfast but on the way down to our aeroplanes I asked Ginger Lacey, 'What's all this "Green 3" business?' Not very reassuringly, he said, 'Well, we're the "Arse-end Charlie Section". When we get in the air, we're the last section behind the other three, and when we get up there you'll see me do a turn to the right. The idea is to have a good look round and make sure the squadron isn't bounced by any fighters. When I turn to the right, you do a turn to the left.' Well, he turned to the right, so I thought, 'Right, here goes', and did what I thought was a very gentle, very short duration, turn to the left, because I didn't want to lose the squadron, so soon turned back, but in the split-second I'd flown at a right angle, they'd disappeared. They had just forged ahead, doing 300 mph plus. I knew that we were going to Hawkinge, so I made my own way there. That was the pattern of each day: get up early, fly down to Hawkinge at dawn, and sit around at dispersal tents, waiting for the telephone to go, scrambling us into the air. I recall being quite on edge, wondering whether the telephone would ring, and if it did when, and if it meant us scrambling and climbing up into what was clearly a dangerous activity.

By 21 August, Bill had recorded the grand total of seven hours and forty-five minutes flying time on Hurricanes in his log book. That day, he took off from Hawkinge in P3397, later recording in his log: 'Scramble to 15,000 feet. Attacked fifty to sixty Do 215s from port forward quarter. Fired six-second burst 800–100 yards range and broke away to starboard, violently. Results unobserved. Return fire heavy. Bombs jettisoned between Manston and Canterbury. Bouquet from Group on turning heavy formation back.' On his first sortie of 24 August, Sergeant Green patrolled in Hurricane V6545:

I remember we were patrolling convoys going through the Dover Straits, and one day we were orbiting over this convoy, when I saw a huge splash in the middle of it. I immediately suspected that a bomber had crept in, over the top of us, but there was no sign of any aircraft at all; I would have been angry if there had been, because we should have seen it. We spent most of our time in the air 'rubber-necking', which is to say looking through an orbit of 360°, up and down, all the time, constantly, especially the rear, to ensure that we were not bounced by enemy aircraft. Anyway, that evening I learned that the splash was caused by the Germans lobbing their first shell from the French coast.

Later that day, Saturday 24 August, we were scrambled and vectored towards Manston, and were then vectored on to some Ju 87s, which were about to dive-bomb that sector station. We were just pulling in behind them, to attack, when I was hit by AA fire. My windscreen immediately became covered with black oil, and the engine was coughing. I turned away, back towards Hawkinge, realising that I was a non-combatant from that point onwards, pumped the undercarriage down and managed to land with a half-dead engine, which was only running some of the time. I put the aircraft down on Hawkinge but discovered that so much damage had been done to my undercarriage that the aeroplane finished up on its nose, with me looking almost vertically down at the ground. Anyway, I was safe and sound, not injured in any way, and continued flying. I must say at this point that I was, and am, no hero. I was very mindful of the very dangerous activity in which we were engaged, and mindful that I could be seriously wounded or killed at any time. My overriding recollection is that whilst in the air I was very vigilant, very aware of the dangers of being attacked from behind or above.

In his log book, Bill recorded the incident, as a 'nasty prang'. On the first sortie of 28 August, his log book records that he 'patrolled Southend at 3,000 feet. Attacked by Hurricane just below cloud base until out-turned same, to see grinning face of Flying Officer (Peter) Hairs. (Bags of cold sweat)'.

Later that day, my flight, 'B' Flight, were tannoyed and given a twenty-four hour stand-down. Flight Sergeant Morfill and I had pre-arranged that as and when we got a day off we would grab the Magister and fly home. He lived near Maidenhead, and would use White Waltham as an airfield, and I was going to Whitchurch airport, near Bristol. Anyway, we just got into the Magister, took nothing with us, were probably unwashed, certainly unshaved, but away we went. I dropped Morfill off, then went home for nearly twenty-four hours with my wife at Bristol. She had given me some socks, and so on 29 August 1940, I left her at Whitchurch, in the Magister, wearing my brand new socks, picked Morfill up, then the pair of us returned to Gravesend, where we had to be by mid-day, to go on readiness straight away, which we did. I recall that there was very low cloud, so I wrote to my wife, telling her how much I loved her, how much I'd enjoyed being with her, how much I missed her, and telling her not to worry because the weather was too bad for there to be any flying that day. I had no sooner written the letter than we were scrambled, however.

That evening, after a day of generally reduced fighting, owing in part to the weather, *Luftflotte* 2 launched a series of fighter sweeps over south-east England, involving some 500–600 Me 109s, in waves. Certain German fighter pilots, probably of JG 51, watched 501 Squadron's progress with great interest.

We went up through the cloud, late afternoon, early evening, about sixish, formated above the cloud and were vectored down to Deal. Once over Deal – code-named 'Red Queen' – at 20,000 feet we were told to orbit and 'Look out for 200 "Snappers"' – 109s – coming in. I remember that when Hogan got the vector, he said, somewhat whimsically, 'Come on, boys, come to Deal with me' – not using the codename. There we were orbiting, vigilantly and vigorously searching the sky all around us, when suddenly there was a crash, broken glass, and a gaping hole in my windscreen, slightly larger than a tennis ball, and immediately I was covered with liquid of some sort. My control column was useless, it was connected to nothing. I realised that the aeroplane was finished. So, I slid back the hood, although I may have already had it back, because I think that at the time we were told that one of our colleagues had been hit and seen going down, on fire, clawing at the canopy, which was stuck fast; he crashed and was killed, so with that in mind, I'm sure my hood was already back. I pulled the pin of the Sutton safety harness, got as far as being on my knees, up on my seat in a semi-crouched position, when I was either sucked out or the aeroplane blew up, I don't know which. But I was suddenly out, rolling over and over, and I heard my flying boots go past my ear. My legs were spread-eagled, so I frantically grabbed around for the ripcord, eventually found it after what seemed like a long time – and pulled it. I saw something white do two eccentric circles, going away from me, upwards. This had no significance until the main canopy came straight up between my legs. I rolled forward, into this unopened parachute. I realised that the parachute should not have come out between my legs but behind me, so I then tried to push the parachute back between my legs. I remember thinking about my wife, who I had seen that morning, and I suppose that I was now contemplating my end, thinking 'I wonder if she will wonder if I wondered, as I was falling, what my end was going to be like'. Then I remember thinking that she would realise, as I realised, that everything would go black, and that would be it. I kept struggling with this parachute until eventually there was a jolt, then a secondary jolt. I grabbed the rigging lines – having seen one part of the parachute disappear I thought the whole lot might be going! I was then hit by this enormous silence that one experiences – having fallen through the air from perhaps 16,000 feet, at 140 mph, with the rustling of the parachute around my ears all that way – when one experiences when floating down by parachute. The silence – caused by my parachute opening at almost literally the last second – hit me more than any noise I've ever heard. I just shook my head and thought, 'Gosh, that was close!' Left and above me there were trees, higher than I was, and there were electricity cables level with me, and I thought, 'Gosh, I'm near the ground!' The only thing I knew about parachuting was that I had to bend my knees, which I did – bang – I hit the ground. I sat there, on this sloping field, full of thistles and cowpats, and there I sat, in my stockinged feet, having lost my boots, thinking, 'Oh dear, I've got to go and walk through this awful field in my bare socks.' I then pulled my parachute towards me, to examine the cords and see what had gone on, and found that the pilot parachute had been severed about nine inches from where it joined the main canopy, the thin attaching cords having been severed by shrapnel. So, when I pulled the ripcord, the pilot parachute shot off into space, leaving nothing to pull the main parachute out of its pack. In 1995, I visited the crash site for the first time since the event, and worked out, from the height of trees and the electricity cables, that my parachute had eventually opened at just 150 feet – or, in other words, 1½ seconds from certain death.

Hurricane R4223 crashed at Ladswood, near Canterbury in Kent; Bill landed at Mill Hill Farm, Elham:

I was rescued, if that's the right word, by two fellows who came running down from the nearby farmhouse with shotguns. They quickly recognised that I was British and took me back to the house for a cup of tea. I was collected by a couple of army people who motored me back to Hawkinge. I had collected some wounds in my right leg, and in my right knee there was a hole where a bullet had passed completely through, a perfectly round hole. I was taken to Station Sick Quarters and the Medical Officer there started to poke around in this hole, with a long steel needle, and I remember just passing out. I was then invited to go into the Officers' Mess by my Flight Commander, Flight Lieutenant John Gibson, or 'Gibbo' as he was known to us, and I learned that he had been shot down at exactly the same time, but that his parachute had opened in the orthodox fashion. He had floated down gently from a great height and was conjecturing where he might land, and thought, 'Oh, I won't be far from Hawkinge', but then thought, 'Oh, I think I should land just about on the airfield.' Then 'Oh crikey, I'm going to overshoot the airfield, looks like I'm going to land in Folkestone, hope I don't hit a church spire and end up suspended 150 feet above the ground ... I'm going to overshoot Folkestone, I'm going to land on the beach. Wonder if it's mined?' Then he realised he was going to hit the water, some miles out, and got picked up by an RAF ASR launch. He would say that he hit the water at 7.30 p.m., and I know that I was in the farmhouse drinking tea at 7.10 p.m. I was about eight miles from the coast, he was some miles off the coast, so that tells you the difference between a perpendicular fall, in a non-operating parachute, and drifting out to sea in an offshore breeze from a height of 20,000 or 16,000 feet. The time difference is also indicative.

The next day, I was taken to Station Sick Quarters at Gravesend, and then to Woolwich Hospital, where my wounds could be attended to. I was then sick for some weeks, and didn't fly again with 501 Squadron

501 Squadron, however, in which AAF unit Bill Green made the quantum leap from engine fitter to fighter pilot, uniquely remained in the front line until the Battle of Britain's bitter end – losing nineteen pilots killed in the process (unsurprisingly the highest number suffered by any squadron). 'The Bristol Aeroplane Company at Filton, near Bristol, had been bombed, however, and 504 'City of Nottingham' Squadron, also of the AAF and flying Hurricanes, had been posted there to defend it. I was posted, compassionately, to 504, on 20 November 1940.' This was, of course, during the night blitz on British cities – and being an important port, Bristol was frequently a target for the enemy bombers. During daylight, reconnaissance aircraft and lone Ju 88s, bent on harassing attacks and making use of cloud cover for preservation, were active over England during daylight. On 28 November, Bill's log book records, 'Scramble to 15,000 feet after Hun over Bristol, who turned and beat it towards Weymouth and heavy front of cloud.' The following day, Bill flew over his home city, noting in his log book, no doubt with a heavy heart, 'Counted at least fifteen fires. Oil tanks at Avonmouth burning.' On 3 January 1941: 'Chased Hun to 30 miles South of Land's End, when bastard found 10/10ths cloud.' By 16 March 1941, Sergeant Green was considered tour expired:

I was then posted to 4 FIS, Cambridge, as an instructor, before also instructing at Weston-super-Mare Airport and Shellingford. In October 1942, I was commissioned, and in June 1943, went to instruct on Masters at Cranwell, before onwards to Tealing, in November, to instruct on Spitfires at 39 OTU. Between March and October 1944, I was at Enstone, flying Tomahawks on fighter/ bomber affiliation exercises with trainee Wellington crews, largely from Moreton-in-Marsh and Honeybourne. Then I converted to Typhoons at Aston Down, followed by Tempests at Thorney Island. Although I had been successful in my *ab initio* training work, and found it rewarding, I had a deep feeling of guilt that my operational experience was so short-lived, and our son was born in August 1941; I dreaded the thought that he would ask, sooner or later in his growing and curious years, what I did during the war: I would have felt ashamed to tell him that mostly I was in a non-combatant role. So, and without telling my wife, I battled to get back into 'Ops' – and won.

In November 1944, I managed, with outside help, to extricate myself from the imprisonment of Training Command and return to operational flying, this time flying the Tempest Mk V with 56 Squadron, at Volkel, in Holland. On 22 February 1945, however, I was the victim of so-called 'friendly fire', when accidentally shot down by an American P-51 Mustang, near Lingen, in Westphalia. Upon landing I was looking down the barrel of a twelve bore shotgun and captured. I was then imprisoned at Nurenburg, walking under escort to Stalag VIIA at Moosburg, near Munich, where I was the Kitchen Officer. It was a short stay but, for a variety of reasons, dangerous and is an interesting story in itself.

Upon repatriation, on VE Day, 8 May 1945, Flight Lieutenant Green instructed at 3 EFTS, Shellingford, leaving the RAF in November 1945. Two years later, however, Bill, by then living and working in Northamptonshire, joined the RAFVR, spending the next six years instructing at 6 RFS at Sywell. He also enjoyed a happy family life, with two children and grandchildren in equal measure, and a successful post-war business career, eventually retiring as chief executive of Crown Paints and director of a unit including Sanderson's Fabrics and Polycell. 'In fact, I escaped another brush with death in 1947: I was in a factory when the floor collapsed, taking all of the heavy machinery and a colleague and I with it. He never walked again, but I only broke a wrist. I've had a few brushes with death, therefore, leading me to conclude that someone watches over me.'

Bill Green was a regular visitor to commemorative events at the National Memorial at Capel-le-Ferne and the Battle of Britain Fighter Association's annual service at Westminster Abbey. He was also a big supporter of the Kent Battle of Britain Museum at the airfield from which once he flew and fought – Hawkinge. Indeed the Museum there, entirely staffed and created by true enthusiasts, is a truly wonderful thing: some, might say, the best and most moving Battle of Britain museum there is.

Bill Green was ever at pains to stress that 'I was only involved in the Battle of Britain for just nine days, during which, largely due to not having attended an OTU, I was shot down twice, so didn't really do much. In my opinion, in fact, the Battle of Britain was not won by the "Few", but specifically by a few of the Few. What I mean to say is that it was won by pilots with experience, for example, on 501 Squadron, pilots like Paul Farnes and James Lacey. It is to pilots like them that the real debt is owed.'

Bill's story, however, is a significant one, because progressing from lowly fitter to pilot was a rare thing – especially so at that early stage of the war, and particularly in an AAF squadron at that time. This is, in fact, a prime example of how the war helped accelerate social change in Britain. Indeed, if not for the war, many young men like Bill, from ordinary backgrounds, would never have had the opportunity to fly. Bill's account also emphasises the frequently *ad hoc* nature of training on occasions, and the often confused state of things, so desperate was the hour, the system in many respects overwhelmed as servicemen and women learned to deal with an unprecedented situation. Sadly, Bill did not live to see this book in print: he died, aged ninety-seven, on 7 November 2014. His chapter in *The Final Few*, however, is an important reminder of how things were, and, indeed, how things have changed – and how, as a result, young people are more able to achieve their potential on the basis of their ability and not just social class. That was not, of course, what the Battle of Britain was directly fought for, but it is arguably a consequence of the ultimate Allied victory. Had Hitler and the Nazis prevailed in 1940, things would have been very different indeed.

6

SQUADRON LEADER G. H. A. 'BOY' WELLUM DFC

On 5 August 1941, *The London Gazette* published a list of airmen awarded the Distinguished Flying Cross. Among them was Flying Officer Geoffrey Harry Augustus Wellum, a Spitfire pilot of 92 Squadron who had celebrated his twentieth birthday only the previous day. The citation read,

> This officer has been with his squadron since the evacuation of Dunkirk. During the recent offensive operations over France he has led his section and flight with great skill and determination. He has destroyed at least three enemy aircraft and damaged several others.

The astonishing fact is that before his twentieth birthday, Geoffrey Wellum had already fought through and survived the Battle of Britain – hence his nickname 'Boy'.

Aged eleven, Geoffrey, an only child from Walthamstow, London, began boarding at Forest, a minor public school in Snaresbrook. When seventeen, this aviation-minded youth applied to the Air Ministry to be a pilot. Six months later, he followed the well-trodden path to Adastral House for selection. In spite of his very young age, Geoffrey was accepted. Before leaving Forest School, Geoffrey achieved another ambition and captained the First cricket XI; the sand of that last summer of peace, however, was rapidly running through the hourglass. On 28 July 1939, Geoffrey firmly left school days behind and entered the man's world that was the RAF. On that day, still seventeen, he reported for *ab initio* flying training at 7 EFTS at Desford in Leicestershire. Flying, Geoffrey immediately decided, was 'absolutely beautiful'. Although learning to fly did not necessarily come entirely naturally at to him at first, his instructor, Mr Hayne, clearly recognised some potential, conceding during a private pep-talk that Geoffrey 'could possibly make a fighter pilot'. After around ten hours of dual tuition, Geoffrey soloed on a Tiger Moth. On that day, Hitler invaded Poland. Two days later, Britain and France declared war on Nazi Germany. The Second World War had begun – and eighteen-year-old Geoffrey Wellum would soon find himself in the very thick of it. Flying had already become an obsession for Geoffrey, his only ambition to be a professional RAF pilot – and a fighter pilot specifically.

Having successfully passed his *ab initio* course, Geoffrey found himself square-bashing at Hastings, learning how to be a serviceman. From there, Acting Pilot Officer Wellum was off to Little Rissington in Gloucestershire, to learn how to fly the North American Harvard with 6 FTS. A single-engined monoplane trainer, the Harvard provided fledgling pilots with experience of a modern fighter-like aircraft, prior to progressing to the types they would fly into battle – namely the Supermarine Spitfire and Hawker Hurricane. Looping and rolling over the Cotswolds, Geoffrey was now 'enthralled' by flying. His ground studies were tackled with somewhat less enthusiasm, though, leading to a dressing down by the Chief Ground Instructor. At Little Rissington, the loss of a friend while flying, Nick Bellamy, was another new experience young Pilot Officer Wellum had to deal with – sadly this loss would be the first of many. Ultimately, Little Rissington proved to be the gateway to Wellum's dream: sporting a new pilot's brevet, he was delighted with a posting to 92 Squadron – to fly Spitfires!

On 21 May 1940, Pilot Officer Wellum, with 168 flying hours, including ninety-five solo recorded in his log book, reported for duty with 92 Squadron at Northolt, London. What his log book lacked was any Spitfire flying. The same was true of another replacement, Pilot Officer Trevor 'Wimpey' Wade. What Geoffrey did have, however, was a passion for flying – and an 'above average' assessment from Little Rissington. A willingness to learn was one thing – time to do so quite another, as the CO, Squadron Leader Roger Bushell, took no time pointing out. It was not an auspicious start. In anticipation of imminent defensive action, 92 Squadron's CO needed trained pilots. Every combat-ready pilot could be needed at any time, so neither time or personnel existed to train replacements. Before the war, new pilots were trained by their squadrons, being taught by experienced hands how to fly the type in which they would be expected to fly into battle. In January 1940, however, it was decided to provide this training at dedicated OTUs, three of which were created. Nonetheless, their combined output of pilots converted to type proved inadequate to make good losses suffered by Hurricane squadrons in France, much less provide a fully trained reserve. This may explain why, unusually at the time, Geoffrey was posted direct to a fighter squadron and not to an OTU.

92 Squadron was first formed in September 1917, flying SE5A scouts over the Western Front and accounting for thirty-seven aerial victories before the Armistice. With no war to fight, 92 was disbanded in 1919 but, with Britain at war with Germany again, reformed at Tangmere on 10 October 1939. Although a regular RAF squadron, unusually the nucleus of its original personnel was drawn from 601 'County of London' Squadron of the AAF. If graduates of the RAF College Cranwell were the service's professional elite, auxiliaries were the socially elite. Hugh Dundas,

who, according to his contemporary Johnnie Johnson, a Volunteer Reservist, 'was related to half the ruddy aristocracy of northern England', joined 616 'South Yorkshire' Squadron in 1938:

> In all the history of arms there can seldom have been a body of men more confident and pleased with themselves than the pilots of the AAF. We wore a big brass 'A' on the lapels of our tunics and no amount of official pressure during the war would persuade us to remove them. The regulars insisted that the 'A stood for Amateur Airmen', or even 'Argue and Answer Back'. To us they were the symbols of our membership of a very special club. The pilots of the AAF were lawyers and farmers, stockbrokers and journalists; they were landowners and artisans, serious-minded accountants and unrepentant playboys. They had two things in common: a passion for flying and a determination to prove that anything the regulars could do the Auxiliaries could do better.

This mixture of regular and auxiliary personnel provided 92 Squadron a unique identity – personified by its CO.

Roger Bushell was a twenty-nine-year-old Cambridge graduate called to the Bar. A practising barrister and exceptional sportsman, he joined 601 Squadron of the so-called 'Millionaire's Mob' in 1932. A huge personality, upon formation of 92, Bushell was the first auxiliary to be given command of an RAF fighter squadron. One of his flight commanders, Flight Lieutenant CP 'Paddy' Green was also a former 601 Squadron auxiliary, the other no less than Flight Lieutenant Robert Stanford Tuck, a professional airman, no less flamboyant, and destined to become a leading 'ace'. Initially, 92 was equipped with twin-engined Bristol Blenheims, which were exchanged for the Supermarine Spitfire in March 1940. Fully appreciating the Spitfire's superiority, and in particular its high altitude capability, Air Chief Marshal Dowding, Air Officer Commander-in-Chief of Fighter Command, determinedly preserved his smaller Spitfire force after Hitler invaded the west on 10 May 1940. While Hurricane squadrons were embroiled with the Luftwaffe on a daily basis across the Channel, the Spitfire squadrons in England watched, waited and made ready for the onslaught soon to come. After the *Blitzkrieg* began, 92 Squadron continued training flights, including night flying, and provided escort to communications aircraft landing at French airfields. There was no contact with the enemy.

On the afternoon of 22 May, Pilot Officers Wellum and Wade attended a radio-telephone procedure course at nearby Uxbridge. The following day, Squadron Leader Bushell led his Spitfires to Hornchurch, from which sector station he later took them on patrol over the French coast. At about 0830 hours, six Me 109s were engaged, all of which 92 Squadron claimed destroyed. Unfortunately, Pilot Officer Pat Learmond, a Cranwellian, was shot down in flames over Dunkirk – worse was to follow. That afternoon, Bushell led his squadron over the French coast once more, intercepting some forty Me 110s. 92 Squadron claimed another seventeen enemy aircraft destroyed – but in the process lost Squadron Leader Bushell, Flying Officer Gillies and Sergeant Klipsch. The remainder of the squadron forlornly returned to Hornchurch – with seven shot-up and unserviceable Spitfires. This was not, in fact, an untypical first brush with what was a very combat-experienced enemy. Fortunately, although Bushell's loss, according to 92 Squadron's diarist, was 'a severe blow', this larger-than-life character was not dead. Having damaged two Me 110s, Bushell had been shot down, possibly by *Oberleutnant* Günther Specht of 3/ZG 76, who claimed three Spitfires that day before being shot up and forced to crash-land himself. Bushell also survived a forced landing but was captured. Incarcerated in the infamous Stalag Luft III at Sagan, 92 Squadron's first Commanding Officer was destined to be among those Allied prisoners murdered by the Gestapo following the ill-fated but so-called 'Great Escape'.

For the next few days, 92 Squadron continued this pattern of operating from Hornchurch and engaging the enemy close to the French coast. On 25 May, the squadron was ordered to Duxford, to 'rest and re-equip', and Squadron Leader PJ 'Judy' Sanders was posted to command. Sanders had been educated at Cheltenham College before going up to Balliol College, Oxford, and being permanently commissioned into the General Duties Branch of the RAF in March 1936. Thereafter, he joined 1 Squadron, flying Hawker Fury biplane fighters, until the unit re-equipped with the modern Hurricane monoplane in October 1938, by which time Flight Lieutenant Sanders was a flight commander. When posted to command 92 Squadron, Sanders was an experienced pilot, but mainly on now obsolete biplanes, and the Hurricane. What he lacked was actual combat experience. Nonetheless, Sanders lost no time in leading 'Ganic Squadron' from the front.

By this time, the military situation in France was catastrophic. To the north the Belgians had collapsed, and to the south *Panzergruppe von Kliest* achieved the unthinkable, successfully negotiating the Ardennes, outflanking the much vaunted but incomplete Maginot Line and racing to the French coast. Moreover, the Me 109 dominated the battlefield in a lethal demonstration of air superiority. Consequently, the BEF found itself in a pocket and in danger of envelopment. Reluctantly, therefore, on 26 May, its commander, Lord Gort VC, took the decision to retire on and evacuate from Dunkirk. Suddenly, Air Vice-Marshal Park, Air Officer Commanding 11 Group, found himself with an unprecedented responsibility – masterminding the aerial cover required for this seaborne rescue operation. The problem was that too few aircraft, the range involved and long hours of daylight meant it was impossible to provide an uninterrupted aerial umbrella over the French coast from dawn to dusk. Hurriedly, Spitfire squadrons left their peacetime bases and deployed temporarily to south-east England, reducing the distance to France. As we have seen, however, Spitfire squadrons had already been in action over the French coast, meeting the Me 109 for the first time. The previous day, among the RAF fighter pilots embroiled with the Luftwaffe was 65, a certain Flying Officer Brian Kingcome destroying a Do 17. The following day, on which Lord Gort made his fateful decision, Kingcome was promoted to Acting Flight Lieutenant and posted to 92 Squadron, to take over 'A' Flight from Flight Lieutenant 'Paddy' Green, who had been badly wounded in the thigh. Kingcome was an exceptional individual by any standards. Born in Calcutta, India, this Cranwell graduate and holder of a permanent commission was six days shy of his twenty-third birthday.

26 May 1940 was also an important personal date for Pilot Officer Geoffrey Wellum:

On that day, 'Wimpey' Wade and I made our first Spitfire flights. It was awe-inspiring, an achievement because it was *the* aeroplane everyone was talking about. And here I was flying one – and I wasn't nineteen years old. There you are, careering around at 300 knots in this thing, just the slightest thought that goes through your brain conveys it to your hands and feet, and the next thing you know the aeroplane is doing it. You feel detached from fellow man, it's clean, it's pure, it gets into the very soul, and you think, 'This is absolutely beautiful.'

Clearly this was a match made in heaven, a love affair lasting a lifetime.

From then on, the two fledgling fighter pilots, Wellum and Wade, embarked upon a programme of training flights in 12 Group, away from the battle raging over France. These were days filled with aerobatics, battle climbs and dog-fight practice: 'wonderful stuff'. Meanwhile, the rest of 92 Squadron flew over Dunkirk, from Northolt, in support of Operation DYNAMO, and, according to the unit's Operations Record Book, 'covered itself in glory'. By 3 June 1940 the evacuation was complete, the BEF having been snatched from the jaws of defeat.

While Geoffrey Wellum clocked up Spitfire hours flying over East Anglia, Flight Lieutenant Brian Kingcome found his opposite number in 92 Squadron, the commander of 'B' Flight, to be Flight Lieutenant Bob Stanford Tuck – good looking, extrovert, and a superb fighter pilot. Of 92 Squadron, Kingcome later wrote that the squadron always had the special ingredient which sets certain groups apart from the rest – a small, indefinable, quality in the alchemy that gives an edge, a uniqueness. This quality can never be duplicated or planned for, but somehow comes into being and is aptly called 'spirit'. It always begins at the top, and 92's exceptional spirit undoubtedly had its origins in the outstanding personalities of the original squadron and flight commanders. It then continued to flourish in the fertile soil of the rich mix of characters who made up this exceptional fighting unit: determined, committed young men, intent on squeezing the last drop of living from whatever life might be left to them at the same time as they refused to take themselves or their existences too seriously.

On 18 June 1940, 92 Squadron, to its surprise, was not transferred into the frontline sector of 11 Group, but sent to Pembrey, in South Wales. From there, the squadron assisted with the defence of Bristol and Swansea, and the posting was not without action. On a number of occasions lone raiders were intercepted, such as on 4 July, when Pilot Officer Saunders and Sergeant Fokes destroyed a He 111 near Weston-super-Mare. A number of night patrols were also carried out that month – without, let us not forget, the sophisticated, computerised, aids pilots have today; Geoffrey Wellum:

> The Spitfire was not a great night-flying aircraft, due to the narrow-track undercarriage, poor forward visibility when taxiing, caused

by the long nose, and the glare from six exhaust ports negatively affected night vision. This aircraft was not, though, designed for night flying, do not forget, but as a short-range daylight interceptor. The lack of aircraft specifically designed for night fighting, however, meant that Spitfires and Hurricanes had to be used in this role.

Geoffrey had yet to fly a Spitfire at night, so upon arrival at Pembrey rapidly found himself practising dusk landings prior to his first nocturnal flight on 20 June. 'Terrifying', he said of the experience many years later. 'Just a black void. I didn't do very well, it must be said. It was disorientating. I ballsed up the landing, thought I was going to kill myself, collided with a Chance light and broke my Spitfire.' Fortunately our hero survived – but was grounded by Squadron Leader Sanders for 'an indefinite period'. Understandably, Flight Lieutenant Kingcome was not best pleased, and incurring his displeasure alone was enough to mortify 'Boy' Wellum, but at least his flight commander talked through the incident and offered sound advice. Ten days later, Geoffrey once more experienced the unparalleled thrill of Spitfire flight – and had no further trouble landing at night.

While the Battle of Britain raged over south-east England, life continued much the same into August for 92 Squadron. On 18 August, Kingcome's 'A' Flight was deployed to Bibury, near Cheltenham in the Cotswolds, to bolster the Midlands' embryonic night defences. More night patrols and inconclusive interceptions followed until Kingcome led his Spitfires back to Pembrey, their sojourn in Gloucestershire over. The tedium, however, was abruptly banished on 8 September 1940: 92 Squadron thundered in formation to Biggin Hill, that most famous of fighter stations on a plateau in Kent, south of London. The scene that greeted Sanders' pilots was a clear indication that things here were likely to be very different from the West Country; as Geoffrey said, 'Biggin Hill was quite badly knocked about'. The previous day had seen an unprecedented scale of fighting as the Luftwaffe pounded London around the clock, but throughout daylight at least this particular Sunday was comparatively quiet, providing an opportunity for fresh squadrons like 92 to relieve those badly in need of rest and refit. Geoffrey Wellum's Battle of Britain was now about to begin in earnest.

9 September 1940, dawned with a nine-tenths covering of cloud over southern England, the overcast remaining until the afternoon and delaying the day's onslaught. At 1630 hours, Pilot Officer Wellum took off, in Spitfire X4051, with the rest of 92 Squadron, led by Squadron Leader Sanders, on a 'Fighter Patrol'. Twenty minutes later, the day's largest raid crossed the English coast, inbound: twenty-six He 111s of II/KG 1, escorted by twenty Me 110s and sixty Me 109s. Although tasked with attacking Farnborough in Hampshire, the enemy formation turned west, south of London, passing through the Kenley, Biggin Hill and Northolt sectors – a gauntlet indeed! Nine RAF fighter squadrons were up, eight of which – some ninety Spitfires and Hurricanes – attacked virtually simultaneously. Other enemy formations, including forty Ju 88s of KG 30, were also on the board, the sky again a mass of twisting, turning, firing aircraft. To 'Boy' Wellum, the scene was 'breath-taking'. 92 Squadron was attacked near Biggin Hill by the Me 109s of III/JG 26. Three Spitfires were soon hit, Pilot Officers Saunders and Watling being wounded while Pilot Officer Wright escaped unharmed. All had fallen victim to that real *Experte*, the *Gruppenkommandeur*, *Oberleutnant* Gerhard Schöpfel.

Squadron Leader Sanders claimed an He 111 and an Me 109 destroyed:

Whilst patrolling over Dungeness at 26,000 feet, I heard a warning of 'snappers' (Me 109s) and turned sharply left. I saw that Green Section, behind me, had attacked, and I got a short burst at one

Me 109 as it broke away from them in a left-hand turn. I could not observe the effect of my fire, as my turn was too tight and I span out of it.

Blue 2 re-joined me and on instruction from Cactus we returned to base. I was told there were bandits at 15,000 feet. At about 13,000 feet I encountered a formation of He 111s in close 'vic', about ten miles SSE of Biggin Hill, heading North. I attacked the left-hand aircraft at about 100 yards. I broke away upwards, turned right and saw that my target had slid out of formation and appeared to be going down in a left-hand turn.

Immediately afterwards I saw an aircraft with a yellow nose and a yellow patch on the front of its fuselage. This turned out to be an Me 109. We circled around each other a few times, and I got in a deflection shot by turning inside it. Immediately after I fired, it half-rolled and dived for cloud, black smoke only came out behind it. I followed and fired several short bursts at about 200 yards, diving very fast. It entered cloud at 8,000 feet and I never saw it again.

At 1705 hours, Flight Lieutenant Kingcome was in action north-east of Biggin Hill, at 15,000 feet:

I lost the squadron whilst proceeding to our objective, but by following the vectors heard, I saw a large formation of enemy bombers. They were already being attacked by a squadron of Spitfires, so I climbed to attack eighteen yellow-nosed Me 109s which were circling in line astern and to the bomber formation's left. I joined in on the end of the formation and gave the last machine a short burst, slight deflection, using normal sighting. He dived away with white smoke coming back. The remainder turned on me so I dived away, climbed back and gave another a very short burst with no apparent effect. They all attacked me again, so I dived into a cloud and returned to base, my oxygen supply exhausted. By this time, the bombers were out of the fighter formation's sight.

At 1830 hours, Pilot Officer Wellum landed safely back at Biggin Hill. An hour later he was up again, for an uneventful 'Fighter Patrol'.

The next day, adverse weather conditions dictated that no major attacks were mounted, although Pilot Officer Wade and Sergeant Fokes caught and destroyed a lone Do 17 near Gatwick. Poor weather the following morning, 11 September, delayed operations until mid-afternoon. At 1500 hours, the He 111s of I and II/KG 26 took off from their French bases, rendezvoused with a 200-strong fighter escort and headed for the Thames Estuary, targeting London. From 1530 hours onwards, Fighter Command's squadrons intercepted the raiders but were unable to reach the Heinkels until after the docklands had been bombed. The Me 110 escorts then formed a defensive circle over Croydon, covering the bombers' shortest exit route: out over the coast between Dover and Dungeness. Flight Lieutenant Kingcome:

> I was patrolling with Yellow 2 when I sighted a very large formation of enemy bombers with a large fighter escort of Me 109 and Me 110 above and behind. They were crossing the coast over Dungeness when I first sighted them. With Yellow 2 I made a head-on attack on the lower layer of the bomber formation. One aircraft, a He 111, started to smoke, but I had no time to notice whether it crashed or not. I broke away downwards, climbed up behind and started a stern attack on the lower layer of the bomber formation when my engine cut, so I broke off the attack.

Pilot Officer Wellum, in Spitfire R6760, was also among the RAF fighter pilots harrying KG 26 over the Kentish coast:

> Having lost the squadron I was flying near the coast at 9,000 feet when I saw and engaged a He 111. The port engine was out of action. I did one quarter attack and was met with fire from top

and bottom guns of the E/A. I did a second quarter attack and this time met with fire from the top gun only. Black smoke began to come from the starboard engine. I did one more quarter attack and then went in astern. White smoke came from the starboard engine and the enemy aircraft lost height slowly. Having finished my ammunition, I broke off the engagement.

This was the first time Geoffrey had fired his guns in anger, and the He 111 was subsequently claimed as destroyed. Out of ammunition, having emptied 2,740 rounds into the raider, Gannic Red Two was heading home when

a flash, bright like magnesium and a sharp, very loud explosion. Something red streaks past the cockpit from somewhere astern ... My own fault. Elementary rule number one: never relax vigilance ... So this is how a fighter pilot dies. Looking back over my shoulder, an Me 109 sitting on my tail thirty yards away ... turning with me. I see the flash from his cannons and puffs of greyish smoke as he tries a quick burst ... more hits ... I keep turning, keep going, the 109 tucks in behind me. Round and round and still he sticks there, glued to my tail. This chap can fly ... an old hand. I hold on to the turn ... and even tighten it. Must be pulling six G. The Spit judders, a high-speed stall ... hold on ... fly her like hell. As I watch the 109, I now know the meaning of the word 'fear', real stark staring fear, the sort of fear that few people possibly ever experience. Round and round we go. The Hun fires again ... Missed me. Maybe I've gained a little on him. I'm starting to calm down and think logically. The German pilot is trying to tighten his turn ... I see the 109 flick. You won't do it, mate ... I can see his head quite clearly, even the shape of his oxygen mask.

Turning, turning, always turning, tighter and tighter; the 109 came out of the turn, pulling up to gain height before turning again. By now, the Spitfire had gained too much, and was behind the 109 – but out of ammunition. Carefully awaiting his moment, the 109 low on fuel, the second the German broke away Geoffrey was rolling out and away in a vertical dive. It was a lucky escape – and a baptism of fire, if ever there was one: 'When that 109 caught me after that Heinkel, I remember thinking, "If you can get away with this, you can get away with anything" – because he should have killed me.'

It was a lucky escape indeed (vividly brought to life many years later, as we will in due course see). Other 92 Squadron pilots were not so fortunate: Pilot Officer Hargreaves was missing, Edwards killed, and Paterson was wounded.

By now, it was abundantly clear that the Hurricane's inability to fight at high altitude was a serious deficiency. In fighter combat, height is everything – and the 109s frequently came in very high, just beneath the stratosphere, meaning that the *Jagdfliegern* had an immeasurable advantage over the Hawker fighter. Fortunately, this did not apply to the Spitfire, which could get up there and take on the 109s. Recognising this, on 11 September, Air Vice-Marshal Park instructed his Controllers to despatch squadrons in pairs, 'Spitfires against fighter screen, and Hurricanes against bombers and close escort'. For the battle Air Vice-Marshal Park was now fighting, like Dunkirk, there was no precedent – so the whole tactical process was a continually evolving one.

More poor weather reduced enemy activity over the next few days, but on 14 September, Me 109s of both *Luftflotten* 2 and 3 flew an increased number of *Freie Jagd*. 92 Squadron became embroiled with some forty Me 109s over Canterbury, as Flight Lieutenant Kingcome's combat report relates:

I was leading the squadron and vectored into the path of approaching bandits. We were still climbing on our vector when I saw several formations of Me 109s passing directly over us in the opposite direction about 5,000 feet above. There appeared to be no bombers, so I turned about and was climbing after the Me 109s when I noticed another formation of enemy fighters (109s) diving onto another squadron of Spitfires which was following us and was about 2,000 feet below us on our right. The squadron apparently did not notice them, so I turned and dived into the 109s. I gave the first one a two second burst, ¾ deflection, and it turned away in a gentle spiral glide to the right, into some cloud below. I gave another one a two second full deflection shot and it pulled up vertically on its back and fell away. When I climbed back again I could not find any more bandits, so eventually returned to base.

Not shackled to escorting bombers but allowed to hunt freely over England, the enemy *Jagdfliegern* won this particular day: twelve RAF fighters were destroyed, offset against four Me 109s. 92 Squadron's Sergeant McGowan had baled out, wounded, over Faversham, possibly the victim of *Feldwebel* Grzymalla of 8/JG 26.

As is well documented, the following day – Sunday 15 September 1940 – is now remembered annually as 'Battle of Britain Day', so great was the scale of fighting. Flight Lieutenant Kingcome's personal Spitfire, however, went unserviceable as he prepared to scramble that afternoon, so he hurriedly took charge of a spare machine and took off in pursuit of 92 Squadron:

I joined a squadron of Spitfires which I found above cloud, and encountered a formation of about thirty Do 17s. There were many Me 109s several thousand feet above. We attacked the bomber formation from the beam. I started firing, almost from the beam, turning until I finished dead astern. The machine I fired at dropped back from the formation, smoking from both engines. I then finished up my ammunition on a second machine, firing from the quarter, and dived away before the 109s came down.

The 92 Squadron Operations Record Book summarised the day's activities thus:

Weather fair but fine. Enemy intercepted at midday, Canterbury Maidstone area. S/Ldr Sanders destroyed a Do 17 and many more were damaged including fighters. Another large formation intercepted at 1430 hours and two He 111s definitely destroyed besides many others damaged mostly bombers. P/O Holland forced to abandon aircraft slightly injured on landing and admitted to EMS East Grinstead. Night activity continues. South Camp appears to be immune from bombing, perhaps London main objective of enemy.

The following day, unsurprisingly following such a massive effort, enemy activity was much reduced. On that day, Air Vice-Marshal Park issued further orders to his Controllers, and, in further recognition of the Spitfire's superiority at high altitude, instructed that in future Spitfire squadrons would specifically and preferably engage the 'very high enemy fighters': 'The Spitfire squadrons of Hornchurch and Biggin Hill are, in clear weather, to be detailed in pairs to attack the high fighter screen, which is normally between 25,000 and 30,000 feet.' This did not mean, of course, that Spitfire squadrons would no longer attack and execute damage to German bombers howsoever and whenever they could, but the advantage of this essential protective screen, enabling Hurricane squadrons to operate lower down without fear of a surprise attack from above, must not be either underestimated or overlooked.

On 18 September, the fighting continued. Firstly, 109s roamed over southern England, destroying five Spitfires against losing two of their own number. At lunchtime, a small formation of Ju 88s, escorted by one hundred Me 109s, attacked Rochester: Major Adolf Galland, the *Kommodore* of JG 26, personally destroyed three Hurricanes. The day's final and most significant raid came in at 1630 hours, when, incredibly, the largely unescorted Ju 88s of III/KG 77 – a unit fresh to the battle – headed for Tilbury Docks. Air Vice-Marshal Park's reaction was swift and decisive: fourteen squadrons were scrambled and intercepted the raiders over the

Thames Estuary. 92 Squadron attacked the bombers at 18,000 feet over Southend, as Flight Lieutenant Kingcome reported:

> I was driving the train consisting of 92 and 66 Squadrons and we were ordered to 30,000 feet. At that height we were still in cloud, however, so I broke away and came down. At about 18,000 feet we encountered a small formation of about sixteen Me 109s. We attacked but they climbed up into the cloud. The squadron was split up after this attack, when I saw a formation of eighteen enemy bombers. I managed to collect three other Spitfires and flew alongside the enemy formation in echelon starboard and peeled off, attacking just forward of the beam. I saw pieces fly off the first one I had attacked but had not time to watch it, so I went straight through the formation and attacked again from the port side. The machine I attacked this time broke away from the formation and spiralled down into the cloud with pieces falling off it. I broke away and found myself behind a bomber which had broken away and was making for a cloud with glycol coming from one engine. I gave it a burst from above and behind, and it spun into the Thames Estuary off the Isle of Sheppey.

When the fight was over, eight Ju 88s had been destroyed for the loss of just one RAF fighter, the pilot of which was safe.

Although the following day was inauspicious from a perspective of aerial operations, due to low cloud and heavy rain over southern England, it was, in fact, enormously significant: British intelligence decoded a German signal confirming that Hitler had postponed Operation *Seelöwe* indefinitely. The threat of imminent invasion had passed, but still the fighting went on.

With the enemy's daylight bombing offensive having failed, the 109s flew frequent fighter sweeps. This was naturally welcomed by the *Kanaljäger*, but such operations could easily be ignored, a fighter only being dangerous to another fighter. All Air

Vice-Marshal Park's Controllers had to do was not react – and let the enemy waste time and fuel. On the morning of 20 September, a German fighter sweep approached London but was ignored – until bombs rained down on the capital. Göring had decided that one *Staffel* in each *Gruppe* would become fighter-bombers, each Me 109 carrying a single SC250 bomb, in an effort to provoke a reaction. The Biggin Hill and Hornchurch Spitfire squadrons were scrambled too late, and were caught on the climb over the Thames Estuary. At a distinct tactical disadvantage, the Spitfires suffered accordingly. At 1134 and 1135 hours, the German *Oberkanone*, Major Werner Mölders, the expert of all *Experten*, destroyed two 92 Squadron aircraft over Dungeness: Pilot Officer Howard Hill, a twenty-year-old New Zealander, was killed, and Sergeant P. R. Eyles was never seen again. Sergeant Alan Wright:

The squadron was split in half due to oxygen failure. The first half was surprised by Me 109s. Howard and Eyles, both of Green Section, were lost. I have a vivid picture in my mind of me leading Green Section on that day. After the split, the front two sections, led by the CO, Squadron Leader Sanders, were left flying in a close formation of two vics in line astern. I happened to glance to my left and was amazed to see a 109 taking the place of the Spitfire that I expected to see there, a glance to the right showed another one! I immediately shouted 'BREAK!' and pulled up and around in a tight turn. The others probably reacted similarly. I noticed that we were immediately above a coastal town. I cannot remember what I did after the break, when flying at 200–300 mph one can, in just a few seconds, find oneself quite alone and unable to re-join the action.

At that time, many squadrons, including ours, would be vectored towards our targets in a close formation of nine, comprising three vics with two weavers criss-crossing overhead and safeguarding the blind area behind the formation. Its advantage was that the eleven aircraft as a whole were very manoeuvrable. The danger was that if anything happened to the weavers and they were unable to use their R/T, the rest of the Squadron would be utterly vulnerable. On this occasion, in the rush to scramble, one or more of the rear pilots could have failed to switch on their oxygen, or it may not have been working properly, so that in the confusion the first half were left unaware that no one was guarding their tails. No oxygen at the height of Everest could put you to sleep without you even realising it. Very sad, especially about Howard Hill who had flown with our Squadron since the previous October.

92 Squadron's Red Two, Geoffrey Wellum's direct contemporary Pilot Officer 'Wimpey' Wade, attacked an Me 109 at 1145 hours, 27,000 feet above Folkestone:

Ganic Squadron was split up due to attack by Me 109s. I got on the tail of one and after a short burst the enemy aircraft dived away steeply. At about 4,000 feet it pulled out and started evasive tactics. After two-three minutes it headed south-east at 5,000 feet. I fired a number of short bursts from astern at 100–150 yards range but was unable to close any further. After doing evasive medium turns for a short period he pulled up steeply into cloud at 2,000 feet, 15 miles from the French coast after which I lost him. I had seen my ammunition going into the wings but without the desired effect.

92 Squadron's boss, Squadron Leader P. J. 'Judy' Sanders, also attacked an Me 109 at 1145, firing 2,450 rounds at it:

As Squadron Leader patrolling Dungeness I knew that there were enemy aircraft about and was weaving. At 27,000 feet, Blue Section, behind me, was attacked, so I broke quickly to the left and saw an Me 109 also turning left behind me. I gave one short burst about 120 yards from above and from the right. The enemy aircraft at once half rolled to the right and dived steeply for about 10,000 feet. He then pulled up and I got a good deflection shot at him from above and slightly behind. He half rolled again and dived. I fired intermittently at him on the way down and he did not pull out. I came out of the dive at 500 feet and he crashed into the sea about five miles south of Dymchurch and disappeared. I tried to re-group the Squadron and received instructions to return to base and land.

Squadron Leader Sanders was also attacked during the combat and his Spitfire was damaged, possibly by *Leutnant* Altendorf of II/ JG 53. By the enemy's retirement to France, four Spitfire pilots had been killed and several others wounded; one Me 109 lay mangled in a field near Orpington, its pilot also dead. Geoffrey Wellum:

On September 20th I flew two patrols in Spitfire K9998. After this length of time I can recall nothing of the action, but I do remember that during September and October 1940, Me 109s were always in the Biggin Hill Sector in numbers, and caused problems. I recall that they were always above us as we never seemed to be scrambled in time to get enough height. Our climb was always a desperate, full throttle affair, but we never quite got up to them. I did manage to get a crack at two Me 109s on one patrol but although I saw strikes I could only claim them as damaged.

After his altercation with Altendorf, Squadron Leader Sanders safely returned to base – but soaked in highly flammable aviation spirit from a ruptured fuel tank. Back on *terra firma*, 'Judy' lit a cigarette – and burst into flame. Fortunately the fire was rapidly extinguished, but not before causing serious burns. Sanders was then hospitalised until October, but did not return to 92 Squadron, going on to command 264 Squadron, equipped with Defiants and participating in Britain's night defence. On 8 November 1940, however, 92 Squadron's former Commanding Officer was awarded the DFC:

Squadron Leader Sanders has commanded his squadron since May, 1940, and his continuous leadership, skill and determination have been responsible for the high standard and morale of the squadron. On 11 September 1940, when leading his squadron on an offensive patrol, he displayed great skill and leadership and was personally responsible for the destruction of two and probably three hostile aircraft. He has in all destroyed at least six enemy aircraft.

As senior flight commander, after Sanders' accident, Flight Lieutenant Kingcome became 92 Squadron's Acting Commanding Officer. Again, however, seniority in the Air Force List dictated this would be short-lived.

Having served with distinction in India during 1937, Squadron Leader Robert C. F. Lister was awarded the DFC for his part in operations over Waziristan. After returning to England, Lister became a flying instructor before breaking his spine in a crash. Proclaimed fit for flying duties, in August 1940 he volunteered to fly Spitfires, converting to that type at 7 Operational Training Unit, Hawarden. After a brief spell with 41 Squadron, during which time he was shot down by an Me 109 and baled out slightly wounded, on 22 September Lister was posted as supernumerary to 92 Squadron. By flying as an extra pilot, officers with seniority in the list were able to gain experience before receiving their own commands. So it was that Flight Lieutenant Kingcome – already a proven and experienced fighter leader – was formally succeeded in command by Squadron Leader Lister. In the air, however, it remained Kingcome who led 'Ganic Squadron' into action – with Lister flying on his wing. The new Commanding Officer made his first sortie with 92 Squadron on 23 September, a patrol over Gravesend at 27,000 feet in Spitfire X4427; it was the first of four such sorties Lister would make that day.

The Luftwaffe continued the pattern of fighter sweeps and small raids by individual or small formations of bombers. Göring had also changed tack again, and was now largely concentrating on targets connected with the British aircraft industry. On 24 September, the day's main enemy effort saw *Erprobungsgruppe* 210 dive-bomb the Supermarine factory at Woolston, killing ninety-eight factory workers and injuring forty more. Further east, two raids were mounted against London, the bombers enjoying protection from a massive fighter escort. That morning, Biggin Hill's three Spitfire squadrons were scrambled, and climbed desperately to intercept bandits heading for Tilbury. Flight Lieutenant Kingcome reported that over Rochford he was

leading the squadron, which was part of a train consisting of 72, 66 and 92 Squadrons. We were flying due south from just north of the Thames Estuary when we sighted a formation of about twenty enemy bombers with a large escort of Me 109s on both sides and above.

The bombers were approximately 18,000 feet. We just managed to get to the bombers before the Me 109s got to us, approaching from ahead and slightly to one side. I delivered an attack on a Ju 88 from almost dead ahead at very close range, but had no time to notice the effect of my fire apart from a piece of cowling which flew off.

I broke away violently, owing to the presence of the 109s, blacking out completely; when I came too, my engine was dead. I came down several thousand feet before I noticed that both my ignition switches were in the 'off' position. As there was nothing in the cockpit which could possibly have touched the switches, I can only assume that the force of the breakaway must have been sufficient to have forced the switches down, although admittedly this would seem impossible. When I climbed up again the formation had broken up and was flying off down the Thames Estuary, due east.

92 Squadron's Pilot Officer J. S. Bryson was shot down and killed in this engagement, and Sergeant W. T. Ellis crash-landed on Higham Marches. Having followed Kingcome into the attack,

Squadron Leader Lister found himself alone and surrounded by a *Staffel* of Me 109s. Suddenly a cannon shell exploded in the bottom of his cockpit, wounding the Spitfire pilot in both legs and wrists. It was now that Lister's skills as a pilot rose to the occasion – and saved his life. Returning to Biggin Hill from his first flight on what promised to be yet another busy day, Lister found only one flap working, which, when applied, sent him into a diving turn. Recovering, he managed to make a wheels-down landing, coming to a halt just ten yards short of the wood situated at runway's end. The pilot survived but was so badly wounded that although he remained in the service until 1954, he never flew again. Once again, Flight Lieutenant Kingcome assumed command.

Two days later, an auxiliary, Squadron Leader Alan M. MacLachlan, was given command of 92 Squadron – another officer lacking combat experience. Having joined the Auxiliary Air Force in 1935, MacLachlan had first flown Hart and Demon biplanes with 600 Squadron, before converting to twin-engined Blenheims when called up for full-time service in September 1939. The Fall of France made it immediately apparent, however, that the Blenheim was unsuited to daylight operations, and so 600 began operating at night and experimenting with Airborne Interception Radar. Quite how such experience, therefore, qualified this officer to lead a highly effective and aggressive Spitfire squadron in the Battle of Britain is difficult to comprehend. Brian Kingcome:

> The RAF was still in a time warp, in which the Commanding Officers of front-line squadrons were selected on a basis of age and length of service, rather than operational experience and ability. It was another policy for which we continued to pay the price until 1941, when sanity prevailed and it was changed.

27 September 1940 proved to be another day of heavy fighting, with major raids launched on targets in the West Country and,

inevitably, London. At 1450 hours, 92 Squadron was scrambled from Biggin Hill with orders to rendezvous over base with 66 Squadron from Gravesend, then patrol the Maidstone Line at 20,000 feet, in anticipation of yet another raid. Pilot Officer 'Boy' Wellum reported:

> Whilst on patrol with squadron we met and engaged about twenty Ju 88s escorted by many Me 109s. I got in position under the bombers and fired a long burst into an 88. I then broke away and about two minutes later observed a Ju 88 leave its formation. Three other Spitfires and myself chased it. They got to the 88 before I did and I gave the 88 a short burst from long range, as it dived into the ground. The crew of the 88 baled out. The aircraft crashed several miles south of the Rochester area.

Geoffrey's claim was for a Ju 88 destroyed, shared with other 92 Squadron pilots. Collectively, 92 Squadron claimed to have destroyed thirteen bombers and damaged a 109. On this occasion the enemy fighter escort having arrived too late to prevent RAF fighters executing great damage to the Ju 88s of KG 77, which, having already lost four aircraft in the morning, actually lost a total of seven bombers that afternoon.

This was actually an exhausting time for Fighter Command, due to the frequency of enemy fighter sweeps – which, due to the potential presence of fighter-bombers – could not be ignored. Consequently it was often necessary for 11 Group to maintain standing patrols at height, from dawn through until dusk. 92 Squadron was frequently up there, sparring with 109s.

On 8 October 1940, 92 Squadron had cause to celebrate: news was received that both Flight Lieutenant Brian Kingcome and Pilot Officer Tony Bartley had been awarded the DFC. Both were well-deserved awards indeed. When gazetted, Kingcome's citation read,

Flight Lieutenant Kingcome has personally destroyed six enemy aircraft and by his leadership has been responsible for the destruction of many others. He has led his flight, and lately his squadron, with judgement, skill and keenness.

This was due recognition for providing both an anchor and inspiration to 92 Squadron throughout a time when Britain faced the realistic prospect of an invasion. It was also a time when leadership was inconsistent: after Squadron Leader Sanders' premature departure, Lister's tenure had lasted just two days; of his replacement, MacLachlan, nothing is known: apart from detailing his arrival to command, the 92 Squadron Operations Record Book makes no further mention whatsoever of this particular Commanding Officer. To Geoffrey Wellum – then as now – Brian Kingcome was an immeasurable inspiration: 'Brian *was* 92 Squadron. A *real* leader, a gifted fighter pilot, popular with all, he was someone to really look up to, to emulate, if at all possible. I modelled myself on Brian – as did we all.'

On 11, 12 and 13 October 1940, Flight Lieutenant Kingcome destroyed 109s. Of the action on the 12, 92 Squadron's Form 'F' reported that

the squadron was ordered to rendezvous with 66 Squadron at 3,000 feet over base, with 92 Squadron leading. Eleven Spitfires took off at 1550 hours, and ten had landed by 1650 hours.

AA was observed in the direction of the Thames Estuary, and on investigation proved to directed at a straggling mass of Me 109s flying westwards in no particular formation at 20–24,000 feet. An average estimate of their number was fifty plus.

F/Lt Kingcome, leading the squadron, was attacked by approximately twelve Me 109s, but after taking evasive action was able to attack the near-most aircraft from dead astern, and shot it down into the sea in mid-Channel. A second machine that he attacked was last seen diving and smoking heavily – claimed as damaged.

P/O Lund made a number of attacks on an Me 109 which he chased down to 2,000 feet in the Dover areas, and was then smoking enough to be claimed as damaged.

A second E/A was destroyed on land by P/O Wade, who made two attacks, the second closing to within fifteen yards, resulting in the pilot baling out. This was confirmed by P/O Mansell-Lewis. P/O Wade then fired from full starboard beam at another Messerschmitt, which immediately started pouring glycol, rolled slowly to the right and dived vertically. With his remaining ammunition, he damaged a third, which dived, smoking, to 4,000 feet, approximately, before he lost sight of it.

A third E/A was destroyed on land by Sgt Kingaby, whose first attack from 100 yards astern evidently killed the Me 109's pilot, as his aircraft was observed by Sgt Ellis to crash near Rochester, although no results of fire were seen by Sgt Kingaby. Before this he had fired a 2/3-second full deflection burst at an Me 109, which crossed his bows, and this machine, pouring glycol and diving away, was claimed as a probable.

After this engagement, P/O Pattinson was missing, but he was not seen to be attacked.

In total, 92 Squadron claimed three Me 109s destroyed, two probables and three damaged; Pilot Officer Pattinson had been killed. It was another hard day's fighting, the high-flying Me 109s and fighter-bombers having come in three waves, there being seven separate attacks, five of which reached London. Since 30 September 1940, though, the enemy had been unable to sustain the level of casualties suffered by its bombers. From that point onwards, only heavily armed and fast Ju 88s operated over England in daylight, either singly, engaged on nuisance attacks, or in small formations. Much safer, although less accurate, was night-bombing, the British nocturnal defences being embryonic. Such activity, however, was not going to achieve aerial supremacy – the dream of which had already been abandoned.

On 15 October 1940, the enemy fighter-bombers – *Jabos* – disrupted London's railway network. For the defenders, even though the days of mass bomber formations were over, responding to this continual high-altitude threat was relentless. At 0945 hours, 92 Squadron took off for the first time that day, with instructions to rendezvous with 66 Squadron and patrol Biggin Hill at 'Angels 30' (30,000 feet). While gaining height over London, the Spitfires pilots saw some fifty Me 109s of JG 26 heading back to France – so gave chase. Over Maidstone, however, Sergeant K. B. Parker was shot down and killed by *Unteroffizier* Scheldt, while the remainder of 92 Squadron pursued their enemy halfway back across the Channel, Sergeants Kingaby and Fokes both destroying 109s. Having landed at 1015 hours, an hour later the Spitfires were off again to patrol Sevenoaks at 30,000 feet. While en route and at 27,000 feet, 92 Squadron was vectored west and engaged fifty more Me 109s – head-on. A running battle ensued, during which Sergeant Fokes destroyed an enemy fighter in flames, and Pilot Officer Holland claimed a probable; Pilot Officer 'Tommy' Lund was shot down into the Channel and was rescued by HMS *Nysan*.

While returning to Biggin Hill, Flight Lieutenant Kingcome, who had again led the squadron, thought that he was alone in the sky. With the airfield in sight, thinking of an uneaten breakfast, the pilot throttled back and prepared to practice forced landing with a dead engine. As Kingcome later wrote,

It was breathtakingly stupid behaviour. It was so irresponsible that it would never even have occurred to me to warn new pilots against it. The skies of Kent were at all times a hostile environment, whatever the illusion of emptiness ... I can only put the action down to an overconfidence fostered by constant exposure to the dawn-to-dusk rotation of 'take off, climb, engage, land, refuel, rearm, take off, climb, engage...' two, three, sometimes four times a day, familiarity reducing what had begun as exciting, adrenalin pumping action to make routine. In other words, I had grown blasé.

The twenty-three-year-old had also shouldered a significant amount of extra responsibility, in the air and on the ground, given the problems experienced by 92 Squadron with two successive inexperienced and ineffective commanding officers. Inevitably, however, in spite of appearances, the sky was not empty: Kingcome's Spitfire was suddenly hit by shot and shell, having become a sitting duck for a marauding Me 109. Wounded in the leg, the flight commander baled out safely and was admitted to the Royal Naval Hospital, Chatham. This was a loss 92 Squadron could ill afford at this particular time, but at least Kingcome had survived, returning to the squadron six weeks later.

On 26 October 1940, Squadron Leader MacLachlan, who does not appear to have made his mark and is unmentioned in 92 Squadron's official record, was replaced as CO by Squadron Leader John Kent AFC DFC – a tough, no-nonsense Canadian fresh from commanding a flight of 303 Squadron's tough Poles at Northolt. Kent was not altogether impressed by his new command, which he considered undisciplined; 92 Squadron, however, disagreed and considered this simply evidence of its unique fighting spirit. Either way, on 31 October 1940, the Battle of Britain was officially considered over – and won by Fighter Command. To the pilots of Fighter Command, however, there was no distinct, abrupt end to the fighting, which continued into the winter months. Certainly the enemy bombing effort was now at night, but still the 109s swept over south-east England.

At 0900 hours on 2 November 1940, Squadron Leader Kent led 92 Squadron in an attack on JG 52, 20,000 feet over Ashford. Pilot Officer Wellum:

The Final Few

Whilst on patrol as Yellow 3 … we attacked fifty – sixty Me 109s. I got on the tail of one, and saw my tracers go into the enemy aircraft, which started a slow glide to the right. I then had to break away because of 109s on my tail. I then fired a long burst at about 250 yards range at another 109, and again saw my tracer going into the enemy aircraft. I was unable to observe the effect of my fire owing to there being so many 109s.

On this occasion, the Spitfire pilots had enjoyed the height advantage – subsequently claiming four enemy fighters destroyed, one probable and the two damaged by Yellow 3.

At 1615 hours on 17 November, 92 was patrolling in company with 74 Squadron at 20,000 feet over Eastbourne:

I was flying as Red 3 in the squadron when we saw and attacked some Me 109s. I observed one 109 in a shallow dive and going very fast out to sea; he was leaving a white smoke trail. I chased him astern and fired a long burst at the enemy aircraft and saw tracer going into him. At once the enemy's aircraft steepened. I fired another good burst, which resulted in the smoke trail thickening a lot, which I think was due to glycol. The enemy aircraft's dive steepened still further to about 70°, and I last saw this 109 going into the cloud, and it seemed to turn slowly onto its back, but this cannot be certain.

I attacked another enemy aircraft and fired one short burst which I observed go into the enemy. This aircraft, which was diving at the time, continued its dive into the cloud out to sea.

Two Me 109s were destroyed, two (including that claimed by Geoffrey Wellum) probably destroyed and three damaged. One Spitfire was shot up in response, but fortunately the pilot, Sergeant W. J. Allison, was unhurt.

As the winter advanced, the *Nachtangriff* on British cities

192

continued unabated. By February 1941, the worsening weather concluded the 'season's' fighting between the opposing fighter forces. A reorganisation, however, was taking place in Fighter Command. Air Chief Marshal Dowding had been succeeded as Commander-in-Chief by Sholto Douglas, and Air Vice-Marshal Park in 11 Group by Air Vice-Marshal Leigh-Mallory, previously of 12 Group. Being supporters of the controversial 'Big Wing' during the Battle of Britain, these officers created wings of three fighter squadrons at every sector station. Each wing was to be commanded by a 'Wing Commander Flying', whose role was not administrative but to lead his squadrons into action. The strategy was an offensive one, the intention being to 'reach out' across the Channel, taking the initiative and war to the enemy in France. Spitfires began replacing Hurricanes in all front-line RAF fighter squadrons, the Supermarine fighter's superiority having been proven. 74 Squadron's Squadron Leader Adolph Gysbert Malan DSO DFC – known universally as 'Sailor' on account of his previous nautical service – became Biggin Hill's first Wing Leader on 10 March 1941.

So it was that when the 'season' of 1941 opened, Fighter Command found itself on the offensive, in a reversal of the Battle of Britain scenario. Now it was the RAF pilots who faced a two-way sea-crossing and action over enemy occupied territory – while the *Kanaljäger* now fought the short-range defensive battle for which their Me 109 had also been designed. On 16 June 1941, Flight Lieutenant Kingcome engaged 'lots and lots' of Me 109Fs over Le Touquet:

I was sub-section leader of a section of four aircraft, and the squadron consisting of seven aircraft was detailed to carry out a sweep over France. 74 Squadron was behind us. We had just crossed the coast at Le Touquet when we were intercepted by a large number of Me 109Fs. In the dogfight which followed I fired at three

E/A, but it was impossible to wait around and watch results, owing to the large numbers against us. Garrick Leader, however, states that he saw the first E/A I fired at (from the beam) pass straight through my tracer, turn slowly on its back, and go down inverted at 45°, pouring black smoke.

The fight lasted about fifteen – twenty minutes altogether. The Me 109Fs were flown well but their shooting was very bad.

On the way back, I was by myself when I noticed two unescorted Blenheims west of Boulogne. There were some 109s in the vicinity, so I stayed with them. The port engine of the rear Blenheim was on fire, and it eventually jettisoned its bombs, landing in the sea about six miles south of Folkestone. The crew climbed out and boarded their dinghy before the Blenheim sank.

Four Hurricanes appeared but did not remain. I climbed to gain height for a voice fix but my R/T was U/S. I was then attacked by two more 109Fs, and phoned Operations, Biggin Hill, to give them appropriate position of the Blenheim crew.

On 8 July, Flying Officer Wellum claimed an Me 109F 'probable':

While flying with the squadron as Blue Leader, I observed two Me 109Fs attacking the bombers in the Desvres area. I chased the E/A and finally carried out a quarter attack on the rear 109, firing both cannon and machine-guns from about 150 – 200 yards. My first burst appeared to go behind the E/A, so I added on another ring of deflection and saw my cannon tracer going all around him, and one went into the cockpit area. The E/A appeared to jerk away from the bombers at the same time as its dive increased, to almost vertical. I finally lost sight of the E/A, diving at terrific speed into the ground haze. On returning to base, Sergeant Warn, my Blue 2, said that he saw tracer hitting the E/A, which turned away from the bombers. He then added that the E/A's angle of dive increased to such an extent, and the speed so great, that he was unable to follow it below 4,000 feet.

The following day, Geoffrey destroyed an Me 109F over St Omer:

> I was flying with Garrick Squadron as Blue Leader when we encountered about fifteen Me 109Fs, in two layers. Red and Yellow Sections attacked the bottom layer of none E/A, while Blue Section attacked the upper layer of six. I noticed five E/A turn and dive right across the rear of Red Section. I at once gave chase with my Section and from 300 yards I gave a long burst from astern at one E/A, with cannons and machine-guns, of about four seconds. One of my cannon shells burst just in front of the cockpit, and I finished my ammunition at 500 yards. E/A's nose dropped and he began to turn slowly over on his back. I last saw the E/A going into the haze at about 6000 feet in a kind of spin, with engine enveloped in flames. The spin was not fast, and the E/A was diving at 45°, out of control.

This was Geoffrey's final combat claim with 92 Squadron.

On 24 July, Flight Lieutenant Kingcome scored his last victory with 92 Squadron, during a coastal raid to Le Havre:

> I was Garrick Leader of 92 Squadron, and Garrick Squadron was top cover for the wing, which was protecting six Beauforts. When the target ship was reached, I saw about twenty Me 109s at about 2000 feet, just inland. We were at about 3000 feet. About six 109s came and circled round us at about 5000 feet. One dived towards the bombers and I followed, and gave it a short burst from astern. I saw it break off its attempted attack and then lost it as I turned around to see what was behind. I did not claim this at the time, but apparently the aircraft was seen to dive into the sea by Beauty Squadron (609), and as no Spitfires were missing from this show, and as I was the only one to fire, it must have been this 109. Garrick Squadron lost the bombers in the mist after this show, but we returned in their track behind them. Some 109s shadowed us for a few minutes but remained well out of range, and made no further attempt to attack us.

For both Geoffrey Wellum and Brian Kingcome, it had been a long, hard road. In August 1941, Geoffrey's well-deserved DFC was gazetted, and that month also saw Brian leave his beloved 92 Squadron, on rest as an instructor. A month later, Flying Officer Geoffrey 'Boy' Wellum DFC also left 92 Squadron, serving as an instructor at 52 Operational Training Unit until March 1942, when he was posted to become a flight commander with 65 Squadron at Debden. This was the end of an intense experience – but there was to be little let-up. In August 1942, Geoffrey was posted overseas, leading eight Spitfires off the aircraft carrier HMS *Furious* to Luqa, on the besieged Mediterranean island of Malta. After three years of combat flying, however, the twenty-two-year-old suffered a breakdown, caused by sheer exhaustion. The young pilot was returned to England, where he recovered and continued flying, first as a test pilot on Hawker Typhoons, then finally instructing aerial gunnery. After the war he married his sweetheart, Grace, the couple having three children, and remained in the post-war RAF until retirement in 1961. Thereafter, he worked as a commodity broker in the City of London before becoming a harbour master in Cornwall and, eventually, retiring to that picturesque peninsula.

Kingcome later resumed his distinguished combat career. In February 1942, he returned to operations, leading 72 Squadron, increased his score and in June, became Kenley's Wing Leader. The following August, Wing Commander Kingcome was awarded the DSO, and after a spell at the Fighter Leaders' School also found himself posted to Malta. There he led 244 Wing, participating in the Allied invasions of Sicily and Italy, after which he was promoted to Acting Group Captain. By the war's end, Group Captain Brian Kingcome DSO DFC was 205 (Heavy Bomber) Group's Senior Air Staff Officer. Like Geoffrey Wellum, he too remained in the post-war service, until being invalided out, suffering from tuberculosis. Recovered and starting a new life on 'civvy street', he first ran a successful garage and car hire business in London, with fellow former Battle of Britain Spitfire pilot 'Paddy' Barthropp, before moving to Devon in 1969, setting up 'Kingcome Sofas' with his wife, Lesley. Many years later, without notes or diary, and possessed only of a 'fading memory', he wrote his memoir, entitled *The Ramblings of a Geriatric Ex-Fighter Pilot*, dedicated to his 'Minder', Lesley Kingcome, whose 'benevolent terrorism', Kingcome maintained, 'controlled' his life. The work was first published in 1999, under the title *A Willingness to Die*, but by that time Brian Kingcome was no more: sadly, he died, aged seventy-seven, in 1994. 'When I visit my old station, Biggin Hill,' he had once said, 'I walk with ghosts'; perhaps now, this very special man is among those august spirits.

Although Geoffrey Wellum did not keep a diary, he did make some notes on his experiences while en route to Malta, and retained his personal pilot's flying log book. Thirty-five years after the war, partially as a means of exorcising the violent and traumatic past, he sat down with these aged references and started writing – and didn't stop until his story was committed to paper. The book, though, would not be published for over twenty years, until produced and distributed by Viking Books, under the evocative title *First Light*, in 2002. The following year, Penguin distributed the title – which leapt on to the bestseller list and catapulted is very modest author into the public eye. The book was lauded as among the most honest, accurate and gripping memoirs to have emerged from the air war, with which assessment I would entirely agree. As the seventieth anniversary of the Battle of Britain approached, Geoffrey's bestseller also inspired film producer and director Matthew Whiteman:

In a way, this was a dream come true – getting the chance to dramatise *First Light* for BBC Two to mark the seventieth anniversary. The book is Geoffrey Wellum's memoir of what it was like to be an eighteen-year-old Spitfire pilot, thrust into the gut-wrenching life-and-death struggle of the most violent aerial combat ever. And it also deals with his mental disintegration in eighteen relentless months on the frontline.

This was one film where we had to get not just the emotional thrust right, but also the historical detail. There are a lot of people out there for whom this really matters – and I am one of them. It's not a question of being 'nerdy' – I believe we all know when something *feels* right; whether it is in the tone of a performance, costume, props, or whatever else clouds the mind of a director trying to truly evoke the time and place of a story.

The conversations started early about getting Spitfires airborne. But what is it they say? Never work with animals, children ... or, in my case, vintage aircraft! We were discussing a scene in which 'Boy' Wellum, the hero of our story, makes his first flight in a Spitfire, and our actor, Sam Heughan, couldn't wait to get into the air. The problem was how to convince the audience that he was actually at the controls of a Spitfire for the first time, rocketing through the clouds. The big snag was that there was no way we could get Sam airborne in a real Spitfire. This scene was crucial to the story, appearing little more than ten minutes after the opening of the film. We had to produce a sequence breath-taking enough to make the audience believe that flying the Spitfire was love at first sight for 'Boy'. We had access to a real Spitfire – and the budget for maybe forty-five minutes' flying time – but the Spit is a single-seater and there was no question of anybody but a very experienced pilot taking the controls of several million pounds' worth of vintage aeroplane. And we also had access to a replica Spitfire, which could be shoved about on the ground, but had no proper cockpit interior. We soon decided that rather than shooting costly air-to-air footage, we would use outtakes from the Battle of Britain movie – and enhance it with CGI.

This was a huge task in itself; viewing around fifty hours-worth of unused and unseen material, but it was great that we could give some of this footage the light of day at last! The old movie footage was lovely stuff, but the code letters and numbers on the side of Spits in the movie footage didn't begin to match our real or replica planes. One plane was brown and green, the other brown and grey. And the real one was based at Wycombe Air Park, whilst our replica was eighty miles away on the drama set outside Dunstable. Bringing the replica down would nuke what little was left of the budget, but if we didn't, Sam could be walking in the rain to the replica on one location, and then climbing into the cockpit (to shoot an authentic start-up sequence) in bright sunshine on the other. It was quite a headache! Somehow we wangled it in the end. New codes and numbers were put on the replica – and the owner was persuaded to bring his baby to stand side-by-side with the real McCoy.

Then we found a friendly pilot, prepared to have the back cockpit of his two-seater Russian YAK trainer converted to look like a Spitfire cockpit interior. Sam leapt in, surrounded by high definition (HD) mini-cams, and took to the sky with his script taped to the instrument panel. Meantime, our real Spit took off with the pilot delivering 'Boy' Wellum's point of view (by way of a specially designed camera mounting on his flying helmet). When we got into the edit, the whole story came together. By combining Sam walking to the replica Spitfire, the real thing taxiing, Sam in close-up in the back seat of the YAK – and then cutting to his point of view, shot in the real Spit, we got the hair-raising images of 'his' first take-off. Once airborne, we started to inter-cut Sam in the cockpit with flying footage from the Battle of Britain movie.

...And that was the easiest of the flying sequences in the film!

Then we had to work out how to create a full-blooded dogfight, and a nightmare flight in torrential rain over the channel – during which 'Boy' shoots down a German bomber. Looking back on it all now, I can't believe that we shot the whole drama, including the flying, in just nine days. We couldn't have done it without the orchestration of the first assistant director Chris Carreras, whose experience spans the *Bourne* movies, *United 93*, *Harry Potter* and many other big films. And Chris was dead right when he took one last long look at the schedule just before we began the shoot, and, having considered the weather and all the other infinitely frightening variables, commented dryly: 'We're going to have to be 100% lucky on this one!'

Geoffrey Wellum didn't have time to visit us on set – but before the shoot, as I was scripting, we spent a huge amount of time together. And afterwards, during post-production, Geoff worked very closely with the CGI artists to make sure we got the tracer fire absolutely correct in the air battles. Geoff explained to the CGI folks that real tracer doesn't fly in straight lines – like *Star Wars*; it curves and snakes across the sky, governed by the motion of the aircraft and the air.

Working so closely with Geoffrey has made *First Light* a unique experience both for me as a director and I think, for the audience. The combination of Geoff's expert eye-witness guidance, and actually getting Sam up in the air – instead of in some faked up studio cockpit – has made the film an incredibly rich experience for everybody. And, I guess, is just about as close as any of us would want to get to the nerve-jangling terrors of air combat, Battle of Britain style.

Creating the tension on the ground, however, was just as important as in the air. I love the waiting scene in dispersal before Geoff's first combat – the tinkling of teaspoons in cups, the rustle of a magazine and flight leader, Brian Kingcome, chewing on his match… And then the sudden shrill ringing of the phone – scramble! Geoff watched these scenes with great interest and said that he felt the film perfectly caught the mood and emotions he felt at the time, both on the ground and in the air. The war literally tore Geoff's emotions apart. If he had not been rested from flying before going back for a second tour of combat, I think he would be the first to say he would no longer be with us now. But at that time – as he reflects in the film – he was desperate to fight on until the bitter end. Geoff still carries a sense of guilt that he survived when so many he knew died. This was the truth for many soldiers – the feeling that they had been taken off the line before the 'job was done', and now were left to watch others die whom they could no longer help or protect.

Geoff hates to be called a hero, but his efforts, and that of all those around him seventy years ago, saved us from the terrors of Nazi occupation. I believe that his war – the Battle of Britain, was the key turning point of World War Two. If England had fallen to Germany, the Britain could not have been used as the launching point for the D-Day landings and the liberation of Europe. I salute you, Geoff – however reluctant you are to be called a hero. I salute you and all those that fought alongside you. And I'm sure the audience will, too.

Sam Heughan, who played Geoffrey Wellum in the drama:

I have always been particularly interested in World War Two and the Battle of Britain. I guess my first contact was through my grandfather; he took me to the Imperial War Museum etc. at an early age, and had himself been called up to fight. I think this influenced my career. I have always been cast in many period productions. My first job leaving drama school was *Island at War*, a big budget ITV drama focusing on the Channel Islands and the German occupation. I did a lot of research; there are a few documentaries and books on the subject. We filmed on the Isle of Man, which in its own way leant itself to feeling like a small community removed from the mainland. I have also filmed several period documentaries and worked on many stage productions set in that period. I guess what fascinates me is the 'spirit' of the time. It seems to me that the British Isles were isolated and the war brought out the 'British' spirit, one where the people were industrious and collaborative, and learnt to survive. Also, the great tragedy, the bigger cause and the personal struggle. I guess everything seems more poignant at wartime, time and life is precious, and should not be wasted. It lends itself to a great setting for drama – I guess that's why there are so many fantastic TV and film productions about the war. I also grew up watching the old 1940s movies, which all had a slight glamour, the uniforms and hairstyles. Only in more recent years, though, has the true grim reality of war been more accurately portrayed. To me, productions based on reality or history are a real gift to an actor, as you have so much research and source material.

When I was asked to audition for *First Light*, I read the script and instantly loved it. I did some research, saw that it was a book and read it. I think I finished it in one day; it was SO good, readable and touching. It became the whole cast's handbook. An insight into the world of 92 Squadron and the characters who fought, lived and died alongside each other. The pictures were evocative and the honesty in which Geoffrey revealed his innermost thoughts were a gift. I *had* to do it!

I met with Matthew Whiteman, the Director (also a pilot), and instantly felt that we got on. He has a great wealth of knowledge of the period, and, more than that, it's his passion. Matthew had also already done some great docudramas on the period (*Double X* is fascinating, I'd love to make it into a film), so had written and produced similar projects. In preparation, we talked, and had rehearsals. I re-read Geoffrey's book (the true inspiration and actually all we needed, it's all in there!), plus I wanted to understand more about Spitfires and what it meant to be a pilot. I found a reproduction of the Spitfire Pilot's Notes, an amazing pilot's aid. It was not a dissimilar way to how pilots learnt in those days. I studied the book and learnt all the controls for the cockpit and the start-up sequence. In the scene where I have my eyes closed and am being tested by the aircrew, I actually found I knew exactly where to find the 'Trim, brake, fuel select' etc. I also visited the Imperial War museum and RAF Museum site at Hendon.

However, again, on set it was Matthew who had the eye for everything. Much of the memorabilia in 'Boy Geoffrey's' home were Matthew's personal toys. I think in many ways, the film married Geoffrey's and Matthew's absolute love of flying. I felt that was the strong message in his book. Geoffrey's joy of flight, the freedom of the air. That's why the first flight in a Spitfire is such a large section of film. The ability to escape the dark goings-on of wartime and be free to glide anywhere, must have been amazing. These beautiful machines, being used for foul purposes. I was fortunate that we had a Spitfire to film in. I spent a large amount of time in the cockpit. It was a magical experience. I am six feet and three inches tall, not the perfect height for a pilot! However, once inside it felt very familiar. You can see what a great design it was, the mechanics beautifully engineered. The smell of grease, the ticking of the engine; I fell in love with the aircraft too. And when it fires up!

We also did some flying, an air sequence where I went up and did barrel-rolls, loop the loops etc. What a thrill! Terrifying also, to know these young men were put in charge of these powerful machines – fitted with guns – given comparatively little training, and then left to see if they'd survive... I remember my first day, watching a Tiger-moth performing some aerial acrobatics and thinking how graceful and brave it was of the pilot. A young man's game, easier if one were less aware of the consequences. How those boys grew up quickly, we wanted the characters to age through the film. Experiencing the terrors and mundane side of the War, fraying our nerves and hopefully doing a little justice to what the real pilots went through. We can only imagine...

The filming schedule was intense, maybe two-three weeks. I remember it was full on. We banded together as a team of young pilots. We drank beer in the evening, smoked cigarettes. The boredom of a filmset, waiting around, maybe not too dissimilar to the wait before being scrambled? (Without the threat!) The heavier themes of being at war were maybe found through our own personal experiences. We would discuss the book, the war, and I think everyone involved had some connection through relatives involved. As filming came to a close, we all felt deeply upset. We had all invested in it and knew how much we wanted to do Geoffrey a service.

Matthew had been working with Geoffrey for some time but thought it best I didn't meet him until after filming, so as not to try and mimic him, but find my own way into the part. Though Matthew knew him very well, and would answer questions or give me occasional insights into his character, I was desperate to meet Geoffrey and a few weeks after filming completed I did. We met at the RAF Club at Green Park. Geoffrey walked in, full of energy and humour. An amazing character, charming all around him, but yet clearly still living with the effects of living through World War Two. It's still with him and he'll never lose that, I also don't think he wants to. We must not forget.

The reason his book works, is his personal account of a tenacious young man surviving on his natural abilities during a time of great hardship. It doesn't feel dated, as it could apply to any period of history, however it was indeed a time of great change and high deeds. These days, challenges are different. I wouldn't say younger generations are forgetting, but I guess it's getting more distant, and more recent happenings (Afghanistan) are focused on.

I feel deeply honoured to have met Geoffrey Wellum. I'm lucky to have been able to work on this project and hopefully make sure people don't forget what these people did for us. Geoffrey wouldn't say he's a hero, he'd say that he and comrades did what they did just to survive. Yet we should be grateful – and celebrate their deeds.

The Lion Television docudrama *First Light* was broadcast on BBC2 on 14 September 2010. Personally, I thought it excellent. The clever cutting between past and present, with Geoffrey Wellum appearing gazing out to sea and, in parts, providing a moving voiceover, produced, in my opinion, a very powerful programme indeed. As a Battle of Britain historian I am hard to please, and, given the limitations of time and budget, every production has to telescope certain events, create, perhaps, composite characters, and use a bit of artistic licence here and there in order to tell a convincing story. Howsoever much of those various ingredients Matthew Whiteman used occasionally and by necessity, he undoubtedly achieved as accurate and moving a tribute to 92 Squadron and Geoffrey Wellum as could be humanly possible. Sam Heughan was perfectly cast in the part – and left a lasting impression. Suffice it to say, *First Light* has raised the bar and set an entirely new standard. There is no doubt, then, that Matthew and his team achieved the tribute they intended to. If anyone wants to get a feel of what life must have been like as a young RAF fighter pilot during the Battle of Britain – watch and read *First Light*.

In 1993, when I was researching a particular engagement in which Geoffrey Wellum had been involved, we briefly corresponded. Publication of *First Light* was both a surprise and treat. After the programme, so impressed by what I had seen, I knew that I just had to meet Geoffrey in person – and include his story in this book. Because he has already documented that so well, the angle I wished to pursue, which came out very well in the film, was Geoffrey's admiration and respect for Brian Kingcome – whom I had also known personally. Arrangements were made, and one splendid autumn day in September 2012, found my wife, Karen, and I enjoying Geoffrey Wellum's company for dinner at his local. Geoffrey is now ninety-three, but it remains easy to imagine this sprightly, charming and energetic man flying Spitfires in 1940. Like most of his ilk, Geoffrey can be quiet and reserved, and a little guarded, but he is possessed of a quiet but powerful subconscious ability to really make you think: to consider not only the war and what was endured, but equally what these men have suffered since. Although Geoffrey would doubtless be embarrassed to hear me say it, I was both deeply moved and very impressed by our meeting – as was Karen. In sum, Geoffrey Wellum is a very special man among the Battle of Britain's last survivors.

It is fitting to conclude this chapter with some of Geffrey's own words, spoken on *First Light*:

People say to me, 'How do you remember these things?' How do you expect me to forget? You can't. I can remember it vividly, see things, see people, see aeroplanes. The experiences of being a Spitfire fighter pilot in the Battle of Britain stay with you forever. You can't do anything about it.

I asked myself, 'Was it worth it?' All those young men I fought and flew with, all those chaps no longer with us. I asked myself that question and I can't answer it. I suppose it must have been. I am still struggling.

7

A KALEIDOSCOPE OF MEMORIES

The following are extracts, randomly selected, from my extensive correspondence with members of the Battle of Britain Fighter Association.

Pilot Officer Harry Whelford, 607 Squadron

'We hadn't long refuelled when we were scrambled that evening. There was no interception, but the following morning we lost six out of twelve Hurricanes. Three sergeants were wounded and three officers killed. One of the latter was my best friend, Stuart Parnall, and the others, "Scotty" and the young South African George Drake, were all lovely people, people like Alex Oblenski and "Ching" MacKenzie, with whom I would have flown to hell in glorious comradeship. Somehow we could not believe it. No one talked about it. Of course we all hoped that news would come through from some remote pub or hospital. When no news came, we hardened ourselves for the worst: "Killed in Action". We bit back our tears and sorrow. It was, "You heard about Stuart and Scotty – rotten luck, wasn't it?" Someone would add, "And young

George, bloody good blokes." After that epitaph the matter would apparently be dismissed with the ordering of another round of drinks, to avoid any further trace of sentiment.'

Squadron Leader Harry Hogan DFC, CO of 501 Squadron

'Some of our Hurricane squadron's replacement pilots were straight from OTU, and these we tried to get into the air as quickly as possible, to provide a little extra experience. We were just too tired, though, to give any dogfight practice at all. They were all very "green", youngsters who were bewildered and lost in action.'

Squadron Leader John Hill, CO of 222 Squadron, in a letter to Mrs Whitbread, the mother of Pilot Officer Laurie Whitbread, Killed in Action on 20 September 1940

'It is with deep regret that I have to write to you from 222 Squadron and offer our sympathy on the very sad loss of your son. He was killed instantly by a bullet from an enemy aircraft when doing his bit in the defence of his country. His passing is a great loss to us; he had been in the squadron since its formation and was always most popular, having a quiet and efficient disposition and charming manner.'

Pilot Officer Roger Boulding, 74 Squadron

'It is astonishing, upon reflection, how many young pilots failed to return from their first sortie; to see was to live, but your "eyes" only grew with experience.'

Flying Officer Frank Brinsden, 19 Squadron

'During late August 1940, I always felt a bit cheated, as we of 19 Squadron in 12 Group always seemed to be ordered off late, and therefore late to intercept; we often arrived over the battle zone to find all gone home.'

Squadron Leader Gerry Edge DFC, CO of 605 Squadron

'They didn't like that head-on attack, you know, but you had to judge the break-away point just right. If you left it to the last 100 yards then you were in trouble, due to the fast closing speeds, but once you got the hang of it a head on attack was a piece of cake. When you opened fire, you'd kill or badly wound the pilot and second pilot. Then you'd rake the whole line as you broke away. On one attack, the first He 111 I hit crashed into the next.'

Flying Officer James Coward, 19 Squadron

'Flight Lieutenant Clouston led us into a copybook Fighter Command No 1 Attack from dead ahead, turning in three sections, line astern, to come up in sections echelon port, behind the enemy, who were in sections of three, in vic line astern. Our fourth section, led by Flying Officer Frank Brinsden, was detailed to climb and intercept the fighters. I got a cannon shell through the cockpit, which shattered my left leg below the knee, also severing the elevator controls, and I had to bale out. I put a tourniquet around my thigh, using my helmet radio lead, and landed by parachute about four miles north of Duxford on the Royston to Newmarket Road. I was admitted to Addenbroke's Hospital in Cambridge and obviously out of the battle from then on.'

Pilot Officer Keith Ogilvie, 609 Squadron

'During the afternoon, things happened on a much larger scale. We arrived in time to engage the He 111s. I did not see any results but found an He 111 and fired from his rear. The rear-gunner returned my fire, but then stopped. I began to pull in for a better target when there was an almighty bang behind me, which destroyed my radio. A hole in the port wing told me that I had company! I was quick to break off, but never did see my attacker, nor indeed any other aircraft after that time. I made for home and landed gingerly but without incident on a flat tyre. As I recall we were so short of aircraft that I had to fly my plane to the Spitfire plant for repairs, and returned to Middle Wallop with a serviceable example. 30 September 1940, was certainly an interesting day, but all I could claim in both engagements was experience.'

Pilot Officer John Bisdee, 609 Squadron

'My most vivid memory of the entire Battle of Britain is coming right down to see that Ju 88 burning on the Downs, with a crowd of yokels waving pitchforks and dancing around it! I did a victory roll over them, then went back "upstairs" to see what was happening.'

Pilot Officer Michael Appleby, 609 Squadron

'I must not forget the time when the invasion was supposed to be imminent, church bells ringing, and we were all sitting in our aircraft awaiting a massed attack. Nothing happened.'

Squadron Leader Duncan MacDonald DSO DFC, CO of 213 Squadron

'Jackie Sing was shot down over the sea and rescued by an American oil tanker. You can imagine his feelings when informed by the captain that the cargo consisted of 100 octane aviation fuel for Fighter Command! The tanker made landfall at Shoreham, Sussex, and I motored down from Tangmere in the early evening to recover this valuable member of my squadron, who was a bit shaken but fortunately uninjured. He was in the air again the next day, none the worse for this most frightening experience.'

Pilot Officer Roger Hall, 152 Squadron

'We saw our own fighters, the 11 Group squadrons, and some from 12 Group in the Midlands, climbing up from the north. There seemed to be quite a number of us. They too were black dots, climbing up in groups of twelve, or thirty-six in wing formation. Most of them were Hurricanes. I recalled for an instant Mr Baldwin's prophecy, not a sanguine one, made to the House of Commons some five years before, when he said that the bomber would "always get through". Now it was doing just that.'

Pilot Officer F. W. 'Taffy' Higginson DFM, 56 Squadron

'I remember thinking that morale might be better if we had a squadron mascot, so I went into the local town and bought a small monkey, which was named "109". He was a great success and was kept in a cage and on a lead. Anyway, the Station Commander gave a cocktail party and suggested that 109 should be present. He was, and went down very well, until, that is, he started to undertake enthusiastic sexual self-gratification! Morals being what they were in those days, we had to remove 109 very quickly!'

Sergeant Jack Stokoe, 603 Squadron

'On 2 September 1940, I was involved with two more interceptions, during the course of which I damaged two enemy aircraft but was myself shot down in flames, fortunately baling out. On that occasion, as I was attacking an enemy aircraft I remember machine-gun bullets, or maybe cannon shells, hitting my Spitfire, followed by flames in the cockpit as the petrol tanks exploded. I thought, 'Christ! I've got to get out of here, and quick!' I undid the straps and opened the hood, but this turned the flames into a blowtorch. I was not wearing gloves, as during our hasty scramble I had forgotten them, but I had to put my hands back into the fire to invert the Spitfire, so that I could drop out (no ejector seats in those days!). I remember seeing sheets of skin peeling off the back of my hands before I fell out of the aeroplane. I was then concerned regarding whether the parachute would function or had it been fire-damaged? I pulled the ripcord and fortunately it opened perfectly. I landed in a field, but the Home Guard queried whether I was an enemy agent! A few choice words in English soon convinced them I was genuine, and thereafter I was rushed into the emergency hospital at Leeds Castle, suffering from shock and severe burns to my hands, neck and face. At the time, we were suffering so many casualties that administration got pretty chaotic. Consequently, for four days after baling out, although quite safe in hospital, I was officially posted "Missing in Action".'

Pilot Officer William Walker, 616 Squadron

'After I was show down and baled out over the Goodwin Sands on 26 August 1940, I was picked up by a passing fishing boat before transferring to an RAF launch, which took me into Ramsgate harbour. With a bullet in my foot, I was carried up the steps to a waiting ambulance, by which time quite a crowd had gathered and gave me a loud cheer. A kind old lady handed me a packet of cigarettes, so I decided that being shot down was perhaps not such a bad thing after all!

Later, after surgery, I was convalescing at the Palace Hotel in Torquay with Flight Lieutenant James Brindley Nicolson when a telegram arrived for him. "Nick's" response was simply, "Well, what do you make of that?" It was, of course, notification that he had been awarded the Victoria Cross for his "signal act of valour" over Southampton on 16 August 1940. He was genuinely puzzled and not a little embarrassed, that of hundreds of brave deeds performed by RAF fighter pilots that summer, his had been singled out for this very great honour. His was, in fact, the only VC awarded to an RAF fighter pilot during the entire war, because due to the speed and height of fighter combat, witnesses are hard to find, supporting evidence being a prerequisite. At first Nick got into trouble for being improperly dressed, because he refused to stitch the maroon ribbon onto his tunic. In the end I think he adopted the attitude that he was accepting the medal on behalf of us all. He was a good sport, in fact, and we enjoyed playing together in the four-piece band that we formed with other wounded pilots down at Torquay.'

Sergeant David Cox, 19 Squadron

'Now you must admit that when we were following Bader on 15 September 1940, all of us arriving together over the capital was pretty inspiring! I well remember the words of Bobby Oxspring, then a flying officer in an 11 Group Spitfire squadron, 66, exclaiming what a wonderful sight it was to see us appear. We must have given the German aircrews, who had been told that we were down to our last handful of fighters, one hell of a shock!'

Squadron Leader Harry Fenton, CO of 238 Squadron

'Our routine was to rise before first light, about 0330 hours, have a coffee and then then go to dispersal. We then spent the day there, being scrambled at intervals in either squadron or section strength. We shared Middle Wallop with 609 Squadron and so took it turns to spend every third day down at Warmwell, undertaking convoy protection patrols. That was during the early days, but I was shot down and wounded on 8 August, returning to the squadron on 12 September. By that time, 238 Squadron had been back to Middle Wallop for two days, but we already had two pilots missing from action over 11 Group: David Hughes, an able flight commander, and a Polish pilot, Duszinski, whom I had not met. The tempo of combat had totally changed.'

Pilot Officer John Greenwood, 238 Squadron

'I remember being with Sergeant Kee and diving for our lives into cloud. As I recall he copped a little enemy fire and we landed together shortly afterwards, having made no effort to locate the rest of the squadron. Kee's Hurricane had a little fabric missing and a few holes. I had stopped an armour-piercing bullet through my head-armour, the point of which bullet lodged in my neck. It had only just penetrated and was as sharp as a needle. I kept it for many years afterwards as a souvenir.'

Sergeant Reg Nutter, 257 Squadron

'For me personally, the Battle of Britain remains a vivid kaleidoscope of memories. I recall trying to warn Pilot Officer Capon that he was about to be attacked by a 109, but my radio was unserviceable; I remember The Hon David Coke returning from a battle over Portsmouth during which a German bullet had nicked him in the little finger of the throttle hand. Once I chased a lone Do 17 reconnaissance bomber in and out of the clouds along the south coast, whilst listening to American jazz music coming over the squadron frequency. Vivid memories all.'

Squadron Leader Robert Stanford Tuck DFC, CO of 257 Squadron

'Of course I knew Pilot Officer Franek Surma very well and there are many stories I could tell you of him. He was a wonderful little chap – but wild! He was also a loyal and thoroughly trusty wingman. Franek and myself were born on the same day – July 1st 1916. On the occasion he was shot down near North Weald, he was wearing a German leather flying jacket, which he had taken from a German bomber shot down in Poland. This did not assist positive identification and a group of Free French soldiers decided that he was an enemy airman and prepared to lynch him on the spot! Fortunately I arrived on the scene in time to stop this nonsense, the French then insisting that we have a drink with them.'

Pilot Officer Jerzy Poplawski (Polish), 229 Squadron

'The Battle of Britain was the most exciting time of my entire war, although later stages, including the Dieppe landings and D-Day period provide me with unforgettable memories. Although I did not shoot anything down in the Battle of Britain, I did fire at several enemy aircraft. I think I was so excited that I trembled too much, and as a result my aim was not good!'

Pilot Officer Valclav Bergman (Czech), 310 Squadron

'In those heady days I was a mere pilot officer who loved flying, loved the Hurricane and was happy to point my guns at any German target. But my English was limited. I have always had the impression that the initial interception was to be by 11 Group, whilst we of 12 Group were to follow the raiders and destroy as many as possible on their return journey. More than once the Duxford Wing was released for lunch when Douglas Bader "pegged" into the dining room and shouted, "Come on boys, we are wanted!" That was followed by the clatter of cutlery on the unfinished plates – rush for the door, transport to dispersals, and in fifteen to twenty minutes all twelve Hurricanes of Bader's 242 Squadron took off in formation from the grass airfield, followed by ours of 310; 19 Squadron's Spitfires, based at nearby Fowlmere, would soon appear overhead. Their job was to protect us from enemy fighters whilst our Hurricanes went for the bombers (not that it always worked out like that, though). In mid-September our squadron was engaging a formation of Do 17s when we were jumped by a swarm of Me 109s: I was shot down.'

Flight Lieutenant Francis Blackadder, 607 Squadron

'We were ordered from Tangmere to Southampton. Just as we reached it the Hun was diving down to bomb the Supermarine works. We came down on top of them in a head-on attack, some say right through the balloons. The Hun disappeared to the south, towards Portsmouth, and we split up. Sergeant Cunnington and I spied another large formation of bombers, which we climbed up to meet. They had fighter escort, and we were only able to carry out a rather stupid quarter attack, hose-piping the formation. I reported on their further movements to Operations, and they were eventually intercepted by more of our fighters over Weymouth.'

Pilot Officer Peter Brown, 41 Squadron

'In October, the pilot of one of the Me 109s I claimed baled out and landed near West Malling aerodrome. As Fighter Command had previously almost always refused to accept my claims, I decided on this occasion to get evidence. I landed at West Malling and went with the Intelligence Officer to see the German pilot, who was in the lock-up. After introductions, we had a friendly chat through our interpreter. Why? Well, he was obviously not a Nazi, but he was a fighter pilot and this made for a common bond. I took as a souvenir his survival jacket, which was superior to our Mae Wests, and wore it for the rest of my time on 41 Squadron. Group allowed this claim to be considered confirmed!'

Pilot Officer Wallace 'Jock' Cuningham DFC, 19 Squadron

'Some six of our Czech had to gain a working knowledge of English. What they learnt was influenced by their squadron associates. I remember one of them, Sergeant Plzak, sitting writing to his girlfriend in Cambridge and asking me, "Jock, what is difference between beautiful and bloody fool?" It was not long afterwards that we received a telephone call from that girlfriend and had to tell her that Plzak was dead.'

Pilot Officer Peter Howard-Williams, 19 Squadron

'I remember Eric Ball landing at Hornchurch during the Dunkirk fighting and stopping in the centre of the airfield. A bullet had gone through his helmet and hair – parting it for him and leaving a small wound'.

Pilot Officer Richard Jones, 64 Squadron

'When we returned from a sortie, anyone who had been successful in shooting down an enemy aircraft might do a victory roll over the airfield, but these were not encouraged, because you didn't know whether your aircraft had some unseen damage to the flying controls. Immediately we landed, the Intelligence Officer took full details from each pilot regarding what had happened, whilst the ground crew, who were absolutely marvellous, did a fantastic job of rapidly preparing the aircraft for another immediate take-off.'

Squadron Leader 'Uncle' George Denholm DFC, CO of 603 Squadron

'We had to learn quickly and rapidly determined not to allow ourselves to be bounced. I therefore decided to fly on a reciprocal of the course provided by the ground Controller, until at 15,000 feet, when the squadron would turn about, climbing all the time. Flying in this way meant that we usually saw the enemy striking inland beneath us, and were therefore better positioned to attack. We also ensured that pilots always flew in pairs, for mutual protection. After an action, though, the squadron would come home individually, in ones and twos, at intervals of about two minutes. In addition to leading the squadron in the air, my duties also included checking who was missing after each action, which I generally did an hour after the end of the patrol. In that time, a call would often come in from a pilot who had baled out or landed elsewhere.'

Pilot Officer Lionel 'Buck' Casson, 616 Squadron

'We were a confident lot. Up north we had chased about after reconnaissance jobs and enjoyed great success during the "*Junkers* Party" off Flamborough Head. We thought air-fighting was pretty straight forward, I suppose. When we were posted to Kenley, the squadron went off, and I just said, "Cheerio, see you later", as I was to follow with a replacement Spitfire we were awaiting. How naive. Very few of us were to survive the next fortnight.'

Flight Sergeant George 'Grumpy' Unwin DFM, 19 Squadron

'I was surrounded by Me 109s and ended up fighting a running battle between Ramsgate and west London. The usual fight ensued, during which I definitely hit at least five of them but only two were shot down, both in flames. I then climbed for a breather and shadowed the third enemy formation when I saw a fourth arriving. By this time two of the other three formations had turned north and the other went straight in a westerly direction. The leading formation turned east and I was at 25,000 feet and above them. As there did not appear to be any of their escorts left, I dived on the rear vic and gave them the rest of my ammunition, about fifty rounds in each gun, and from 450, closing to 50 yards range. The bomber at which I fired wobbled a bit but otherwise carried on. Without ammunition I returned to Fowlmere.

At the time I felt that we of Fighter Command had done nothing out of the ordinary. I had been trained for the job and luckily had a lot of experience. I was always most disappointed if the squadron got into a scrap when I was off duty, and this applied to all the pilots I knew. It was only after the event that I realised how serious defeat would have been, but then, without being big-headed, we never even considered being beaten, it was just not possible in our eyes, this simply was our outlook. As we lost pilots and aircraft, replacements were forthcoming. We were never at much below full strength. Of course the new pilots were inexperienced, but so were the German replacements, and it was clear by the end of 1940 that these pilots had not the stomach for a scrap with a Spitfire.'

Epilogue

FOR JOHNNY

It is interesting to consider whether Operation *Seelöwe* could have succeeded had the Luftwaffe wrested aerial superiority from Fighter Command during that epic summer of 1940. Legend has it that Britain's army was in a poor state after Dunkirk, and was therefore no match for a German invasion force. This, however, is not entirely true. Immediately after the Fall of France, having left behind its heavy weaponry, the Army would certainly have had difficulty in repelling a determined enemy landing, but things had improved by September: four infantry divisions were fully equipped, eight more nearly so. Fifteen more divisions were lacking in equipment, particularly motorised transport, but they would undoubtedly have played a part. Three armoured divisions, equipped with 350 medium and cruiser tanks, backed up by 500 light tanks, would have assured Hitler's thirteen divisions of a bitter battle had they landed. Bomber and Coastal Command fielded nearly 1,000 aircraft collectively, which could have overwhelmed the German fighter screen, which, lacking radar, would have had to fly constant, exhausting standing patrols over the beachhead.

Moreover, the Royal Navy stood by with a counter-force much stronger than the German navy, which had been depleted during the invasion of Norway. The only capital warship available to the enemy was the *Admiral Hipper*, which, supported only by three light cruisers, nine destroyers and twenty-seven U-boats, would somehow have to defend some 155 cargo ships, 2,000 barges, 470 tugs and 1,200 motor boats of Hitler's invasion fleet. The Luftwaffe's torpedo-bombers amounted to thirty He 115 floatplanes, and conventional bombing was notoriously ineffective – indeed, the Germans had no bomb capable of penetrating a battleship's deck armour even when dive-bombing. Moreover, even in perfect weather conditions it is unlikely, given the resources available, that the Luftwaffe could have prevented the Royal Navy's decisive intervention. True, the Germans had successfully used airborne troops against Norway, Holland and Belgium, but in the process had lost half of their transport fleet. This, therefore, was not a viable option, and of course there was also the insurmountable question of supply. It is also important to appreciate that the Germans did not even possess the benefit of surprise: due to the 'Enigma' cipher machine, British intelligence decoded enemy signals. This, of course, provided Air Chief Marshal Dowding with essential and otherwise unobtainable information throughout the Battle of Britain.

Today, academics debate the mythical status of the Battle of Britain, now firmly cemented in our national popular memory of the Second World War. Myths, of course, are not necessarily untrue; how these stories are portrayed and perceived, however, is important. Myth does not always reflect historical accuracy, though, and nor can it resist rigorous historic analysis. Many have written on this subject, among them Angus Calder (*Myth of the Blitz*) and Malcolm Smith (*Britain and 1940: History, Myth and Popular Memory*). All are agreed that the myth was created during the war, and has since been maintained and reshaped to suit Britain's changing place in the world. In the years since 1945, Britain has undergone massive social change, suffered economic depression, coped with large-scale immigration, and arguably become mortgaged to the United States. The heroic memory of Britain's part in the Second World War, therefore, has become an increasingly important reminder of when Britain was centre stage. Indeed, the Spitfire – during the war years a symbol of courage and defiance – has now become a patriotic icon of English excellence (and rightly so). Calder, though, rightly said, 'It is no legend that Fighter Command, by staying in the air, preserved England from invasion.' He was right.

Arguments abound regarding the actual importance of the Battle of Britain, new interpretations being ever aplenty, or so it seems. On balance, there seems no doubt whatsoever that the Battle of Britain was a critical event in this country's long and proud history. Certainly Churchill's rhetoric, partly to bolster Britain's morale, and partially to appeal to America, immediately cast the Battle of Britain as a life-or-death struggle between freedom and democracy, good against evil, in a David-and-Goliath context. In truth, the opposing air forces were actually pretty much numerically matched – but the way the defenders fought the battle, preserving precious fighters, gave rise to the impression that hordes of enemy aircraft were being assailed by the last few RAF Spitfires and Hurricanes. All of this, the facts, the insatiable historical analysis, misses the absolutely crucial and only real point: the British people, reeling in the wake of the catastrophic Fall of France and the BEF's evacuation from Dunkirk, and given Hitler's unprecedented record of conquest, *believed* that invasion was imminent. Virtually all involved, however, faced this violent assault with tenacity and great courage – even though the odds appeared overwhelming and the chances of survival slim. Lord Dowding wrote about 'a grandeur of human endeavour of that time, which lingers in the mind'. It is that, and that alone, that *spirit*, that refusal to surrender to or negotiate with Nazi Germany, that will forever make the Battle of Britain an extremely special, indeed unique, event. Because of this, it is entirely right that we remain proud of the achievement and hand the story down to future generations, pay tribute to survivors and remember those who died.

After the First World War, local communities remembered those who died by way of memorials on which the names of those who fell were inscribed. Following the Second World War, the names of casualties from that conflict were added to these. On 17 October 1953, Queen Elizabeth II inaugurated the Runnymede Memorial, bearing the names of 20,547 airmen from the British Commonwealth and Empire. Among that number, of course, were those reported 'Missing in Action' during the Battle of Britain – although a number of these unfortunates have since been recovered from their crash sites and now have more appropriate graves. The RAF, in fact, already had a specific monument, the RAF Memorial, unveiled in 1923, on the capital's Victoria Embankment and dedicated to the First World War's dead and those of subsequent conflicts. The 2,408 Polish airmen killed flying with or alongside the RAF during the Second World War are remembered separately by the Polish Air Force Memorial in Western Avenue, Northolt – close to that famous sector station from which some had made their last flights. A selection of names (1,241) were included on this monument, including some Polish Battle of Britain casualties, but nowhere did a monument exist specifically to the Few. To one man in particular, this was inappropriate; his name was Wing Commander Geoffrey Page.

Geoffrey Page had been a twenty-year-old Hurricane pilot with 56 Squadron in the Battle of Britain, during which, on 12 August 1940, he was shot down and terribly burned. Like Pilot Officer Richard Hillary, Page too became a 'Guinea Pig', and many years after the war founded the Battle of Britain Memorial Trust – the aim of which was (and remains) to preserve the memory of 'Churchill's Few'. Page's tireless campaigning ultimately led to the (now late) Queen Mother unveiling the National Battle of

Britain Memorial on 9 July 1993. Located at Capel-le-Ferne in Kent, on the white cliffs overlooking Folkestone and the Channel – and firmly, therefore, in what was once appropriately known as 'Hellfire Corner' – the tribute's centrepiece is a seated fighter pilot, gazing towards France, by sculptor Harry Gray. Around the base are Churchill's inspired words: 'Never in the field of human conflict has so much been owed by so many to so few.' Further, in 2005, following a project initiated by the Battle of Britain Historical Society, London's Battle of Britain Monument was unveiled by the Prince Charles and Duchess of Cornwall on Westminster's Embankment. Work to commemorate the Battle of Britain, however, continues.

In July 1999, Lady Aitkin unveiled a wall at Capel-le-Ferne bearing the names of the Few, this tribute having been donated by the Beaverbrook Foundation. Lord Beaverbrook, of course, was the highly energetic Minister for Aircraft Production, responsible for maintaining the flow of fresh fighters to Dowding's squadrons; Lady Aitkin was the widow of Beaverbrook's son Sir Max Aitkin, who had commanded 601 Squadron during the Battle of Britain and whose name is, therefore, included. Appropriately, this new memorial was named 'The Foxley-Norris Wall' – after Air Chief Marshal Sir Christopher Foxley-Norris, another Hurricane pilot during the battle, and long-time Chairman of the Battle of Britain Fighter Association (Sir Christopher died in 2003, aged eighty-six). Adjacent to the Foxley-Norris Wall is a plinth inscribed with a poem, appropriately called 'Our Wall', by one of the Few, Flight Lieutenant William L. B. Walker. On 26 August 1940, Pilot Officer Walker of 616 Squadron was shot down over the Channel, by Major Werner Mölders; when I identified this fact and told him so in 1995, William's reaction was, 'Well, if you are going to be shot down, it might as well be by the top man!' After bobbing around in the Channel, William was rescued, albeit with a bullet lodged firmly in his ankle. A remarkably warm and friendly man, we spent many hours together over a number of years; sadly 'Bill' died in 2012, aged ninety-nine – and at which point he was the oldest surviving Battle of Britain pilot. Indeed, on the Wall appear the names of many survivors I likewise knew well but who are now deceased, so for me personally this is a particularly moving commemoration.

The Battle of Britain Memorial Trust is, in fact, considered by the Battle of Britain Fighter Association to be the appropriate organisation to continue with its objectives – at the time of writing, there are only twenty-seven members of the Association currently still alive, hence why it is necessary to think in these terms. Although the Trust has already achieved much, its work continues – with an eye very much on the future. 'The Wing' education and visitor centre is, to me, the most inspirational and significant development in the commemoration of the Battle of Britain since the National Memorial was unveiled at Capel-le-Ferne over twenty years ago. This features a building in the shape of a Spitfire's wing, behind the Foxley-Norris Wall, featuring a 'Battle of Britain Experience' – using cutting-edge technology. Today, in our computerised, online, age, traditional museums are not enough – although they too remain essential – so the provision of such a facility, if the Battle of Britain is to be portrayed in such a way as to inspire younger generations of both today and tomorrow, is absolutely crucial. The objective is to provide the visitor with some clear idea, through the use of 'video walls and other special effects', with what it was like to be an RAF fighter pilot during the summer of 1940. Importantly, The Wing includes a classroom, and a central 'cockpit' area providing views across the Channel to France. Excitingly, a high-tech screen superimposes historical film of incoming German aircraft over today's 'real-time' view of the same scene. This kind of innovative multimedia experience is exactly what is required – and the Battle of Britain Memorial Trust is to be entirely commended for this spectacular vision. Appropriately, The Wing was opened by Her Majesty The Queen on 26 March 2015 – marking the Battle of Britain's seventy-fifth anniversary year. We can all, in fact, help keep the flame eternal – simply by becoming a 'Friend of the Few' and joining the Battle of Britain Memorial Trust (www.battleofbritain. org.uk, or information available by post: BoBMT, PO Box 337, West Malling, Kent ME19 5QS).

In this seventy-fifth anniversary year, 'The Final Few' – the last twenty-seven surviving members (at the time of writing, August 2015) of the Battle of Britain Fighter Association – can be entirely confident that the memory of 1940 is in very good hands, and that their deeds will be remembered. This book contextualises and relates the experiences of five pilots who survived the Battle of Britain. For some survivors, like Tim Elkington, the Battle of Britain was a brief occurrence at the start of a long career, punctuated by more significant personal events; for others, like Geoffrey Wellum, the experience of being a fighter pilot in the Battle of Britain was a defining, unforgettable moment. For all, the summer of 1940 was one they would never forget.

However, the survivors, to a man, do not trumpet their august exploits. Masters of the understatement, when they are persuaded to talk, detail is frequently omitted regarding their own exploits and combat successes – which would, to them, be seen, God forbid, as 'shooting a line'. Despite this, all believe that by recording, howsoever reluctantly, their experiences for posterity, the deeds and sacrifices of those who *died* will be appreciated and remembered. It is not, therefore, for themselves that the 'Final Few' speak – but for those long lost comrades who cannot. In this book, survivors have spoken of their attitude to casualties at the time, that these were briefly acknowledged – then summarily dismissed. Although this was clearly a coping mechanism, I am not convinced that *anyone* could be entirely unaffected by the loss of such young comrades. When Richard Hillary's *The Last Enemy* was published on 19 June 1942 – his is a deeply moving memoir of hedonistic pre-war days as an Oxford undergraduate, of the coming of war, and his experience of being shot down in flames and badly disfigured during the Battle of Britain – he became famous overnight, receiving innumerable letters from readers paying tribute to *his* courage, *his* endurance and *his* ideals. Upon reading these, Hillary, according to his biographer Lovat Dickson, 'despaired'. Hillary was appalled that the public had not grasped that his book was *not* written to promote his own experience, but as a tribute to the dead: fellow Spitfire pilots like Noel Agazarian, Colin Pinckney, and, of course, Peter Pease, his 'very parfit knyght'. Sadly, on 8 January 1943, Flight Lieutenant Hillary was killed in an accident, flying a Blenheim, while training to become a night-fighter pilot; having left behind his written legacy, 'our amazing Mr Hillary' had gone to join his friends – the loss of whom had so clearly and deeply affected him.

One of those who did not survive the Battle of Britain, and is therefore among those 'The Final Few' would wish to be remembered, is one Wing Commander John Scatliff Dewar DSO DFC.

'Johnny' Dewar was born in Lahore, India, where his father was a Civil Servant, on 10 August 1907. Later he was educated at King's School, Canterbury, where he became a sergeant in the Officer Training Corps (OTC), and entered Cranwell as a flight cadet in 1927. Tours as an army and naval cooperation pilot followed, the latter partially at sea, at home and abroad, with the FAA. On 10 July 1937, Johnny Dewar married Kay Bowyer, the daughter of Southampton alderman Percy Vincent, the couple having met ice-skating in Southampton a year previously. Soon afterwards, the couple moved to Martlesham Heath, where Johnny was posted to test armament with the Aeroplane & Armament Experimental Establishment (A&AEE) at Martlesham Heath, contributing to the development of both the Spitfire and Hurricane prototypes. On 1 February 1938, Dewar was promoted to squadron leader and became Senior Operations Officer (SOO) at RAF Thorney Island in West Sussex – where Kay Dewar became a code and cipher clerk. Soon after the outbreak of war, on 10 November 1939, by which time Squadron Leader Johnny Dewar was amongst the RAF's most experienced pilots, he was posted to 11 Group for reassignment to a fighter squadron; three weeks later he took command of 87 Squadron, which was flying Hurricanes in France. This was, of course, the so-called 'Phoney War' period, during which Squadron Leader Dewar and 87 Squadron received various important visitors, including both His Majesty The King, and British Prime Minister Neville Chamberlain – who had tried so desperately hard to avoid war, or at least buy time for Britain, through his ill-fated policy of appeasement. When the German attack on the west began on 10 May 1940, 87 Squadron was, needless to say, heavily engaged. Two weeks later, its airfields overrun, the unit was evacuated back to England. On 31 May, the *London Gazette* announced that Squadron Leader Dewar was among the first officers to be awarded the 'double' of the DFC and DSO for his services in France. The citations respectively read,

> This officer has shot down five enemy aircraft and led many patrols with courage and skill ... Before intensive operations started, this officer injured his right shoulder in a severe flying accident. Despite this, he flew regularly and led his squadron with skill and dash, more than sixty enemy aircraft being destroyed by them. He remained in command of the squadron throughout the operations, in spite of the injured shoulder, trained his new pilots well and continued throughout to be a very efficient commander, inculcating an excellent spirit in his squadron.

Upon returning home, of his shoulder injury Johnny simply told his wife, 'Oh, don't worry about that...' The fact is, though, that Johnny Dewar was clearly both an exceptional fighter pilot and leader – and it seems that COs with both abilities were in short supply at the time.

87 Squadron was withdrawn briefly to Church Fenton, in Yorkshire, to rest and refit. During that time, on 5 June 1940, Squadron Leader Dewar and Pilot Officer Dennis 'Hurricane' David, also of 87 Squadron, were called to an investiture at Buckingham Palace to receive their decorations gazetted for their courageous service during the Battle of France. The pair flew down to London, stayed overnight, and lunched with David's mother: 'She fell under his spell,' he later wrote, 'as did everyone who knew him. Altogether it was a much-needed break from the stress we had been under. We returned to Church Fenton refreshed and in good spirits. We did our best with the fresh pilots to get them as much flying practice as we could before the air battles which we knew lay before us, because we were aware that although our boys had more than enough courage and dedication, they were as yet no match for the experienced German pilots.'

On 5 July 1940, Squadron Leader Dewar led 87 Squadron from Church Fenton in Yorkshire to the new 10 Group station at Exeter, on Devon's south coast. As the squadron's ORB commented, 'By this time the capitulation of France had completely altered the whole strategic situation of this war, and the South West of England suddenly found itself vulnerable to attack, instead of being a safe assignment. There was therefore considerable speculation as to when the *Blitzkrieg* would be launched against England.' Exeter was, in fact, a civilian airport procured by the RAF and in the process of changing over to a war-and-service footing. 213 Squadron had arrived a fortnight previously, 'and naturally had occupied the best parts of the station. The officers were billeted at the Rougemont Hotel in Exeter, and the men at Farringdon House, not far from the aerodrome.' Recognising the significance of the phase of air operations 87 Squadron was about to be engaged in, the charismatic and popular Squadron Leader Dewar addressed his pilots:

No one is going to stop the Huns invading this country in the next month or so – except us. When we have cleared the bastards out of the skies over the Channel and the south coast, they won't be able to invade by sea – so we are going to stop them. There's nobody else and we are in a proud position and the luckiest people at this time. This is what we are here for, so now let's get on with it!

It was a busy time for 87 Squadron's CO, 'the first bit of excitement from the operational point of view' occurring on 11 July.

Just after 1100 hours on that day, 601 Squadron was scrambled from Tangmere, and half an hour later sighted around fifteen Stukas escorted by forty Me 110s, approaching Lyme Bay from Cherbourg. More RAF fighters were hurriedly sent off, including nine Hurricanes of 213 Squadron, and three of 87 – among them Squadron Leader Dewar. Although these reinforcements arrived too late to prevent the bombing of Portland at 1153 hours, 601 Squadron disrupted the Stukas' attack, only one merchant ship consequently being hit. Johnny Dewar reported that he was

leading a flight of three Hurricanes at 5,000 feet west of Weymouth; sighted nine enemy aircraft approaching Portland from south at 15,000 feet. Commenced climbing south, to get in between E/A and sun. Saw nine more E/A and one group of twelve Me 110s as we were going up. Got level and up-sun of enemy at 12,000 feet. As we approached, some aircraft dived to attack shipping. Enemy did not appear aware of our presence. Saw two other Hurricanes attacking and swung into Me 110s, which seemed to be flying to form, a circle. Saw a Hurricane diving and turning slowly with 110 on his tail, so put four bursts into 110. On last burst the port engine appeared to blow up. Aircraft flicked onto its back and dived almost vertically. Owing to presence of numerous E/A, I did not watch this aircraft hit the sea, but feel certain it must have gone in, four miles east of Shambles. Method of approach was line astern, then 'free for all'.

The Me 110 concerned is believed to be the aircraft of 9/ZG 76, which crashed onto the Verne's chalk cliffs with such violence that no trace of the crew has ever been found. The pilot was actually *Reichsmarschall* Göring's nephew, *Oberleutnant* H. J. Göring – whose *Zerstörer* was the first enemy aircraft to crash in England during the Battle of Britain. It was also the new RAF station at Exeter's first 'kill'. The action, however, was not yet over for 87 Squadron's CO:

> I went into a full turn to review progress of battle and remove two other E/A trying to get on my tail. Saw a bomb exploding by shipping in the harbour and two E/A diving for ground. One E/A still pursued me. My Hurricane turned easily onto his tail – he was vertically banked. He then dived for ground, going east – I followed but withheld fire as I was getting short of rounds. E/A pulled out about 1,000 feet and continued in 'S' turns. I gave him a burst from about 100 yards and vapour came out of both engines. I had to slam throttle back to avoid over-shooting. Vapour then ceased to come from one engine and he gathered way again. I was very close and there was no rear gun fire, so I held my position and took careful non-deflection shot, using all ammunition. E/A at once turned inland, going very slowly. Seeing me draw away, he turned seawards again. I went to head him off and he, apparently thinking I had more rounds, turned for land again, sinking slowly. At about 200 feet, another Hurricane came up and fired a short burst at him. He immediately turned and landed on Grange Heath (or near). Both crew got out, wearing yellow jackets. Army was close by. Number of other Hurricane was UW-F (I think).

This was another machine of 9/ZG 76, which had previously been attacked by 238 Squadron's Green Section; the Hurricane that Dewar reported as having also attacked was Flying Officer Hugh Riddle of 601 Squadron (and whose Hurricane was more likely UF-W). The enemy unit's *Staffelkapitän*, *Oberleutnant* Kadow, and his gunner, *Gefreiter* Scholz, were both captured unhurt having forced-landed at Grange Heath, near Lulworth. In total, the enemy had lost four Me 110s – an early indication that the type was generally no match for Hurricanes and Spitfires, in spite of its much vaunted heavy armament – and two *Stukas*. Fighter Command suffered no loss, although, as the 87 Squadron ORB reported, the Australian Pilot Officer Richard Glyde 'had a near escape from a bullet which pierced his central panel of his hood and struck his armour plating – close to his head'.

The following day, 12 July 1940, Johnny Dewar was posted – and became RAF Exeter's Station Commander. This did not, however, prevent him continuing to fly operationally on occasions with 87 Squadron, now commanded by the New Zealander Squadron Leader Terence Lovell-Gregg. This may have been because although 87 Squadron's new CO had joined the unit in June 1940, he lacked operational experience, sensibly relying upon his flight commanders to lead the squadron in the air, while gaining the necessary experience himself. On the other hand, it was also because Johnny Dewar was undoubtedly a 'press-on type'. On 13 August, for example, the Exeter Station Commander made up a section of 87 Squadron Hurricanes, with Pilot Officers Glyde DFC and Jay, for an early patrol over the Channel. Twenty miles south of Selsey Bill, a lone enemy bomber was sighted, attacked and shot down into the sea. This was shared by the section as a Ju 88, but was actually an He 111 of III/KG 27, the crew of which remain missing. Unfortunately, during the engagement Glyde's Hurricane was hit by return fire, his aircraft streaming white vapour while returning to Exeter. The next time Squadron Leader Dewar looked the damaged Hurricane had disappeared, and a search of the Channel proved fruitless. It was a sad loss: only the previous week, the twenty-six-year-old had joined his CO and other 87 Squadron pilots at Buckingham Palace, where all received gallantry awards at an investiture held by King George VI.

On 15 August 1940, the enemy attacked Portland in strength, and a great air battle developed over the south coast – in which Squadron Leader Lovell-Gregg was killed. Three days later, on 'the Hardest Day', Squadron Leader Randolph Mills DFC arrived at Exeter and took command of 87 Squadron. On 25 August, Johnny Dewar – now promoted to Wing Commander – once more led 87 Squadron (a formation not including Squadron Leader Miller) when both Exeter Hurricane squadrons were scrambled at 1730 hours to intercept a raid of over one hundred Ju 88s, Me 110s and Me 109s bent upon destroying Warmwell airfield:

Led squadron to patrol Warmwell at 10,000 feet, as ordered. Sighted AA bursts over Portland, but no aircraft. Then sighted a large enemy force coming westwards, along coast. Selected squadron of Ju 88s least escorted, and led in on a quarter attack. Fired about 800 rounds. As I pulled away, I saw the E/A smoking. Flight Sergeant Badger, who was following, saw it burst into flames. It must have fallen near Lulworth. Later confirmed by Observer Corps that one fell there.

I continued my turn on pulling away, and met about ten 110s head-on, taking a fleeting burst at the last one. By the time I had turned around again, I could see no aircraft near me. Beyond Lulworth there was a huge circle of wheeling aircraft. Every now and then, one dropped out, smoking. The bombers seemed to be making out to sea. Very high over Portland way a white 'Verey' light was fired. I flew, climbing towards the coast, turning now and again, to sweep the sky above. During one of these turns I almost collided with an Me 109 turning in the opposite direction. I started to pursue as he went past me, and saw that he was the leader of four. They did not appear to have seen me, so I joined them in the rear. Unfortunately their high speed prevented me from getting closer than about 600 yards, and although I had +9 on the boost, I could not catch up. As they turned, however, I slowly gained. When about

300 yards away, I opened fire on the rearmost in short bursts. He immediately turned more steeply than the rest, and increased speed, but not before vapour came pouring from him. His manoeuvre carried him to the front of the others and I had to break off action with him. Last seen, he was diving at about 45°, slightly banked, and may also have come down near Lulworth, on land or in the sea. Fumes were pouring from him. I suspect he carried armour, as I fired at least 800 rounds, with almost dead astern shots. The others quickly climbed out of reach. I was greatly handicapped by lack of speed. Seeing no further activity and being short of ammunition, I returned to base without seeing any of my squadron since the first encounter.

I consider that greater effect would be achieved from an attack, and less losses suffered, if we patrolled in larger numbers, if possible two squadrons going together. Twin-engined bombers can take terrific punishment from the rear and their own shooting has greatly improved. I consider it a mistake to attack from the rear if any other method is possible. With fighter escorts, only fleeting attacks can be made, making it difficult to obtain conclusive results.

During this engagement, two Ju 88s of II/KG 51 crashed into the sea, along with two Me 109s of III/JG 2; whether any of these were those attacked by Wing Commander Dewar is impossible to say. At Warmwell, two hangars were damaged, the station sick quarters burnt out, and communications disrupted until the following day.

On 12 September 1940, the 87 Squadron ORB recorded that 'Wing Commander Dewar set out from Exeter for a visit to Tangmere and was not heard of again. He had been informed of enemy activity on the route over which he was to pass, and no doubt must have run into more trouble than he could cope with by himself. A very sad loss to 87 Squadron.' An anonymous airman later wrote, 'One afternoon we lost our Station Commander, Johnny. He had borrowed one of our machines to fly to Tangmere for a conference. He was in excellent spirits when he took off. Just after he had left, "Ops" told us there was a *Blitz* in that sector. They warned Johnny on the R/T. He gave the usual answer: "Message received and understood." Then nothing more.'

A letter dated 23 October 1940, from the CO of 87 Squadron, Squadron Leader R. S. Mills, to Exeter's new Station Commander, confirms, however, that 'Acting Wing Commander J. S. Dewar on 11 September 1940 gave orders that he would be flying to Tangmere and the normal procedure for advising Operations at this Station was carried out. This officer took off at 1500 hours in Hurricane V7306, and before doing so was advised of enemy activity over Selsey Bill. The route, however, to be flown was from Exeter, via Winchester, then to Tangmere, thus avoiding the balloon barrage over Southampton.' Such a course would also have avoided the coast – and the enemy. A lone aircraft is, of course, potentially vulnerable to attack, and could confuse defenders. It must be remembered that radio-telephony at that time was comparatively limited, communication being possible between individual pilots and their Ground Controller and within their own squadron but not with other airborne units. This was, however, essentially a routine domestic flight, unofficial, some have said, the purpose of which was visiting Mrs Dewar at Thorney Island. If so, that may explain why details were not released by Exeter until the following day, in the hope that the Station Commander had come down over the sea and would be rescued, or would turn up from an area of remote countryside – as often happened – thus saving unnecessary trouble.

Earlier that day, the German precision bombing unit *Erprobungsgruppe* 210 had arrived at Cherbourg-Ost airfield, tasked with destroying Southampton's Spitfire production capacity. The main location concerned was, naturally, Supermarine's Woolston-based factory, on the banks of the River Itchen, with final assembly and test flying completed at Eastleigh airport, seven miles to the north. At 1530 hours, the unit's Me 110 and Me 109 *Jabos* took off from Cherbourg-Ost bound for Eastleigh, escorted by Me 110s of ZG 76, and Me 109s of JG 2. At 1540, 213 Squadron scrambled from Exeter and vectored to Selsey Bill, followed over the next ten minutes by 602 and 607 Squadrons from Tangmere. While the latter patrolled base, the Spitfires of 602 Squadron headed out to sea, the Hurricanes of 213 following slightly below and behind. Just before 1610 hours, about forty Me 110s were sighted incoming at 15,000 feet, with an unspecified number of Me 109s some twelve miles behind the main German force. Both RAF squadrons attacked the Me 110s before the Me 109s arrived, but nonetheless bombs began falling on Eastleigh at 1613 hours – not, as intended, on the Spitfire Final Assembly and Flight Hangars, but on the Cunliffe-Owen Aircraft factory – just 400 yards away – where Lockheed Hudsons from America were assembled and parts made for the new Stirling bomber. Spitfire production was, therefore, unaffected by this raid, but forty-nine civilians were killed, thirty-eight badly injured and fifty-four more slightly so.

During the engagement off Selsey Bill, at 1605 hours, 213 Squadron reportedly claimed the destruction of five Me 110s, and two damaged; 602 Squadron claimed, at 1610 hours, three Me 110s destroyed and one damaged, one Me 109 destroyed and another probably destroyed. It was a fine bag,–but somewhat over-exuberant: the available evidence confirms that only one Me 110, of II/ZG 76, was shot down (this aircraft ditching in the Channel); no Me 109s were, in fact, lost. It appears, however, that the RAF fighters engaged the escorting Me 110s and Me 109s, while the fighter-bombers of *Erprobungsgruppe* 210, reached Eastleigh, at low level, and withdrew safely without being intercepted. 602 Squadron, however, suffered a pilot missing, one slightly wounded, and another landed back at Tangmere with a damaged Spitfire. 213 Squadron lost two Hurricanes: a Polish pilot reported missing, and a flight commander who baled out but was fortunately rescued by a passing ship.

Frustratingly, the details of German combat reports available are incomplete, in many cases simply relating the unit, pilot, type of enemy aircraft claimed, time and location. Frequently, however, certain of these essential details are missing from the record, owing to the vast amount of documents destroyed during the death throes of Nazi Germany in 1945. What we do know regarding the action with which we are now concerned is that the following claims exist:

Leutnant Kurt Votel	3/JG 2	Hurricane	1646 hours
Oberfelwebel Hans Tilly	3/JG 2	Spitfire	1650 hours
Oberleutnant Hans Hahn	4/JG 2	Hurricane	1615 hours
Unteroffizier Kurt Bühligen	6/JG 2	Hurricane	1635 hours
Leutnant Heinz Bolze	4/JG 2	Spitfire	1700 hours
Oberfeldwebel Siegfried Schnell	4/JG 2	Spitfire	1705 hours
Oberfeldwebel Siegfried Schnell	4/JG 2	Spitfire	1712 hours
Oberfeldwebel Franz Willinger	8/JG 2	Hurricane	1727 hours
Oberleutnant Wilhelm Herget	6/ZG 76	Hurricane	1700 hours

The only known location is for Herget's claim, which is recorded as five to ten kilometres east of the Isle of Wight, and at 5,000 metres. Clearly both sides, as ever, over-claimed, a not uncommon scenario given the speed and confusion of fighter combat. In all probability, Wing Commander Dewar was en route from Exeter to Tangmere, when, contrary to his flight plan but typical of his 'press-on' spirit, he joined in this air battle near Selsey Bill. The likelihood is that one of the *Jagdfliegern* listed shot down V7306, which crashed into the sea. Indeed, a 'file note' in this outstanding officer's Casualty File, dated 8 October 1940, states, 'Spoke to Adjutant Exeter. He stated that Wing Commander Dewar had been warned before taking off to keep away from the coast, as enemy aircraft had been reported in the vicinity. If he had kept to his course, he need not have gone near the coast. The Adjutant was of the opinion, therefore, especially as Wing Commander Dewar had failed to bale out, that he had left his course purposely to encounter enemy aircraft and had been shot down.' In his letter of 23 October, Squadron Leader Mills wrote that 'at 1600 hours intense enemy activity developed over Southampton area and it is presumed that Wing Commander Dewar decided to engage the enemy, although there is no definite evidence to support this supposition'. Significantly, however, he added that 'a pilot of a rear protective section reported later that he noticed a lone Hurricane that followed his squadron just before the enemy aircraft were engaged'. Indeed, having 'examined the Raid Tracings of sector station Tangmere', Mills 'formed the opinion, in view of anti-aircraft gunfire over Southampton and intense aircraft activity north of Southampton, that Wing Commander Dewar followed one of the operating squadrons and definitely sought engagements as he would have been in the operational area at about that time'.

Following Exeter's reluctant signal reporting their valuable Station Commander 'missing' on 12 September 1940, nothing further was heard of Wing Commander Dewar until 30 September, when, again according to Squadron Leader Mills, 'a body clothed in a shirt was washed up on the beach at Kingston Gorse, Sussex, and subsequently identified as Wing Commander J. S. Dewar by means of laundry marks'. Curiously, 'a tunic was also found nearby the body, marked "JSD" and had the ribbons of DSO and DFC. It was established that this officer was killed by machine-gun fire, there being bullet wounds in the back of the head, and the left leg was practically shot off.'

The final moments of Wing Commander Dewar's life, however, will never be known. Although the evidence of his character and air operations at the time undoubtedly supports the view that the lone pilot 'had a go', many questions remain unanswered.

For example, even if the badly wounded pilot had inverted his Hurricane, dropped out and taken to his parachute, given his grievous wounds it is unlikely, I would suggest, that he would have been able to extricate himself from his parachute and harness once in the sea – and yet the body was free of such encumbrance. Was, therefore, the Wing Commander killed in the actual attack, or so badly wounded as to make abandoning his machine impossible? That being so, perhaps his body was flung clear upon impact with the water, or rose to the surface later – if either scenario was the case, why was he not wearing a parachute, and how had his tunic independently ended up close to the body? So many questions, all concerning points of essential detail that will forever remain a mystery. At the time, a rumour circulated that Wing Commander Dewar had baled out only to be machine-gunned on his parachute by the enemy, although there was no direct evidence, then or now, to support such an accusation (and is contrary to the File Note of 8 October 1940 stating that the pilot had 'failed to bale out').

As Group Captain Dennis David rightly wrote of his friend, 'A man of his calibre, leadership and character cannot be replaced – and all who knew him felt this.' Another distinguished 87 Squadron pilot, Wing Commander Roland Beamont, remembered that Wing Commander Johnny Dewar was 'a super chap, a marvellous commander and leader who inspired us all with his calm, totally unflappable manner – he seemed to take the view that it was all rather a joke and certainly not good form for any of us to be in any way concerned about it!'. Whatever happened in the final moments of Exeter's distinguished Station Commander's life, two things are clear: once he knew that the Luftwaffe was active in his area, there was no hope of him maintaining his intended flight plan, and his was a loss Fighter Command could ill afford.

Wing Commander J. S. Dewar DSO DFC was thirty-three, and the highest-ranking RAF officer to die in the Battle of Britain.

Today, his grave can be found in the peaceful country churchyard of St John the Baptist at North Baddesley, near Southampton – the Commonwealth War Graves headstone incorrectly recording the date of death as 12 September 1940. Sadly, he joined his twenty-seven-year-old brother-in-law, Pilot Officer Richard Bowyer, who had lost his life in a training accident at Hullavington on 18 September 1939 and was also buried in this Hampshire churchyard.

At Easter 2014, my wife, Karen, and I visited these graves – all but forgotten except by those who maintain the churchyard and worship at St John the Baptist. Somehow, especially with the Battle of Britain's seventy-fifth anniversary year impending, that did not seem right at all. So it was that my friend Adrian Saunders and I began working with Sally Kerson at the church to arrange a commemorative event – set, poignantly, for the eve of battle: 9 July 2015. Taking our inspiration from the 'Flower Children' who lay floral tributes annually on graves at the Arnhem-Oosterbeek Airborne Cemetery, it was agreed that Year 5 pupils from William Gilpin School near Lymington would pay a similar tribute at the graves of Wing Commander Dewar and Pilot Officer Bowyer. It was a real pleasure, in fact, to visit the school and tell these wonderfully enthusiastic children about the Battle of Britain, so that they appreciated the significance of this very personal act of remembrance. On the day, Wing Commander Jon Whitworth of RAF Swanick led the RAF presence, whilst Squadron Leader Chris Fopp and friends passed overhead, paying their own tribute with a formation of Chipmunk and Bulldog aircraft. As the haunting notes of 'The Last Post' faded across the rolling fields, the children placed their flowers alongside the grown-ups' wreaths. When we left the churchyard, both graves were covered in floral tributes – and Johnny Dewar was very much back on the radar. Appropriately, during the service, my personal reading was John Pudney's famous poem 'For Johnny' (superbly recited by Sir John Mills is the 1945 film *The Way to the Stars*):

Do not despair
For Johnny-head-in-air;
He sleeps as sound
As Johnny underground.
Fetch out no shroud
For Johnny-in-the-cloud;
And keep your tears
For him in after years.

Better by far
For Johnny-the-bright-star,
To keep your head,
And see his children fed.

Flight Lieutenant Denis Robinson, a Spitfire pilot with 152 Squadron and who survived being shot down by II/JG 53 over Swanage on 8 August 1940, once wrote to me and said, 'Telling my story helps me to deal with my "survival syndrome". In a difficult-to-describe way, it is though I am speaking for other chaps who did not make it. Their final story would have been more readable than mine. One constantly asks, "Why did I survive ... why did others not?"' More recently, and in conclusion, Geoffrey Wellum movingly and succinctly summarised how 'the Final Few' now feel: 'Nobody wants a medal. Nobody wants a "thank you". But it would be nice to be remembered, because then you must think of all of us – and not just those of us who survived.'

BIBLIOGRAPHY

Books

Allen, H. R., *Who Won the Battle of Britain?* (2nd edn; London: Granada Publishing, 1976)

Calder, A., *The People's War: Britain 1939–1945* (12th edn; London: Pimlico, 2008)

Calder, A., *The Myth of the Blitz* (London: Jonathan Cape, 1991)

Caldwell, C., *The JG 26 War Diary, Volume One, 1939–1942* (London: Grub Street, 1996)

Campion, G., *The Good Fight: Battle of Britain Propaganda and The Few* (London: Palgrave MacMillan, 2010)

Clapson, M., *The Routledge Companion to Britain in the Twentieth Century* (London: Routledge, 2009)

Connolly, M., *We Can Take It! Britain and the Memory of the Second World War* (1st edn; Pearson Longman, 2004)

Crook, D. M. C., *Spitfire Pilot* (London: Faber & Faber, 1942)

David, W. D., *My Autobiography* (London: Grubb Street, 2000)

Dickson, L., *Richard Hillary: A Life* (London: MacMillan & Co Ltd, 1950)

Foreman, J., *RAF Fighter Command Victory Claims of World War Two, Part One: 1939–1940* (Walton-on-Thames: Red Kite, 2003)

Francis, M., *The Flyer: The British Culture and the Royal Air Force, 1939–45* (Oxford University Press, 2008)

Franks, N., *Air Battle for Dunkirk: 26 May – 3 June 1940* (3rd edn; London: Grub Street, 2006)

Handel, M. I. (ed.), *Intelligence & Military Operations* (Abingdon: Frank Cass, 1990)

Hillary, R., *The Last Enemy* (2nd edn; London: MacMillan & Co, 1950)

James, T. C. G., *The Battle of Britain* (London: Frank Cass, 2000)

Kent, J., *One of the Few* (Stroud: The History Press, 2008)

Kingcome, B. F., *A Willingness to Die* (Tempus, Stroud, 1999)

Lane, B. J. E. (ed. D. Sarkar), *Spitfire! The Experiences of a Battle of Britain Fighter Pilot* (Stroud: Amberley Publishing, 2009)

Long, A., *The Faithful Few: Worcestershire's Fighter Boys* (Worcester: Victory Books International, 2007)

MacKenzie, S. P., *The Battle of Britain On Screen: 'The Few' in British Film & Television Drama* (Edinburgh University Press, 2007)

Mason, F., *Battle Over Britain* (2nd edn; Bourne End: Aston Publications, 1990)

Moseley, L., *Battle of Britain* (London: Pan, 1969)

Moss, N., *Nineteen Weeks: America, Britain & the Summer of 1940* (New York: Houghton Mifflin, 2003)

Overy, R., *The Battle* (London: Penguin Books, 2000)

Ponting, C., *1940: Myth & Reality* (London: Hamish Hamilton Ltd, 1990)

Price, A., *The Hardest Day: 18 August 1940* (London: MacDonald & Jane's Publishers Ltd, 1979)

Ramsey, W. (ed.), *The Battle of Britain Then & Now* (fifth edn; London: After the Battle, 1989)

Ramsey, W. (ed.), *The Blitz: Then & Now, Volume I* (London: After the Battle, 1987)

Ramsey, W. (ed.), *The Blitz: Then & Now, Volume II* (London: After the Battle, 1988)

Robinson, A., *RAF Fighter Squadrons in the Battle of Britain* (London: Arms & Armour Press, 1987)

Russell, C. R., *Spitfire Odyssey: My Life at Supermarines 1936–1957* (Southampton: Kingfisher Railway Productions, 1985)

Sarkar, D., *A Few of the Many: Air War 1939–45, A Kaleidoscope of Memories* (Worcester: Ramrod Publications, 1995)

Sarkar, D., *The Few* (Stroud: Amberley Publishing, 2009)

Sarkar, D., *The Last of the Few: Eighteen Battle of Britain Pilots Tell Their Extraordinary Stories* (Stroud: Amberley Publishing, 2010)

Sarkar, D., *How the Spitfire Won the Battle of Britain* (Stroud: Amberley Publishing, 2010)

Sarkar, D., *Douglas Bader* (Stroud: Amberley Publishing, 2013)

Smith, M., *Britain & 1940: History, Myth & Popular Memory* (London: Routledge, 2000)

Vasco, J., *Bombsights Over England: The History of* Erprobungsgruppe *210 Luftwaffe Fighter-Bomber Unit in the Battle of Britain* (Norwich: JAC Publications, 1990)

Walker, O., *Sailor Malan* (London: Cassell & Co, 1953)

Wallace, G., *RAF Biggin Hill* (London: Universal Tandem Publishing, 1969)

Wellum, G. H. A., *First Light* (2nd edn; London: Penguin, 2003)

Wynn, K., *Men of the Battle of Britain* (1st edn; Norwich: Gliddon Books, 1989)

Unpublished Sources

Author's personal papers, including correspondence and interviews with the Few

Sarkar, D., 'Was the Leadership Ability of RAF Fighter Squadron Commanders in WW2 Compromised by Pre-War Socio-Educational Prejudice?', undergraduate dissertation, University of Worcester (2010)

Pilots' Flying Log Books

Wing Commander J. F. D. Elkington
Flight Lieutenant W. J. Green
Squadron Leader M. T. Wainwright AFC
Squadron Leader G. H. A. Wellum DFC

The National Archives

AIR 27/743   92 Squadron ORB
AIR 27/748   As above, Appendices

AIR 50/40   92 Squadron Combat Reports
AIR 27/1/18   1 Squadron ORB
AIR 50/1   1 Squadron Combat Reports
AIR 27/2088   605 Squadron ORB
AIR 50/62   605 Squadron Combat Reports
AIR 27/712   87 Squadron ORB
AIR 27/1315   213 Squadron ORB
AIR 27/1949   501 Squadron ORB
AIR 50/162   501 Squadron Combat Reports

Films

Gossage, J. W. & Twist, D., *Angels One Five* (Templar, 1952)
Salzman, H. & Fisz, S. B., *Battle of Britain* (Spitfire Productions 1969)
Whiteman, M., *First Light* (Lion Television, 2010)
Willis, J., *Churchill's Few* (Yorkshire Television, 1985)

Websites

www.battleofbritain.org (Battle of Britain Memorial Trust)
www.92Squadron.org.uk (92 Squadron Association)
www.1fsa.org (1 Squadron Association)
www.raf.mod.uk/battleofbritainbunker (11 Group Underground
    Operations Room)
www.bentleypriory.org (The Bentley Priory Battle of Britain Trust)

ACKNOWLEDGEMENTS

Firstly, I must thank all of the Battle of Britain pilots featured in his book, and their families, for their continued friendship and support of my work.

In 1979, I read what I still consider to be the best book ever written on the Battle of Britain: Dr Alfred Price's superlative *The Hardest Day*. That work continues to be an example and inspiration to us all – thank you, Alfred.

I would also especially like to thank, in no particular order: Geoffrey Wellum for his permission to quote a short extract from *First Light*; Deborah Scarfe (Geoffrey's daughter); Geoff Simpson; Group Captain Patrick Tootal OBE DL, of the Battle of Britain Memorial Trust and Battle of Britain Fighter Association; Liz Collins; Andrew Long; Eric Young; Matthew Whiteman; Sam Heughan; Sally Kerson; Adrian Saunders; Heather Collinson; Etienne Bol, Sue Johnson; and Ray Cobern.

As always, Jonathan Reeve, Alex Bennett and the team at Amberley Publishing made producing this book another pleasure.

Last but not least, my wife, Karen – for everything.

LIST OF ILLUSTRATIONS

23. Ken Wilkinson, snapped while a sergeant pilot flying Spitfires with 19 Squadron at Fowlmere during the Battle of Britain.
24. Pre-Fighter Course, Montrose, June 1940: Sergeant K. A. Wilkinson second row, second right; many pictured went on to fly, fight and sadly in some cases die in the Battle of Britain.
25. The 19 Squadron operations caravan and bell-tented squadron office at Fowlmere during the Battle of Britain.
26. Sergeant Bernard 'Jimmy' Jennings DFM, Ken Wilkinson's closest friend on 19 Squadron, who taught the fledgling fighter pilot the skills of dogfighting: 'He was a hard taskmaster.'
27. Warrant Officer Ken Wilkinson, on wing, left, pictured with 'A' Flight on 165 Squadron at Church Stanton in 1943.
28. Warrant Officer Ken Wilkinson with 165 Squadron Spitfire Mk IX, Church Stanton, 1943.
29. Ken Wilkinson and the author, pictured at a book signing in 2009.
30. LAC Bill Green – a newly qualified pilot but not yet promoted sergeant – upon his marriage to Bertha Louisa Biggs, 3 June 1940.
31. A 501 Squadron Hurricane pictured at Kenley in September 1940.
32. A well-known photograph of 501 Squadron pilots at Kenley during the Battle of Britain. Seated at right is Flight Commander John 'Gibbo' Gibson, who was shot down in the same action as Sergeant Green on 29 August 1940. Gibson, however, made a parachute descent from 16,000 feet, drifting out to sea, while Green's parachute opened a mere second from certain death.
33. The way it was: pilots of 501 Squadron at readiness, Gravesend, August 1940. From left: Sergeant Tony Pickering, Sergeant R. J. K. Gent, Flight Sergeant Peter Morfill, Sergeant Paul Farnes, Sergeant Anton Glowacki (Polish), unidentified, Sergeant W. B. Henn, Sergeant Tony Whitehouse, Sergeant James 'Ginger' Lacey, Pilot Officer Bob Dafforn.
34. Sergeant Anton Glowacki (Polish) makes his after action combat report to a steel-helmeted intelligence officer during the Battle of Britain.
35. Squadron Leader Harry Hogan (centre, in forage cap) with pilots of 501 Squadron – which was in the front line throughout the Battle of Britain, losing nineteen pilots.
36. 501 Squadron Battle of Britain survivors at Colerne, 1941; from

left: Pilot Officers James 'Ginger' Lacey DFM, Ken MacKenzie DFC (later a long-serving Chairman of the Battle of Britain Fighter Association), Tony Whitehouse, Bob Dafforn and Vic Ekins. Of this group, only Dafforn would not survive the war.

37. Warrant Officer Bill Green serving with 504 Squadron at Filton in 1941. Commissioned the following year, Green had achieved a rare feat: the transition from lowly engine fitter on an AAF squadron to commissioned fighter pilot.

38. A 22 OTU Hurricane in September 1944, from the pages of Bill Green's log book.

39. Flight Lieutenants Bill Green (right) and 'Shag' Hellens with a 1682 BTD Flight Tomahawk in March 1944.

40. Bill Green, photographed at his West Country home by the author in 2012.

41. Pilot Officer Geoffrey 'Boy' Wellum (right) at Biggin Hill with his flight commander and mentor, Flight Lieutenant Brian Kingcome DFC, for whom Geoffrey has only the greatest respect and affection: 'Brian Kingcome *was* 92 Squadron.'

42. On 14 September 2010, BBC2 broadcast Matthew Whiteman's docudrama *First Light*, based upon Geoffrey Wellum's best-selling memoir of that title. Here Ben Aldridge (left) and Sam Heughan are pictured during filming as Kingcome and Wellum respectively. (Courtesy Etienne Bol)

43. Flying Officer Alan Wright with his 92 Squadron Spitfire at Pembrey in the Battle of Britain.

44. Pilot Officer Desmond Williams of 92 Squadron, illustrating 1940 flying kit – excluding the all-important 'Mae West' life preserver worn when operating over water. Williams became an ace in the Battles of France and Britain, but was killed on 10 October 1940 when he collided with another Spitfire while attacking a German bomber near Tangmere; he was twenty years old.

45. Flight Lieutenant Brian Fabris Kingcome DFC, drawn by Cuthbert Orde in 1940. Kingcome rose to Group Captain, also awarded the DSO, and after the war ran a chauffeuring business with fellow Battle of Britain Spitfire pilot 'Paddy' Barthropp before setting up a furniture-making concern in Devon; he died in 1994.

46. Sam Heughan, as Pilot Officer 'Boy' Wellum, in the excellent BBC2 docudrama *First Light*. (Courtesy Etienne Bol)

47. Squadron Leader Geoffrey Wellum DFC, pictured by the author with his latest model ship project at his Cornish home in 2012.

48. Wing Commander John Scatliff Dewar DSO DFC, Station Commander of RAF Exeter and the highest-ranking RAF officer to be killed during the Battle of Britain – a very experienced and successful fighter pilot and leader, the thirty-three-year-old would doubtless have achieved great things in the service.

49. Johnny Dewar's grave at North Baddesley, Hampshire. Although the date of death is recorded as 12 September 1940, Wing Commander Dewar was actually killed the previous day – as explained in this book.

50. The 2013 service of remembrance at the Battle of Britain National Memorial, situated on the cliffs overlooking Folkestone in Kent. (Courtesy Barry Duffield, via Geoff Simpson)

51. Sally Kerson leads the commemoration of Wing Commander Johnny Dewar at St John the Baptist, North Baddesley, on 9 July 2015. The event was initiated by Dilip Sarkar (right of headstone), Wing Commander Jon Whitworth (centre) leading the RAF presence. (Author's collection)

52. Children from William Gilpin School place flowers on Wing Commander Dewar's grave, watched by Sally Kerson and Dilip Sarkar – who drew inspiration for this moving act of remembrance from Arnhem's 'Flower Children'. (Author's collection)

OTHER BOOKS BY DILIP SARKAR (IN ORDER OF PUBLICATION)

Spitfire Squadron: No 19 Squadron at War, 1939–41
The Invisible Thread: A Spitfire's Tale
Through Peril to the Stars: RAF Fighter Pilots Who Failed to Return, 1939–45
Angriff Westland: Three Battle of Britain Air Raids Through the Looking Glass
A Few of the Many: Air War 1939–45, A Kaleidoscope of Memories
Bader's Tangmere Spitfires: The Untold Story, 1941
Bader's Duxford Fighters: The Big Wing Controversy
Missing in Action: Resting in Peace?
Guards VC: Blitzkrieg 1940
Battle of Britain: The Photographic Kaleidoscope, Volume I
Battle of Britain: The Photographic Kaleidoscope, Volume II
Battle of Britain: The Photographic Kaleidoscope, Volume III
Battle of Britain: The Photographic Kaleidoscope, Volume IV
Fighter Pilot: The Photographic Kaleidoscope
Group Captain Sir Douglas Bader: An Inspiration in Photographs
Johnnie Johnson: Spitfire Top Gun, Part I
Johnnie Johnson: Spitfire Top Gun, Part II
Battle of Britain: Last Look Back
Spitfire! Courage & Sacrifice
Spitfire Voices: Heroes Remember
The Battle of Powick Bridge: Ambush a Fore-Thought
Duxford 1940: A Battle of Britain Base at War
The Few: The Battle of Britain in the Words of the Pilots

Spitfire Manual 1940

The Last of the Few: Eighteen Battle of Britain Pilots Tell Their Extraordinary Stories

Hearts of Oak: The Human Tragedy of HMS Royal Oak

Spitfire Voicxes: Life as a Spitfire Pilot in the Words of the Veterans

How the Spitfire Won the Battle of Britain

Spitfire Ace of Aces: The True Wartime Story of Johnnie Johnson

The Sinking of HMS Royal Oak

Douglas Bader

Spitfire: The Photographic Biography

Hurricane Manual 1940

River Pike